The Price System

David Michael Beechwood

ISBN 978-1-64258-036-5 (paperback)
ISBN 978-1-64258-037-2 (digital)

Christian Faith Publishing, Inc.
832 Park Avenue
Meadville, PA 16335
www.christianfaithpublishing.com

Printed in the United States of America

Introduction

Perhaps a catchier title to this book would be *How to Lie, Cheat, and Steal without going to Jail*. I have to admit that title does sound more interesting. However, just because certain things are done legally doesn't make them right. My title also sounds like it might be a very arduous read; it's not.

You will find that I have avoided using confusing economic spreadsheets or complicated tables. Actually, the title subject is laid out in a fashion that does not require you to have any special training to gain understanding. Basically, this book is written in a story form so it is easy to follow.

While this book is easy to read, I should prepare you for what you are about to read. For someone who hasn't been exposed to any of this material before, you are in for an adventure. However, that adventure may be emotionally painful at times.

Remember, as a child, your disappointment when you first realized that there was no tooth fairy or Santa Claus? Well, now you're in for several new rude awakenings, on a much grander scale. These would be economic delusions that most people are unaware of or consciously avoid, as in denial.

I believe you can handle this more enlightening version of the story behind our current system of commerce. However, giving up old beliefs can be painful. On the up side, your awareness of the things contained in this book will ultimately make you stronger and better able to protect yourself, in the future.

This book was not written to help anyone to lie, cheat, or steal. I would not want to encourage anyone to do that, so a title suggesting that would be inappropriate. What this book does do is expose some ways in which those terrible things are done.

It does this by disclosing the price system for what it really is. That system was designed and continues to be modified by a privileged few. They shape and mold it to their own personal benefits. This allows them to do those deplorable things suggested above excessively. Crazy as it may sound, the price system that we cherish so much is a lot more diabolical than you might have suspected.

This book I believe might shock and amaze you at times. That is, if you have not had the time to really think about how things actually work. The learning experiences here can be pretty depressing.

However, this book should also provide you with knowledge, inspiration, and hope. Still, in order to secure those attributes, you likely will need to expand your current vision of what the price system is. This is because it isn't as benign as most people think. Unfortunately for us, this price system is not always the friend we think it is. It hurts the majority of us, much more than you might have possibly imagined.

So, to start with, I ask you, what do you think the price system is? You likely have been taught a mostly superficial answer to that, which is it is just our system of commerce. However, there is a lot more to that system than what most of us are led to understand.

It is a system that the general public assumes it has nearly complete understanding of. After all, we have used it all of our lives. We pay our bills, we go to the store, we do our banking, and sometimes we even invest in the system. However, there is a lot more mystery to it than we typically would think. In fact, most of the underlying activity, for these transactions, we never see or even think about.

Honestly, most times when we use the system, don't we just use it without knowing the exact details of how it really works. We operate in it every day, and despite our lack of complete knowledge, we are very comfortable with it. We are so comfortable that we seldom even ask questions about it anymore.

We just accept the simple, dumbed-down explanations provided by the vendors. In fact, during the course of our daily transactions, we rarely take the time to ask if this "price system" has a dark underside. We just trust in the system. Why not? Everyone else does. You might be saying, "Hey, it's been here forever. What's to know? Our parents or grandparents must have checked it out, so why should we worry?" But what if they didn't really have a good opportunity to challenge the system? What if hardly anybody really did? Is it possible that for generations now, people never really vetted this system to any real depth?

Could a system based on the accumulation of money really cause us problems? I think you know deep down that it certainly can. Those ancestors of ours that pointed out, "Money is the root of all evil," were typically rebutted with, "Yes, but money is a necessary evil."

Somehow we chose to believe the rebuttal turning a blind eye on common sense. Despite our knowledge of the ills of money with its built-in problems, yet to be discussed, we continue to follow the price system. We typically minimize, in our minds, the role that *money* has on these problems, blaming everyone and everything else instead, when things fall apart.

Various price systems existed prior to the system we use worldwide today. Frankly, the morphing of the price system took a very long time to reach its current form. Apart from the basic initial flaw of the system, which is money itself, there has been a multitude of incremental corruptions along the way to today. These corruptions are represented by the great number of self-serving events in history. Those events occurred to ultimately give us the system we see today.

Regarding those events, oh where should we start? You could pick from many points in time and place during the system's development to find corruptions. I however will start our exploration during the feudal times of Europe. That was a time that we, here in the Western world, can easily draw comparisons to, even today.

The people back then that had any real money and or wealth were royalty. The common people of those times didn't like the inequality of wealth that existed. There was a huge gap between the wealthy and the poor. The writing was on the wall that the idea of certain families always being the kings and queens and thus the rulers was becoming very unpopular. The nobles understood that they could lose their lands and wealth by a populous overthrow of the kings.

They fashioned a plan and a strategy to give the appearance of a shift in control. While still in the driver's seat as leaders of their day, they moved toward the system we use today. Today, you can still find members of those same wealthy families who are lords of business, banking, finance, and government. The kings of those realms are still represented today by the most affluent in their particular dynasty. Today however they normally do not use the title of king; except for a few.

The old kings and nobles were clever enough to fashion a price system that afforded their families the maximum opportunity to retain their control. Their design allowed their small group to continue to control key economic strongholds in banking, education, politics, and religion. That basic system is still working to this day on a continual basis.

Do you think that this small group may have set their new system up in their favor? There should be no doubt about that. Their system only requires a small group of people to administrate, and there, they control that high ground. Yes, even today, a very small group, in terms of percentage, still maintains the controls over the system.

We have given this group authority over our lives without truly knowing exactly what they do. We have given them our complete faith. Most people simply trust that "old established system" without question. Yes, the one that has been found to be corrupted time after time and year after year.

We have given that system power to lay out the defining strategy for the control of everyone and everything on earth. That may sound like an overstatement, but is it? This system controls the money, and if you control the money, you control nearly everything. Simply stated, the economy is money, and as you might have come to understand, money controls us to a great extent. With the economy worsening for the majority of people on earth, perhaps it is time for us to ask a few questions.

Today with most of us anxious to improve our lives, doesn't it seem strange that we really haven't tried to find a more honest system of commerce, perhaps one that is fairer to the 90%, or more, who are clearly left wanting? They are left behind, because, to a substantial degree, they don't have equitable access to an unprejudiced share of the world's wealth. They don't have access because, in part, they are not included in the controlling segment of the system. Yes, I am suggesting that more than 90% of earth's population is not truly represented.

It almost seems like we are forbidden to entertain the idea that the system might not be fair to everyone. Even when we are told that less than 10% of the world's population has over 90% of the world's wealth, we do not see the problem. Somehow, our attention is drawn to other things. Perhaps, this result is not an accident.

The idea of allowing more people to share in the wealth is not a welcomed thought to many people in the 10% group. Ideas for more economic fairness have ended up suppressed for centuries now, by the price system. In fact, the basic concepts for this price system are so old its roots existed perhaps even before religion came on the scene, thousands of years ago. It has defended itself against those compassionate ideas, which often offered a wider distribution of wealth.

Today, most of us have come to believe that there isn't anything wrong with someone making 300 million dollars or more a year. This is because we are taught that great wealth has no negative impact on those people that have next to nothing. We are in fact encouraged to believe this falsehood by the media.

The media promotes a line of reason that you can never have too much. This then allows those that have excessive wealth to have even more excess. The price system has sold us their nonsharing idea through marketing. This is just one way for those in charge of the price system to protect themselves and their *system*.

Consider this—many people now seem to put more faith in this money system, than they do in their religion. More troublesome is that many people know less about this money system than they know about religion. That statement is even more worrisome because for the past several years now, there has been a falling away from the Christian religion. Money, it seems, has instead become a deity to more and more people. It shouldn't be.

This causes me to ask, how could we possibly believe that there isn't a better system to try? Still, we plug along doing the same old thing without question. I can guarantee you that in the coming months, numerous scandals involving the price system will be uncovered. Why? This is because every year, millions of scandals are uncovered; why should this year be any different?

I hope you are starting to see a need for us to learn a little more about the price system. Could it really be that we don't know as much about it as we thought we did? Getting to know more about it might help us improve our national economy and our personal situations. After all, the price system works in nearly every aspect of our lives, through variations of its design.

Since this system is tied to almost everything we do, you would think we would all be experts on the subject. Unfortunately, only a few people are, and they are generally working the system to advantage themselves. The rest of the population, it seems, simply accepts the system as the only way of doing business; and well, that's just the way it is; so why ask questions?

What if there was another way, other than the price system, a better way, but we never truly were allowed to find it? Could we be hurting our families and ourselves by not seeking a more just system? We need to ask, does the price system work to hurt more people than it helps? Is it really designed so that ultimately, only a relatively few selected people end up controlling almost everything?

With this in mind, I ask for a little leeway to present some thoughts for you to consider. Some of my thoughts might seem a little circumstantial at first. However, I hope that they will prove themselves as more supportive information is presented in the upcoming pages.

Consider what *the system* has control over. Aside from controlling the prices of most of our food, clothing, and shelter that we use, it also does much more. It controls the stock, bond, and commodity markets on a worldwide basis. Through its control of the world's economics, it also subtly manages the education, political, and religious sectors.

Many things that we normally would not think to be under its control are. For example, the odds that are paid out at the gambling facilities are. Even our local, state, and federal elections are under its influence.

In fact, nearly everything we do is under price system controls in one way or another. Even those minor annoyances such as those louder television commercials are a product of *the price system*. In fact, all those more than abundant television, newspaper, radio commercials, and spam ads are necessary for its operation. Then, there are the billboards, trucks, buses, and buildings with their advertisements, not to mention those neon signs that imprint on our brains each day. This system touches all of us, in sometimes unnoticeable ways, some trivial, but others are much more bothersome.

We also have to consider that it is the price system that makes it possible for some sports figures and entertainers to be more highly paid than most scientist, engineers, and doctors.[1] Many people labor for their whole life in redundant but important and necessary jobs. Yet their level of pay never comes close to what a well-known sports figure or entertainer might make, even in the first year of their stardom. Is vanity and ego somehow built into this system to allow this? I wish I could say no, but both play a huge role in the inequitable treatment of laborers.

Most of us, deep down, believe in fairness. How should the value of a person who performs daily redundant services for thirty years be considered? Shouldn't that service be at least as important as that of a person who plays baseball extremely well, but for perhaps only five years? You and I know that most common redundant jobs rarely make anyone a multimillionaire, but a good entertainer can be one in no time.

The price system is not built to support those common daily workers in that excessive way. It is designed to minimize their value so that the wages can be held down. Those savings can then be redistributed to those who are in charge—the lucky few. Redundant jobs are more likely to be treated as menial for that reason. Popular singers, actors, and sports figures on the other hand are hyped and treated as if they are extremely more important.

By promoting of the careers of certain people, excessive profits for a select few can be assured. Yes, extreme profit can also be made off their fame. We know this because celebrities get paid extremely well, but their owners and managers often do even better. We are all conditioned to accept this as being just and fair. If you really stop to consider what happens here, you come to understand that the system has crafted our opinions to favor their goals. Again, I hope to justify this last statement to you in the upcoming pages. Could a more equitable system exist? I think so.

What about the work of the scientists, engineers, or educators? We know that their work is important as well. However, very few of these professions achieve celebrity status. Why? This is because the price system isn't designed to hype these more common daily jobs. There generally isn't a marketing department behind these people to glorify them to excess. In my opinion, there are a number of professions that should rank higher in economic priority than singing, acting, or sports. Don't get me wrong, there is a place for the arts in our lives; but the excessive income that some performers, players, and owners receive is wrong.

Many artist, as well, never receive the recognition they deserve, because the *system* isn't designed that way. There is room only for a limited few. It is designed this way so that those in control make larger profits. Allowing more artists a chance at stardom would saturate the market, dilute profits, and cause those in charge to work harder.

The price system controls these unfair and unjust practices. It allows them to occur so that shortages can exist. Shortages create demand, and demand creates profits. It is the controllers of this system who generally reap those rewards. This unfairness works to their advantage in most cases. That is, it works to the advantage of those who control the process. The price system not only sets these conflicts of fairness up but also encourages them.

Here is a short list of other attributes of the system:

1. The price system provides the opportunity for the military to pay $640 for a toilet seat.[2]

2. It provides the means for the pharmaceuticals to charge $100 or more for a single pill.[3]
3. It supports the hospitals when they charge $200 or more for an aspirin.[4]
4. It supports a system of extreme debt as a legitimate way of running an economy.

I would bet that you know of a few more things to add to this list.

Wait just a minute. Are any of the above price system's policies logical? Those doing those things of course have good explanations for doing them; and we, as a group, usually agree. That is, we agree after they show us the symbolic three cups and the little red ball. Yep, they all look good; it must be okay.

You would think we would learn, but look around; it still goes on. Despite the explanations that these magicians give to cover their trail, those figures of theirs still don't add up, unless you figure that they are fixing the game, the price system game, in their favor. They have gotten their system to the point where they are allowed to do the fix, without it being illegal. Yes, the price system is their game, and we play it like zombies. Sleepily, we trudge along, never waking and seldom questioning. I hope this book helps to wake at least some people up.

If each individual citizen were able to fix their prices, in the magnitudes just suggested above, that strain would expose the system's true colors. As you know, we as individuals are not allowed to do that. That right is reserved for a privileged few, mostly for large businesses or corporations, under the law.

We understand that those laws provide them with advantages over the general public. With those laws, we are told that those businesses won't go overboard in their pricing, so we shouldn't worry. Still, reports of corporate excessiveness, in pricing or in executive pay, occur almost daily.

In fact, there are so many reports that we have just given in to thinking that there isn't anything wrong with it. It is business as usual. There is no unified voice demanding that these atrocities stop.

Instead, there is usually only a whimper of objections that quickly die out and the mischief continues.

Many times, we are told that the prices we pay reflect the current cost of business. Could you imagine going to your boss and explaining that the roof repair on your house added additional cost to your budget, so now you have to charge him an extra 10 cents an hour to cover those cost? No, you could try, but you most likely would not be successful. Larger businesses however do have that option, and the larger the business, the more likely that they will get their way on that. Why do we just accept that? Shouldn't the system work the same for everyone?

The answers to those questions above point to a stunning realization—the game, called the price system, is rigged. It has different rules for different people. There are rules for those on top, those in the middle, and those on the bottom. We are all told that we are playing the same game, but that is hardly the case. The rules for those on the top level allow them to do many more things that you, as an individual, cannot.

If this game were a board game, those on top could be said to be able to move their pieces, which are in play, in multiple directions and for any number of spaces. Those on the bottom however can only move one direction and only one space at a time. If you are content being a lower-level player, then you have to play within that set of rules. These are rules that do not favor you.

If by fortune you could move to that next level, you may not want to go there. This is because that choice to jump to the next level can sometimes cause you to have a moral conflict. Here in lies the rub for all of us. For if we do jump to the next level, especially that corporate level, we will have rewards; but we might have trouble dealing with the things we have to do to keep those rewards.

If we were a large business, for example, we might start charging more for our services than is really necessary, that is, if we intend to have a better lifestyle than the people we service. After all, the stated goal of all large businesses is to make the largest possible profit. All things being equal, if we don't charge enough, we will not be allowed to stay in that higher-income level. This can easily cause people to do things they may not otherwise do. Yes, the system is set up this way. The lure of money causes many moral corruptions.

Generally, at the first few levels of business activity, a greater degree of fairness exists in the system. All too often, when businesses grow, the level of fairness fades. Greed can take hold, and then, corruption grows. This makes it much more likely that when we get to the higher levels, we may be one of those who charges $640 for a toilet seat.

But not to worry, our peers will no doubt reward us for such achievements. We might receive a price system award of the year; many businesses have some reward system. This then becomes their gold star for taking excessive advantage of someone, though they wouldn't put it that way.

In a very strong way, the price system tends to put the leadership, of its designs, into the hands of what we could call its agents or managers. The agents don't make the rules they administer and enforce the orders. This group of leaders falls within that 10% group I spoke of earlier. These agents are normally put in charge of the people who are usually more practical or intellectual in nature than perhaps even themselves.

Very often, price system agents do not share the same intellectual mind-set of the people they manage. That is, they don't understand the science or mechanical processes completely, yet they are given control over those that do understand it. This is like putting the cart before the horse. This process doesn't always work well for the earth, but it works well enough in the price system. The experts in engineering and science are many times ignored by the agents of the system.

These experts would be better at making stronger and more stable decisions. However, the price system's controllers want people that can think shrewdly as their agents. This allows their profit-driven goals to rule in the decision-making process. While this brings in money for the price system rulers, it is far too often at the expense of the planet. That is, the environment is polluted.

This pollution however becomes a further benefit to the price system. This is because the system builds itself on debt. Thus, the cleanup that follows has a built-in bonus attribute for their system. However, the bonus mostly serves the few at the expense of the many.

You see, cleaning up these corruptions here nearly always benefits some other sector of the price system. This is because normally, this part is paid for by the public not the system rulers. How extremely clever and diabolical is that? Perhaps, we shouldn't be too surprised as this system has been running for thousands of years now. It has learned how to feed itself very well.

One goal of this book is to demonstrate that a relatively small group of controllers, I will call them that for now, has the means of manipulating everything.[5] By everything, I mean the many forms, applications, or faces of the price system that affect us. Those controllers work to create our biggest problem—*debt*. Why? This is because it is in the best interest of their price system to do so.

When the general public is in debt, this works to produce profits for the controllers in the form of interest, fees, fines, and more. However, debt is bad for us because debt steels our freedoms. The controllers do worry, a little, about taking us too far into debt, so they try not to overdo it. Every once and a while, however, their greed does get so extremely excessive that it can bring their entire system down.

Proving to you that these controllers exist will not be easy. Your orientation year after year, almost from birth, tells you that people, like me, who make these claims, are not to be paid attention to. In addition to this obstacle to my credibility, the systems long life seems to grant it a favored status. Then, there is the fact that we all seemingly have a vested interest in keeping it, the price system, going. We are all tied to it, like it or not, so we tend not to make waves.

Investigating the charges I am making here is a form of making waves. People thus are generally averse to believing these claims from the start. That way, they do not have to investigate them. I wish I had some special pills, like in the movie *The Matrix*, that I might use to open those minds and cause them to see things in a different way; but that is only in the movies.

So let's get started. You might already understand that the gambling casinos have a programmed mathematical formula that they use to operate under. It allows them to collect more money than they pay out in the slot machines. It is in the software that is built into the machines. If gambling truly was a game of chance, then why set the machines to only pay out a predetermined amount? In a sense, you can say the system is rigged. You can say that, but they wouldn't; to them, they are just making a profit.

In reality, both positions are correct; it is rigged, and this design provides them a profit. This indeed seems to be the case, and we as the general public just accept it. Is it okay to rig something to get a profit; oddly enough, we seem to think so. Perhaps, this is because we assume that they would never rig it too much in their favor. By giving them the benefit of the doubt, we wrongfully accept this practice as a necessary evil. We think of this kind of fixing as doing something wrong to do something right, if indeed it is right.

I suggest that we carry this practice of price fixing forward into the other areas where the price system is operated by the controllers. If we do, we can make the same observation—the whole system is rigged. It seems to me that under this price system, everyone, who can, has to rig the game or they wouldn't make money. Since common ordinary citizens cannot fix their price as easily, they are at a disadvantage.

Price fixing sets up moral conflicts for us. This conflict occurs when we have to set up our business model. We will tend to control the following things: wages, services, taxes, and product quality. Each of these can cause us anguish if we have to lower any of them.

Well perhaps, this is a problem for us, but not for the controllers. Lowering wages or product quality isn't a problem for them. In fact, they wouldn't call it price fixing, but rather setting a proper profit margin. Basically, we accept this, so we go along with it. We know no other way. We are convinced that there is no better way, so why look?

Price fixing is a problem because the prices always have to favor the businesses over the people. In the game of price fixing, the bottom rung of this ladder is the common person running his or her own personal business—that would be his or her own life. Next comes the small business with one or two employees, then larger companies, and at the top very large corporations. In this hierarchy, the large corporations have it the easiest when it comes to price fixing, and then, it goes downhill from there.

In a very real sense, you can say the game is rigged in the large corporation's favor. They have all the advantages that the price system affords to them, which those lesser companies, businesses, and people do not.

You normally wouldn't see the corporations as having advantages, because we are trained, or conditioned, not to look. If we were to look more closely, we might find the following. Those advantages allow them to operate under a different set of rules that give them a competitive advantage.

The word "rules" is actually misleading, as it implies fairness; but there isn't a lot of fairness here. The controllers understand this so they define their game in terms of laws. The word "law" causes our minds to think "justice", because laws are there to protect us, and we do have some good laws; right? Our mistake is in assuming these business laws are all good laws; many are not. I will point out a few of the bad ones as we go along.

It can be useful to use analogies when we have complex issues to understand. I realize they are not always perfect, but then, what is? So with that in mind, consider this rough analogy of the *price system* as it relates, this time, to the housing market.

> *Suppose that while visiting California, you decide to buy some vacation property. You tour a condo at the bottom of a beautiful valley. The company had multiple sites along the hillsides surrounding the valley that you could build on. The model was very nice, and the price seemed right too. So you picked out a site on the hillside and arranged to have the condo built for you.*
>
> *You later find out that the unit you purchased was actually located on a windy ridge. That site was much colder than the model you toured on your visit. Its location further up from the valley floor*

was partly to blame. This was something you had not thought about.

To make matters worse, you quickly find out that the unit wasn't well insulated either. In addition, there were numerous construction problems where substituted materials were used. The quality did not match the impression you received from seeing the model. A review of the contract indicated that those features were not standard, but custom features. You begin to have second thoughts about your purchase. Of course, you're told that you are legally bound to the agreement and cannot back out.

On top of all this, you find that the neighborhood association forbids you from insulating that condo unless you use their contractors. Their choice, of course, cost a good deal more than the company you had picked out. Their contractors would also have to be used for any other custom changes that you might want to do; to correct those shortcomings.

The moral here is that buying into the price systems can be like buying vacation property—you don't always get what you think you are getting.

Granted this situation above shouldn't normally happen, however, it happens far more than it should. The point here is that contracts with fine print do exist and are valid under the price system's rules. These faulty contracts, in an honest and sane world, would not exist; so in this sense, they really are corrupt.

In our world, you have to read the fine print. Yet often because the salesman was so nice, you might feel you don't have to. That being said, when you do read it, honestly is not it a little confusing at times. These human tendencies can easily be exploited.

Granted not all transactions are corrupt, yet a very alarming amount of these corruptions occur each year. Our court systems are overflowing with them. So much so that it often takes years for cases to go through the system.

So this corrupted version above, of how the price system can work, is thus understandably a likely situation. I bet you know of someone who has had similar confusions in transactions they may have had. In a way, this happens so much we are not even surprised that something like this could happen.

If we allow the mask of credibility to be removed from that price system, we understand that things like this happen. With the mask off, we can see that the system is far from completely honest. Secondly, we can see that there are not always sufficient laws to protect us from such unscrupulous contracts.

Right now, you might be saying that I am wrong and that there are laws that do protect us. True, there are some laws, but they don't always seem to help. For example, take the overpriced mortgages that were handed out just before the housing bubble burst in 2008. Many people lost those homes to contracts they could not economically honor. They painfully found that laws don't always protect you.

In an honest price system, why should you bother having a lawyer or real estate expert look over your contract? The strong need for a professional implies that there is room for wrongdoing in any contract. That should signal a red flag that the price system, which governs this process, should not be trusted.

In fact, we all know that contracts are often so complicated that teams of lawyers and other professionals are sometimes required to protect oneself. Not to repeat myself, but those complicated contracts are a valid practice used within the price system. They are designed to provide loopholes.

Loopholes are used by the price system to generate money. For example, the mortgage industry sure worked their magic to bring us the housing bubble. The fine print, loopholes, and crafty planning here caused us all pain.

If we chalk up that mortgage fraud to stupid people who didn't read the fine print, we then must admit that contracts can have unfavorable conditions in them—fine print conditions. Contracts, as we have seen, are not necessarily always honest. While the simple analogy above doesn't truly get into all the vile corruptions that the price system allows in, with any luck, it should begin to open our eyes.

Now, mortgage contracts are just one of many other contracts that the price system brings to us.

The confusions, as stated earlier, built into contracts require additional assistance in the form of professional people. Once again, the price system has allowed additional avenues for expenses to be brought in. This complexity is there by design; it generates wealth for the system controllers. Any increase in the use of money supports the system—by working to promote and create debt.

In a sense, our expenses make them wealthy. Thus, they are anxious to continuously invent new ways to create the need for money. Things such as taxing the sky, air, or even the temperature are not out of their reach. Nothing is out of bounds or outside the price system's sphere of influence.

You may have never really stopped to question the very system that you have allowed to have nearly complete control over your life. Most of us, in the past, would have considered it rude and perhaps even unpatriotic to question it. I suggest here that it is your patriotic duty to take a good look at it. In this book, I will hopefully, over its length, bring about a more complete understanding of just what the *price system* is.

Please do not construe this book as coming from an author who has all the answers to our price system problems. I confess that I do not understand all of the problems that it causes, completely. In my defense, nobody really does. The price system is a vast system. On top of this, it has been filled with unnecessary confusions in an attempt to hide its dark side. The price system's dark side helps to promote a false picture of our world.

In my opinion, most of our problems stem from, and are based, mainly on how we perceive the world. There is a strong consensus out there that we are given our view of the world from a surprisingly few people. It is believed by many that roughly 2% of our population controls our views. Currently, that would mean about 140 million people, worldwide, control our views. Do they control our views completely? No, they don't, but enough to make a difference in their favor. One hundred and forty million people equates to roughly about 35 million families that have extreme influences over the way we see things, worldwide.

There are some people out there who say that the 2% figure is too high. They say it is only 1% of our population or about 18 million families that control things. This latter figure is perhaps a more valid guess, in my opinion. When you consider there are about seven billion people in the world, this extremely small size of controlling families should cause us some alarm. It should be of no surprise that the worldview that these families promote is a view that provides them with the lion's share of the world's wealth and power. It is a fact that they use the price system to retain that wealth and power.

In all fairness, each of us also has our own views and opinion on things. If each of us were given control to do our own thing in this world, the result would be absolute chaos. For the sake of some order, it is preferable to have people of like thinking set up the basic rules for living in this world. The trouble is that the only like-minded people to come forward so far are those that selfishly run the system. There doesn't seem to be any other opposing group to challenge. Are there other people of like mind in the world who might form a new and fairer consensus to start a new system?

It is likely there are quite a number of smaller groups that are of like mind, but these groups individually do not have enough power and wealth to raise an opposition. It may be that humanity is not mature enough to put aside their small differences and work together for a just system. While it isn't always obvious, we have to accept that we do have a small group of strong-minded people in power. However, it is unfortunate that these strong-minded people are selfish in nature.

I plan to prove to you over the course of this book that the most powerful group of people, to be of like mind, are those selfish people that control us today. Note that they also have enough money to continue their leadership—thanks to their price system. The easiest part of this for me to prove is that they are selfish.

One only has to consider that this group is, by its nature, getting smaller and smaller, as their selfishness makes some of them richer and richer. Proving to you that they control us is not as easy, because who really wants to admit that someone else controls them, especially when you believe that you are free? However, some of the examples in this book should make it a little clearer that they really do control us, more than they should. You might just have to agree with me, by the time you finish reading it.

Members of this controlling group come from all disciplines. Their system has existed for centuries, and its methods have been woven into all aspects of our lives. One could easily argue that even some religious leaders of the past and present were and are really just members of this same organized group. In the past, if anyone wanted power to push their view, they had to use religion to garner support. To some degree, this is still true today.

I believe that the reason we still have these unscrupulous people in charge today is that they share a common attribute—selfishness. This behavior gives them unity through shared convictions. Having something in common results in them being of like mind. People working together with a common purpose can accomplish many things. With this thought in mind, we need a new group, a group of unselfish people to lead us.

In the United States, the next strongest opposition group, to the current group that is in charge, was the Christians. I say "was the Christians" because those who control our economy have found ways to divide and fragment this group. The Christian like-mindedness has literally been fractured into thousands of pieces. This is true not only for the Christian religion but also for "religion" itself.

Religion, in general, no longer poses a threat to those in charge. Even ISIS is a huge money-maker for those in charge of us, but not for the common person. It is clear that Muslims are also a terribly divided group. Their religious tenants have been corrupted so much that confusion is leading to their ruin.

Worldwide, the Jewish and Muslim religions do not believe in Jesus as the son of God or even as an example of God with us. To them, he is only perhaps a secondary prophet, if he existed at all. Those views have worked against the idea of God becoming a unifying spirit in our world. With the major religions minimized, God's importance has been diminished and thus contained by the price system. Just to be clear, the price system sponsors and supports those ideas that fracture the religious programs.

It is true that here in the United States, the Christian view is still the strongest of faiths and has influenced the minds of the bulk of the population. Unfortunately, the strength of Christian unity has been broken into pieces through the numerous denominations that have come into existence. There have also been a number of scandals that have worked to condemn religious influence.

Further, over the years, the printing presses have turned out a multitude of confusing new versions of the Bible. Each new translation has, in some small ways, increased the rift between Christians and on occasion has even widened the gap between the major faiths. All the squabbling and confusion has driven away many potential believers.

While all three major religions are said to believe in the same God, the diversities within each of these religions cause many of us to wonder if that really is the case. So religion seems to lack the ability to present a unified voice of unselfish like-mindedness. That is a voice that would be able to overtake the current leadership. Is there any hope for increased solidarity? I will leave that for you to answer.

These divisions within our populations have allowed a relatively small number of people with selfish intentions to rule us with their strong influence—the promise of money. Despite our obvious lack of control over things, we still have trouble questioning why things do not work in our favor. It doesn't even seem strange to us that we grew up being given mostly the views of a very few select people. These views end up being taught to us in school and in our news, and we then even teach them to our children.

Since most of us are easy-going folks, if what we are told seems reasonable, we generally go along with it. The funny thing is that this existing worldview, their view, on the surface does make sense. It is only when we get to the fine print that we begin to question their motives. Those that don't go along with the controllers are marginalized, demonized, or made to look silly. In the worst cases, they are put in prison or killed.

Consequently, the existing worldview is something that we do not directly have much control over. In fact, we have very little influence on those that we sometimes call the movers and shakers of this world. Again, only a very small percentage of the earth's population controls our worldview. I would like to add, if we let them; unfortunately, we do. This small segment of our population works together with each other to drive their own agendas at our expense. The price system is the vehicle they use.

This book offers the essences of several interesting views that could create an alternative worldview for us to consider. Most of these ideas that could generate a new view of the world are not really new, in that variations of them have been voiced for thousands of years. Some have even been tried; unfortunately, the mainstream worldview usually attacks them adversely when they are tried. The controllers of the current system push most of us away from accepting the alternate concepts through the training we received, reinforced by their embedded news programs.

In general, those ideas that oppose the current view are suppressed or hindered so much that they lack the strength to succeed. Where they have been tried, they quickly become perverted by elements from the price system itself. Thus, they have never been given a real honest chance at solving the world's problems.

The most common alternative worldview is socialism. It is based on, or drawn from, the writings of thousands of people over time. It is our common understanding that it looks good on paper, but the countries that have tried it have failed miserably. In other words, why try something that is likely to fail? Why are we encouraged to believe this? Is it possible that socialism threatens the wealth of those in charge of the current system? You better believe it does, hence their great fear of it. So we have been taught to hate it.

Several countries have had some successes with socialism. We see this in countries where it was not allowed to run wild and over-dominate the citizens. Deep down inside, we know that many of the ideas within this alternate view are indeed righteous and true. However, here in the United States, the common citizens just do not seem to have the will to push for those truths. We generally cave in to our training, which tells us that the price system's strong capitalist style is the only true way. In this way, the price system retains its control.

Perhaps, a more social view of socialism would be more easily accepted. However, most of the time, we are taught that socialism is as vile as communism, so who would want that? Is it possible that a form of socialism keyed to coexist with a capitalistic system could work better for us? Truthfully, all systems of government hold good and bad ideas in them. We need to find a modified version that will work for the bulk of the population instead of for just a few.

As Christians, we can certainly find elements of socialism that we should already be following. In fact, as you will see later on, our government has always incorporated a bit of socialism and very successfully at that; but it isn't a pure form of socialism. Perhaps, that is why that form of it works so well. However, those features are under threat from the private sectors.

One example of good social behavior is simply just trying to do what is right. You might recall that for a long time, helping someone in an emergency was often considered a bad idea. That was because it likely led to a price system lawsuit. It is hard to believe that the socialistic idea of helping one another was punished. While new Good Samaritan laws have lowered the number of lawsuits, we are still suing each other more than we should. What is not so apparent is that lawsuits make the price system wealthier. This allows our controllers to feed off their system on a whole other level.

It would be easy to solely blame those few who are taking advantage of their power to take advantage of us. If I were to do this, I would be denying our obvious individual shortcomings. Those shortcomings would be our human weaknesses.

These are weaknesses that in part provoke us to pass up our chance to enjoy much more freedom than we have today. We are to blame when sometimes we allow our weaknesses in character, such as our lack of honesty, compassion, or fear of hard work, to take hold of us. We also have weaknesses in body, as at times we lack physical strength and mental abilities and in the worst case have addictions.

These shortcomings may not all be directly our fault; nevertheless, they are human flaws that have to be considered and owned up to. Is it a design flaw in our individual nature that causes us to have our shortcomings? Perhaps at times, we pass up our chance at freedom, in a form of unconscious self-punishment. After all, we humans make mistakes, and this might be our way of paying for our sins.

Whatever the reason is, we seem to have let the price system happen, so in part, we are all to blame. Fixing the blame thus, on those of us who are responsible, helps to prevent future violations. That is, it helps if we try to correct ourselves. However, it does not fix the main problem itself. In regard to the price system itself, we still need to try and develop our own worldview and discard their selfish view.

For the most part, as stated earlier, when ideas that were detrimental to the price system were tried, they were never free of the adversity brought upon them, from the existing worldview. Those loyal to the price system were quick to criticize nonprice system methods. If those methods had any problems, the loyalists were equally fast in calling for the return of the price system solution.

Still, in our efforts to fix things, we should acknowledge that just because something has not been given a real chance doesn't automatically make it a good idea. Undoubtedly, some of the things I have written in this book may not be good ideas, as mankind may not be ready for them yet. As with any effort to fix things, one must have their heart in it or their efforts will not succeed. We may not be mature enough to succeed.

Our human tendencies today still seem to be tied to an animal nature that is embedded in our psyche. This animal nature has in part given us our current worldview. It seems that our animal emotions often override the common sense of our God-given human nature.

We may not be ready to adopt truly civil codes as many of these codes require us to give up some of our subhuman animal tendencies. The idea of a pecking order is one example of such a tendency. Some of us will have to give up thinking that they are excessively better than anyone else, based on their physical or mental strengths.

True, there are differences between us; however, the price system's worldview allows some people to think of themselves as extremely better than everyone else. This is perhaps part of that primitive concept of "might makes right," which still exists in our animal natures today. The controllers seem to revert to this animal "ism" easily as it helps to unite them in their efforts to control others. This strong, but ancient concept, and some other tactics, which we will talk about later, have often prevented the trial of some of the alternative economic ideas that will be discussed in this book.

Many times, they have stifled potential progress because it was, and still is, necessary for them to maintain their price system's worldview. Consequently, many possibly good ideas where never really given a chance to be discovered. Today, some of those ideas might appear to be wrong headed at first (because of our conditioning), but if we were to give them a real unbiased trial, perhaps they would work. We have to remember our training tells us certain ideas are bad. Are those ideas bad or is our training bad? We should be in favor of doing test cases, where possible, to see if the ideas we come up with really have value.

While reading this book, you may see a few ideas that you strongly disagree with. Please don't discard the whole book based on those few ideas that you disagree with. Why? This is because I believe there will be ideas that you will agree with. Remember that the primary goals of this book are to help design a better worldview and economic system. The way to do it is to get ideas out, even if they turn out to be unworkable at this time.

This book offers solutions, but does not confine our ultimate solutions to the ideas presented here. My interest here is in the making of a better world. As you read this book, remember that the Founding Fathers of the United States also had critics. Some of their ideas were as well outside of the box for their time. Yet they were able to make positive changes to their world.

So I ask you, is it possible that we could do the same? We may never be perfect in this world, but we can be a whole lot better, if we try. "Therefore let us not sleep, as do others, but let us watch and be sober."[6]

CHAPTER 1

A Review

Right now, you might be saying to yourself, "A review, shouldn't that be at the end of the book?" Well in this case, it is a review of a few basic definitions. These definitions will assist in getting us on the same page, so to speak. They might possibly help us to understand, a little better, why we may not be of like mind to begin with.

The review is also helpful because we are not all walking dictionaries. That is my way of saying that most of us do not have total recall. To make matters worse, we sometimes bend the definition of what we think a word means, only to find out later we were off a little. Even the price system itself has tampered with these definitions to further corrupt our understanding.

One further pitfall is the multitude of meanings for the same word. Many times, we have quite an array to pick from. Because of these difficulties, we need to make the effort to brush up or review a few words that will be touched on in this book. However, before I provide those definitions, I will present a short backdrop of events and the necessity for a book such as this.

Here in this book, when I speak of the price system, I am referring to the main feature of the economic plan, which unfortunately most of the world shares, even China, Iran, and Russia.[1] It is a plan that allows a small percentage of the world's population to control the whole world's economy, and they do so in their favor.

Rarely does anyone, in the main press, talk negatively about it. However, this book is devoted to pointing out a good number of the problems that the price system forces on the world. By pointing those problems out, it is easier to see the need for a better economic system.

For example, in the recent past here in America, we witnessed the fear generated by the U.S. Treasury Department and the Federal Reserve during the severe financial crisis of 2008–2009. The Treasury Department, headed by a former Goldman Sachs chairman, called for massive bank and large business bailouts. These were fearfully spun on the public through the proceedings there in Washington DC. The former head of a major corporation was running our Treasury Department at that time.

That department, which is supposed to be working for the public, was being run by a major player from the private sector; for many people, this was a conflict of interest. The conflict however was smooth over by a very accommodating president, congress, justice department, and press. Each of these entities, I hope to demonstrate, is tied heavily to the price system. This is why conflicts like these continue even to this day.

Many of us that watched those events in Washington DC, felt our stomachs turn as the troubling fragility of our system of economy was explained to us. Of course, they didn't tell us the whole truth as to how the economy works. We were given cover stories, which only represented half-truths—only what we needed to know so that they could get the money. Those half-truths were, of course, frightening enough to get the citizens behind their bailout scheme.

Consequently, great haste was generated to repair our economic wounds. Fear was used to create that haste, which left those that indirectly caused the problems in a controlling position. The measures, which they put into place to strengthen and protect the economy, were said to have done little to nothing to tackle the real problems. Some people have said that many of those so-called corrective actions have actually made things worse.

Those real problems behind the economic meltdown were left majorly unaddressed or untouched. These are the issues that were hidden behind the price system's veil. If discussed, they would have explained why our economy really began to unwind in the first place.

Here is something even scarier to consider—very few people went to jail. On top of that, some of them that did go to jail only received very light sentences. This was amazing considering the extent of the damage they caused is still painful to us today.

Trillions of dollars were lost, and heavy debts were imposed on the common people so that the economy could be fixed. Why then did so few go to jail? That question should force you to consider that perhaps, there really is a group of controllers in charge, protecting their own.

Their cover-up stories are springing leaks. Even today, bits and pieces of the truths continue to materialize as facts are exposed. Their lawyers however are clever enough to spin new stories, but even those don't line up. The principles explained in this book, concerning the price system, should help you to better understand our economic woes and just why things don't always add up.

I hope to show you that the reason our economy got into trouble is because of the price system itself. It is also the reason that little was done to fix the problems. This is because the price system needs those loopholes and many other tricks to function.

The lack of effective corrective action and the lack of truths point a finger at what I am trying to say. While the foxes control the henhouse, we may never know what really happened. This means it can all happen again, and it is likely just a matter of time. If the failing support columns in our economic structure have only been temporarily supported, should we not consider other economic options in the event of that potential future failure?

Many people believe that a major overhaul of economy and government is necessary for progress to be expected. There is no question that none of our existing leaders have the ability to change the existing economic system or government. They can't, at least head on, correct it in a major overhaul fashion.

Perhaps, the issue of the debt ceiling reflects the extent of their ineptness the best. These are the fearful words of former Michigan

Representative John Dingell in regard to a question on the federal debt ceiling:

> Obviously, on the debt ceiling, you're going to have to raise the debt ceiling. If you fail to do so, you're going to have a massive problem. Interest rates will skyrocket. The dollar will lose its privileged position as the world currency. The market will go down and we will be very, very, sorry.[2]

The price system thus has its tentacles wrapped around almost everything and almost everyone, so it seems impossible to get out from under this monster. Judging from Mr. Dingell's response, he also thought so; and I would venture that the majority of congress agrees, or will ultimately agree, each time the debt ceiling is brought up for a vote.

It also stands to reason that given the current mischief going on within the monetary system, the collapse of our economy is inevitable. It is simply a matter of time. Only a few people know when that might occur, and how hard the system will fall. I am hoping that it is several years away so that this book might be of some value to those who might want to prepare a new way forward.

I suggest here in this book that instead of wasting our time fretting over when the system will collapse, we use the time to explore our options. This is something we can do ourselves. If we let the perpetrators of this existing corrupt price system do the planning again, for their new system, then we will get more of the same.

This would be more of those same selfish ideas that are designed to fail at our expense and not theirs. However, in order for us to do some initial planning, we need to try and bring ourselves up to speed on a few concepts. We need to attempt to align our minds somewhat. Why? So that when we discuss these issues, we will be together on the basic understandings of the terms we are about to talk about.

I am about to present to you some definitions that are important for us to at least have a general idea of. These definitions will be used in our discussion of the various options we will consider in building a new economic plan. It is good to be familiar with them. You don't have to commit them to memory. Consider this a light refresher.

One goal of this book is that you have a clearer idea of what is going on in our world. Then, when our leaders explain to us why we cannot pay our bills, we will see behind their veiled attempt to mislead us again. They might coarsely say to us, "It's the economy stupid," meaning it's not their fault. The information in this book should help you to know it is more likely the stupid economy's fault. That is the price system's fault not yours.

As you will see by the definitions below, *economies* are more or less wrapped up in *governments* of one type or another. This adds more confusion to the process and an increased need for the under-standing of terms. For planning purposes, we need to have a basic consensus on the following terms. This will allow us to consider alternatives to government and economic styles.

Funny thing about definitions—they don't always line up with the ones you were taught in school. If you are confused a little by some of these definitions, don't worry because you're not alone; for our purposes here, however, they will do for a start. They are here to put us on the path to a general understanding. Many of these definition vary, depending on where or who you source or talk to. Not to worry, because getting a concrete standard is not the purpose here; just a simple awareness will suffice.

I picked the following definitions more or less at random off the Internet. You more than likely might have picked others as the sources are numerous. The point I am trying to make here is that even the diversity of sources can cause the subjects of governments and economies to become a little confusing. Which one do you choose?

Holding a conversation with someone, who unknowingly has a different meaning for the words you use, can cause frustration. Let us try to fix that a little, if possible. The following definitions should be viewed as just general definitions, not necessarily exact and not necessarily all inclusive.[3] Consider them a primer that allows us to start the discussion.

Economy

1. The system of production and distribution and consumption. (Wordnet)
2. The efficient use of resources; "economy of effort." (Wordnet)
3. Frugality in the expenditure of money or resources; "the Scots are famous for their economy." (Wordnet)
4. An act of economizing; reduction in cost; "it was a small economy to walk to work every day." (Wordnet)
5. The management of domestic affairs; the regulation and government of household matters; especially as they concern expense or disbursement; as, a careful economy. (Webster's)
6. Orderly arrangement and management of the internal affairs of a state or of any establishment kept up by production and consumption; esp., such management as directly concerns wealth; as, political economy. (Webster's)
7. The system of rules and regulations by which anything is managed; orderly system of regulation the distribution and uses of parts, conceived as the result of wise and economical adaptation in the author, whether human or divine; as, the animal or vegetable economy; the economy of a poem; the Jewish economy. (Webster's)

Well, those are basic enough for the definition of the word economy, but as I said, economies are wrapped up in various forms of government. The following terms represent most of the forms of government and a few non-governmental "ism's" that exist in the world. We may not draw from all of them here in this book, but it helps to know that so many exist.

Communism

1. A form of socialism that abolishes private ownership. (Wordnet)
2. A political theory favoring collectivism in a classless society. (Wordnet)
3. A scheme of equalizing the social conditions of life; specifically, a scheme which contemplates the abolition of inequalities in the possession of property, as by distribution all wealth equally to all, or by holding all wealth in common for the equal use and advantage of all. (Webster's)

Democracy

1. The political orientation of those who favor government by the people or by their elected representatives. (Wordnet)
2. A political system in which the supreme power lies in a body of citizens who can elect people to represent them. (Wordnet)
3. The doctrine that the numerical majority of an organized group can make decisions binding on the whole group. (Wordnet)

Despotism

1. Dominance through threat of punishment and violence. (Wordnet)
2. A form of government in which the ruler is an absolute dictator (not restricted by a constitution or laws or opposition etc.) (Wordnet)

Dictatorship

1. A form of government in which the ruler is an absolute dictator (not restricted by a constitution or laws or opposition etc.) (Wordnet)
2. The office, or the term of office, of a dictator, hence absolute power. (Webster's)

Individualism

1. Belief in the primary importance of the individual and in the virtues of self-reliance and personal independence. Acts or an act based on this belief. (Yahoo's dictionary)
2. A doctrine advocating freedom from government regulation in the pursuit of a person's economic goals. A doctrine holding that the interests of the individual should take precedence over the interests of the state or social group. (Yahoo's dictionary)

Monarchy

1. An autocracy governed by a monarch who usually inherits the authority (Wordnet)
2. A state or government in which the supreme power is lodged in the hands of a monarch. (Webster's)

Oligarchy

1. A political system governed by a few people; "one of his cardinal convictions was that Britain was not run as a democracy but as an oligarchy"; "the big cities were notoriously in the hands of the oligarchy of local businessmen". (Wordnet)

2. A form of government in which the supreme power is placed in the hands of a few persons; also, those who form the ruling few. (Webster's)

Plutocracy

1. A political system governed by the wealthy people. (Wordnet)
2. A form of government in which the supreme power is lodged in the hands of the wealthy classes; government by the rich; also, a controlling or influential class of rich men. (Webster's)

Republic

1. A political system in which the supreme power lies in a body of citizens who can elect people to represent them. (Wordnet)
2. A form of government whose head of state is not a monarch; "the head of state in a republic is usually a president". (Wordnet)

Socialism

1. A political theory advocating state ownership of industry. (Wordnet)
2. An economic system based on state ownership of capital. (Wordnet)
3. A theory or system of social reform which contemplates a complete reconstruction of society, with a more just and equitable distribution of property and labor. In popular usage, the term is often employed to indicate any lawless, revolutionary social scheme. (Webster's)

Technocracy

1. A form of government in which scientists and technical experts are in control; "technocracy was described as that society in which those who govern justify themselves by appeal to technical experts who justify themselves by appeal to scientific forms of knowledge". (Webster's)
2. Technocracy (as defined by their organization)
   1. An alternative social system.
   2. Not a political party or financial racket
   3. A technological continental design, functional governance for North America.[4]

Theocracy

1. A political unit governed by a deity (or by officials thought to be divinely guided) (Wordnet)
2. The belief in government by divine guidance. (Wordnet)

Here are two other definitions that are helpful to us:

Price System

The fundamentals of any Price System are the mechanics of exchange and distribution effected by the creation of debt claims or the exchange of property rights on the basis of commodity valuation irrespective of whether property in that system is individually or collectively owned. Hence any social system whatsoever that effects its distribution of goods and services by means of a system of trade or commerce based on commodity valuation and employing any form of debt tokens, or money, constitutes a Price System. It may be added in passing that unless it be in some very remote and primitive community, none other than Price Systems exist at the present time.[4]

Realism

When limited to this simple definition, I believe this "ism" should also be considered in any discussions of politics or economy:

1. Interest in or concern for the actual or real, as distinguished from the abstract, speculative, etc.
2. The tendency to view or represent things as they really are.

Capitalism

1. An economic system based on private ownership of capital. (Wordnet)
2. An economic system based on private ownership of the means of production. Under capitalism, individuals, companies or corporations invest in, own, and share in profits (or losses) of the entities that produce goods, distribute products or provide services. (Webster's)

These definitions give us our rough starting point as we attempt to study our problems. They can be used to help us design our new economy. In doing this, we will explore newer ideas for governments as well. The potential mixtures of these systems could provide solutions that might surprise you. There are a few interesting options to consider here.

One of our definitions was for the word technocracy.[5] That definition did not provide a detailed description of the process. So, I will attempt to add some depth to its understanding.

It is likely that many of you will not be familiar with technocracy, at all. Its structure and basic concepts intrigued me to the degree that I felt that it should be included in our discussion. We should after all explore all of our options in designing our new system.

With that said, I will present to you a scaled-down version of its concepts. I will also present some possible modifications to technocracy. Those changes I feel would be required in order to get a variation of it started, if the changes warrant the attempt.

Technocracy never took off, because in my opinion, it has a number of huge roadblocks to overcome. Even in a modified version, there will still be a number of problems to overcome. If the obstacles to getting this plan to work are that difficult, you might wonder why I am even trying to present it to you. The answer is technocracy to me represents a fairer and more just platform to build a new governmental and economic system off. At the very least, their system has some interesting ideas that we could use in our new design.

The system has several good ideas that I believe would be useful in trying to set up a new system of economics. It also allows us a view of the world that counters, or at least limits, the power of the price system. In addition, technocracy is a system that holds to a truer definition of economy.

In the current price system economy, everything is based on "buy, buy, buy" and "sell, sell, sell." Remember that our definition of economy was supposed to have something to do with frugality. Our current system seems to downplay that attribute. The price system does this, because it is based on growth through spending. Technocracy on the other hand does have that principle of frugality. It holds to a truer measure of economy.

This principle of economic frugality is extremely important in that we live in a finite world. True, we have the possibility of invention that could help us if used for the good of all. However, the process of invention, under the price system, has been far too often turned against us.

Technocracy points out that "machines" should have made everyone's lives more economically stable. However, because of the private ownership of those machines in factories, they have led to a widening class economic gap. That means there are fewer people with more, and more people with less.

Does our personal greed allow this excessiveness to happen? Perhaps, it does because we believe that we are likely to be one of those excessively rich persons. However, the odds of that happening are very much against it. Achieving excessive wealth is roughly as likely as winning the lottery. Those odds are stacked against us.

Are we betting against ourselves and allowing the rigged game to continue? After all, aren't there more poor people today than there were just a few short years ago? Is it possible that we would be a lot better off not playing their game, the price game?

Truthfully, there really are not a lot of new economic ideas out there that you haven't heard about. Technocracy however is one that is not as well-known and has not been tried. I believe it might have been thought of as communistic in nature and not given the chance to be heard.

Many of its ideas are, however, very realistic. The people involved in its planning were not necessarily politicians, but rather scientist and engineers. This is another plus for their plan; after all, who really likes politicians these days?

I think their plan requires a fresh look. This is because there are many parts of it that make perfect sense. You might want to visit their Web site and watch their old videos, which explain the plan very well, despite their age. Hopefully, they will still be available by the time this book gets published.

The real question is, why would we not explore all of our options? The definitions you read earlier pretty much cover the governmental worldviews that mankind has held up to this point in time. Many of those concepts contained individual items that would have worked well for the general citizens. However, because those ideas would not work so well for the rulers of the current economic system, they had to be nixed. When the existing system breaks down, those older stifled ideas might come to light again. If so, those ideas will be available for our review and possible use in our new system.

I believe that a review of the various programs that worked, even a little bit, would be a good starting point for the United States or any country that wants to improve. It may be possible and beneficial to use pieces from a few of these systems of government to create a new hybrid system.

This hybrid system could work if safeguards were put into place. Those safeguards are required so that those systems of government could not be turned against the general citizen and then in favor of a few aggressive evil doers.

Changes to the systems of money, politics, justice, and government will all have to be made. This is required to protect the general citizen from those that would want to rule from their existing pedestals. Without those reforms, we would just be setting up a system of corruptions like the one we already have.

Now, let us proceed to a better understanding of the word technocracy. Basically, technocracy is presented as an alternative social system. It would, in its pure form, do away with the current money system completely. Their ideas, as I understand them, would take us out of the control of the international central banking system.

Technocracy explains that the current money system uses what is called the price system to operate. That system allows for a great number of corruptions to enter into its process. The price system, in technocracy's definition, is any social system that exchanges goods and services by trade or commerce based on commodity evaluation and then uses debt tokens or money to trade. This kind of system requires two conditions to function—first, goods and services must have "scarcity," and second, it must have "growth or expansion" to work.

Today, we have machines that can produce items so efficiently that the price of things should be very inexpensive; but they are not. The private ownership of these machines allows individuals to use the two conditions listed above to unfairly improve their position over everyone else. At times, these individuals will create scarcity to influence the price. They can do this in two ways—either by reducing the supply, that is, by cutting production, or by adding more customers. Cutting production is not the preferred method as this is generally only employed in hard times, where they have pushed the system to far.

With private ownership of machines, growth or expansion has to occur or the price system will not work for them. However, this leads to all sorts of ill effects for the general citizen and for the resources of the world. When populations don't grow fast enough, then food or products must be destroyed or production curtailed in order to bring up the price. Conversely, if populations grow too much, then resources are depleted. Either way, the world's resources

suffer. One other method employed by private producers is to manufacture products that have a limited life so that people will buy the
product more often.

To enable and encourage citizens to purchase their things, a
banking system to support credit was established. The bank system
enabled the price system to mask many of its shortcomings and in so
doing flourish. In such a system, money or debt is its lifeblood, and
new debt must always be created to allow it to survive and validate
the existing debt. This is how the system extends its life cycle. The
cycle appears to be nearing its end. When it does, it will be time for
us to face the music, and it is a song we don't want to hear. However,
for the controllers, well they will be eager to start the whole process
all over again, given the chance.

Their system has put a huge strain on the planet. Just in the
last two hundred years, we have witnessed man's ability to change
the landscape of the planet in major ways. For one, we witnessed
"the Dust Bowl" out West; before that, we saw the loss of the fur
trade, the depletion of the buffalo, and the deforesting of parts of
California, Michigan, and other states. More recently, the strip mining projects for coal in the West have seen whole areas turned into
giant pits. Mining projects in the East have caused whole mountain-
tops to be removed and leveled. There are so many of these events
that have happened that the face of our landscapes or vistas has been
changed in alarming ways, perhaps even epic ways.

The noticeable planet-wide changes involving the melting of
the glaciers may very well be caused in part by the price system's
methods.[6] Those melting glaciers, after all, do help to substantiate
the possibility of climate change occurring. Many scientists agree
that the science required to answer this question conclusively will
take more time. Still, more scientists agree that for whatever reason,
climate change appears to be real. If it is, isn't it possible that the price
system's methods have helped to bring it on?

I tend to look at the climate change problem this way. Almost
everyone has had occasion to say, "Oh, what a small world we live
in," for one reason or another. It might be that you were vacationing
in Africa, Asia, Australia, or Europe and you ran into someone from

your home area; or it might be that you realize that you can actually travel to any place on earth by plane within a few hours.

I like to think of climate problem this way, *the diameter of the earth is only 8,000 miles.*[7] That really is not a big number. Our travels around the world today take place in the matter of hours instead of months. Perhaps, the earth really is a small place after all.

Just what are the consequences of over seven billion people digging, building, and moving around on the earth? We cannot forget that we are constantly growing food, building roads, mining, foresting, and doing hundreds of other things as well. These things have effects; to think otherwise is, in my opinion, denial. The size of our fishbowl is limited. If we do not accept that, then we deserve our fate.

What would technocracy do different? By having the machines owned and operated by the public, along with a few other changes, the public can bring about full employment. Technocracy would also abolish "the price system" as we know it. For our labor in the public sector, we would receive what they call energy certificates, instead of money. These certificates would be divided between the citizens.

The certificates don't have value like money, but are only a measuring system. They are issued in each individual's name and cannot be sold or transferred to other people. The certificates being issued in each person's name would prevent other people from wanting to steal your certificates, because they couldn't use them anyway. Crime would go down for this reason alone. What's more, they cancel out or expire if not used in a certain time frame. These certificates would be used to produce and purchase the basic needs of our lives.

The technocracy plan, as I understand it, is set up to operate regionally; and the first area they had mapped out on the globe was called the North American technocracy.[8] All the resources required to have a functioning society are contained in the territory that they define. Those resources would be shared more equally among the people of the nations involved.

Their plan would eliminate the private ownership of any of the primary resources. Technocracy's division of resources makes more sense in that we would as a whole have to decide how we want to prolong the life of the various resources that exist. Private operations all too often deplete the resources wastefully just so that they can gain as much profit as possible. They are not as interested in the big picture; that is not their primary concern.

The technocracy plan is extensively planned out, and there is a multitude of literature on it. I confess I am not an authority on this plan, nor am I their spokesman. I am just giving you my interpretation of some of the ideas as I understood them. Why? This is because I have observed that there are a number of good ideas there that we should study for incorporation into whatever system we built. Technocracy therefore might be a good starting point to build off.

Unfortunately, as with any system, this system has some obstacles that might hamper its implementation. The most obvious is that countries, such as Canada, Mexico, and others, would first have to agree to join the system. It is hard enough getting the people of the United States to agree on things. To try and get other countries to agree would likely be even harder. However, we really do not know what they would do if their economic conditions fade to zero in a worldwide price system collapse; they may be willing to try it.

Even if international agreements cannot be made, I still believe that some of the ideas of technocracy could be applied to our new economic system here in the United States. This system might be, in this case, a true hybrid. It would have capitalism, democracy, individualism, realism, socialism, technocracy, and perhaps even the ideas of a republic as well.

If your back has reared up and your blood has started to boil at the suggestion that we employ socialism, don't worry; like me, you have been trained well. Before you throw down the book and storm off, consider this—our American system already employs socialism and has almost from the time of its founding. The media doesn't like to point these things out.

It is true that not all of the aspects of socialism here in the United States have been good. For example, its use in our educational system has been taken to excess or extremes. It worked a lot better up until the central government jumped in. In addition, while there are problems with the military, this use of socialism has generally worked well. Other aspects of socialism are found in our police and fire departments and in our government operations themselves. When not taken to extremes, they have also worked well, only failing when they are taken over by price system manipulators.

Wouldn't you say that bailing out private business with tax payer dollars is a socialistic action? Tax payers bailing out the very price system that says, "Socialism is evil"; go figure. These examples of socialism in America don't get much attention.

Our training has been that we should privatize everything and that socialism is bad. This attitude would put the price system fully in charge and us fully at its mercy. I think you can see that just as socialism can be bad, it can also have good qualities. We should not throw the socialist baby out with the water, no matter how much training we have had to do just that.

A Brief Description of the Use of Democracy and Socialism in Our Plan

Under our new plan, the major resources would be owned by everyone equally. If the common citizens are to be treated fairly, private industry should not be allowed to control these things. They would surely take our government back into the price system.

Our ownership however would likely use a republic form of the democratic process to establish the distribution of these resources. Income levels, or limits, would be set for the various trades and professions and then voted on. These levels of aspiration provide a means to keep the work ethic part of the American dream alive.

Those that work can get rewarded in proportion to their effort and developed skill. The major resources that we vote on might include all mineral, oil, water, and land rights. This means that mining operations, freshwater sources, lumber, and major food operations would be owned and operated by the public. That seemingly appears to be a major culture shock for private industries; but perhaps, it would not be that bad. There are things that can be done to minimize the change and lessen the impact on them.

Private land ownership or perhaps stewardship would likely be restricted somewhat under our new plan. This is necessary so that excesses, which can cause corruptions in the new system, can be avoided. There may be provisions set up for some sort of grandfathered stewardship clause. This might be done on behalf of some family farms. Ideas like this would have to be considered. Those excessive lands that were secured in there abundance by citizens who capitalized off the old price system will have to be returned to the public to be used appropriately.

Yes, this is a form of nationalization. It worked for Saudi Arabia; it could work for us, the common citizens, as well. However, in Saudi Arabia, the royal families retained most of the nation's wealth; we don't want that here.

Vacant lands might be used as national, local, or state parks or used for resources for the general public. We would rely more on scientists to help govern us and much less on politicians, if at all. Rules to regulate the ownership or stewardship of land would have to be flexible enough to support the idea of an American dream. Since many people have a concept of achieving the American dream, there should be some latitude here in their ability to acquire land use, within reasonable limits.

Those that work hard, physically or mentally, and prove their worth should have an opportunity to acquire land. Just how much land can be acquired is something we have to vote on. I would suggest no more than perhaps fifty or a hundred acres for families that excel to the top levels in the new system.

However, without knowing our full design yet, it is hard to determine what is possible. I really only know that the greater the excess, the greater the potential for corruptions. Still, the American dream would not be possible unless some opportunity exists. Some of us will have to scale back our excessive dreams to more reasonable levels.

Now, remember that the old price system often encouraged huge population growth. This was needed in order to make their system of debt work. Our new system will be asking people to be more responsible.

They will be asked to think about the resources that are available and not deplete them rapidly. One way to not use up the resources to quickly is to avoid having excessive populations. This can be done rather simply by just us controlling our own lives, that is, by controlling ourselves.

It should be obvious that in any national economic system, the total resources available will always be limited. We will have to be careful to monitor our immigration limits so that our American dreams actually have a chance at coming true for future generations as well. Naturally, we don't want to deplete the available resources too quickly or those future generations will suffer. If our scientists can find new ways to create new resources for us, then we will be able to expand immigration, if we so desire.

In the same vein, it will be our responsibility as citizens to limit our family sizes to a reasonable amount. Remember that we have all been conditioned to dislike control over our personal lives in respect to the number of children we have. This is because the old price system, again, encouraged large families. This is how they were able to create low-wage labor.

Minimum-wage labor, under the price system, prospers businesses, but not the society as a whole. Now, under our new system, we will be asking people to drop hundreds of years of constant teaching that we should be able to have as many children as we like. Anyone who tells you otherwise is evil, right?

What is more evil, a system that produces excessive people, who then live in squalor, crime, and abuse, or a system that curbs excessive population and works to reduce those very same ills? Wages less than a living wage, by the way, cause people to become desperate to the point that they can be easily manipulated into doing things they would not have otherwise done—shameful things.

The price system's low-wage structure, imposed on the growing populations, causes atrocities that are contemptible. Their system brings about things like organized crime, drug lords, the sex trade, and child pornography. These are all products of desperate people having to live by any means necessary. Desperate because there are millions of people just like them, poor and out of work in the price system.

The price system fuels these bad behaviors. Its design creates the environment for these things to more likely occur. Their design allows excessive money to be funneled up to those at the top of the hierarchy.

Money in this system becomes very, very, important. It is far too often even more important than the misfortunes of others. Sadly, there is little concern at the top for the terrible by-products that "their" system creates. It cannot be stressed enough that the price system by its design promotes these terrible behaviors. They justify their system through their animal attitudes that only the strong should survive and "might makes right." One other justification that I have heard a lot from them is, "Who says the world has to be fair?"

I know it will be hard to rid ourselves of all of the negative price system brainwashing that we have been exposed to. However, to make a new system work, we will have to try. We should not continue to live for today with little regard for tomorrow.

Let's face it—none of us knows exactly when this world will end. The Bible tells us that when it comes, it will come as a thief in the night. No one knows the time. It may be thousands of years from now, even though the signs might suggest otherwise.

I believe it is fair, to those who might live in the future, for us to consider their needs. To this end, we will have to manage our population with concern for the amount of resources that will exist for them. Limits are necessary until our science can advance resources. In any event, it is generally the best policy to plan for all contingencies. Planning for the future is therefore a prudent idea. If you ever inherited anything, you should understand the wisdom in this.

Our science has to find a way for the plants and animals on the earth to have nourishment, in the habitats that they will need as well. Our forethought will be greatly appreciated by future generations. Their world will be improved based on the self-restraints that we place on ourselves today.

Our efforts should work toward finding a way so that earth's animals and plants will be around for future generations to take pleasure in. Do we really want to continue to be selfish and deplete the earth of its inhabitants and resources and possibly destroy the planet in so doing?

Resources, whether found or created, are necessary to provide the work that we all need, now and in the future. If we use the resources that we have too quickly or fail to create new resources, the future will suffer. What we build for them today will determine their fate. We want them to have lifestyles that would allow them to live full healthy and rewarding lives.

Our science could open up a means to support a larger population. However, we need to have a holistic plan in hand before we push for larger populations. Today, we know that we can produce the food required to support a larger population, but at what cost? Food is only one resource.

If we exist just to eat, without all those other things that are important to happiness, what good will we really be doing? In the future, as it sometimes has in the past, our science can make life better for all of us. For now, we have to be both patient and austere. This is required to heal ourselves from the devastating effects that the price system has put us through.

There is a need to agree on just what is a proper family size. This might be three children, although I really am not sure. This seems calloused, but after the next economic meltdown, it may be necessary; at least for a while. Besides, when people want more than three children, they might be allowed to adopt as it is also calloused to ignore orphaned children who need our help.

Once our new system is up and running, efforts will be made to employ every able bodied-person. That is part of the American dream—to have an opportunity for work. Work then allows us to pursue our happiness. Thus, happiness requires some effort or some work on our part. The extent of this happiness, as noted above, hinges of our available resources. Those resources are critical to providing work. You see how things tie together?

Doing away with the current central banking system puts controls on a number of corruptions. Further, the use of energy certificates in lieu of money for the basic resources we purchase will solve still more problems. Those problems, which the current pricing system created, are embodied in the four dynasties.

These dynasties are the political, financial, education, and religious dynasties. Examples of some of the problems within these dynasties are excessive taxes, excessive unemployment, banking or financial fraud, lower academic scores, and religious deceptions. These are only a few examples. Just how our new system should work to help cure these problems will be addressed further on.

In an amended technocracy plan, we could use certificates to purchase our basic food, clothing, and shelter requirements. The certificates are given to everyone based on their work status or handicap status. Jobs will be available for every able-bodied person.

Those unable to work or chose not to work will also receive certificates. However, their distribution will be at rates determined by the situation. This will eliminate the old welfare system. Homelessness doesn't have to exist because certificates will provide basic housing and all other basic needs. In addition, these certificates would work to reduce the criminal acts of steeling, illegal drugs, illicit sex, and other potential painful human experiences.

The issuing of certificates will be based on the success of our capitalist enterprises. With full employment, these work opportunities will be much less stressful. This is because work hours and even work days would be reduced.

Full employment works for us because we, the public, own the machines and we can run the machines around the clock to create the necessities of life. We can employ the efficiencies of scale to provide food, clothing, and shelter for everyone in our nation. However, we only would provide the basic needs, not all of the bells and whistles that a person might want.

In limiting the socialism to just the basic needs, we leave room for individual capitalism to enhance the lifestyles of those who seek more. I believe most of us will want to seek more, and that is a good thing. This provides an expanded path to the American dream for more and more people.

Better yet, these ideas work to decrease the ability of those deviant individuals from the price system who have been exploiting the unfortunate in our population. This is because now, those unfortunate citizens will at the very least have their basic needs covered. They will be in a better position to refrain from being encouraged to perform deviant behaviors in order to make ends meet.

Under the price system, you do not always have to be jobless or desperate to be exploited. Shaving economic resources off a larger working labor pool is also a price system tactic. For example, when a CEO reduces wages by a dollar a day from each of his or her employees and then keeps it for himself or herself, that CEO could end up with a substantial raise.

The manipulation of people in this way should not be considered normal. Some might say it is justified because managers have the authority to do that. However, that doesn't make it right, fair, or even honest.

Using your brain to take advantage of others excessively is really just an animalistic tendency. The price system allows this. If we realize this, then we can start acting like humans instead of pretending to be humans.

Technocracy might provide us some of the ways to improve the world. In doing so, it might also improve our own personal lives. Should animal behavior rule the world or should a system of honest and humane reasoning rule?

A Brief Description of the Use of Capitalism in This Alternative Plan

In our new system, there will be a need for a barter system, so this leaves the door open for individual capitalism to continue. This is not necessarily a bad thing, as capitalism with controls is really a great idea. It is only when the controls are removed and it is allowed to go to its extremes that it is bad.

History has given us ways to control these extremes; we just need to reimpose similar rules and build in safeguard so that they cannot be removed. I agree this is easier said than done, but we have to try again. Safeguards, such as limits on the amounts of land we can own, the size of the businesses we can own, and the size of the incomes we can achieve, should be implemented.

With those things implemented, we should be able to allow a national currency based on gold and silver or other tangibles to be brought back into use. This currency would be owned and produced by the public, not a private company. Those limits of land, business, and income would be large enough so as to be accepted by the majority of the population. However, those limits should not be large enough to foster corruptions as the price system does.

A Brief Description of the Individual as He or She Relates to the Plan

Each of us has to respect ourselves enough to respect others. Said another way, before you can love your neighbor, you have to be able to love or at least like yourself. Many of our parents taught us that you should love yourself and then your neighbor the same as yourself. This is represented in the golden rule—do on to others as you would have them do to you.

When we love each other, then helping one another should follow. Helping each other thus becomes just simple teamwork. Under our new plan, there exists a means for us to employ this teamwork. We will work together, as a team, to produce the various major life support items we use. Now, along with this increased teamwork come several benefits.

It provides a greater opportunity for individualism to flourish at least when compared to the price system. Our new plan should allow for a reduced work day, work week, and even a means to retire much earlier in life than under the price system. Further, instead of working for the *man* who owns the business, you will be a part owner of the business.

Controls put on both socialism and capitalism should work to increase the opportunities for individualism to occur. However, even individualism can be bad if taken to extreme, so each discipline should work to control each other so that a balance can be set.

Our new plan should allow everyone to have a lot more free time. This free time could be used to pursue our individual talents. Our individualism however has to be restrained so that we respect the rights of others. Our restraint will thus protect their individualism and in so doing fold back to mutually give us respect. This is a loop we should try to perpetuate.

If we hold this respect, then we will think about those of us who have not been born yet. I believe that at least 90% of us are able to do this. There are a few who really don't care—they don't care about you and your children, and regretfully, they don't even care about their own children. This seems like a harsh charge to make, but I believe that the next few chapters will help to confirm that possibility.

The Challenges of a Multistyled Plan

Many of the ideas contained in technocracy provide hope that a countersystem to the price system might be possible. Technocracy is an old idea that has been around for decades, but has never been tried. Again, I am not an expert on its methods; however, I do not believe we could use this plan without considerable changes.

However, a great many parts of it make perfect sense. As with any social system, it has things that we will not all agree with; we should understand that before we start. This should not deter us and cause us to sit idle. As stated before, nothing is perfect.

I believe that a new multistyled plan could be implemented. It would incorporate ideas from various plans such as socialism, capitalism, individualism, and more. The ideas we choose should be able to coexist in a hybrid system.

I believe that if there is a will, there is a way. Perhaps once our plan is up and running, the other nations would see the value in it and choose to participate. This however is jumping ahead a little too far. We first need to see if technocracy could act as the platform to build our new system on.

In going through some of the material on technocracy, I got an unsettling impression. This plan, in its efforts to remove the human corruptions of mankind, might go too far and try to remove our humanity. I want to stress the word might here, because I again am not an expert on that discipline.

The impression I received might be an unfair assessment, but if it turns out to be a problem, our job is to tone down the excesses it brings. It seems every system that man comes up with has excesses that need to be controlled. With caution in mind, technocracy is a plan that is well-worth investigating. We need to find a way to avoid any extremes it might contain; we need moderation.

The next chapter will deal with some of the shortfalls of our existing U. S. economy. We need to study those shortfalls so that we can plan corrective measures. If we understand how the price system worked to create certain problems, we will be more apt to build in safeguards to protect ourselves.

CHAPTER 2

How Our Economy Is Negatively Affected by the Price System

If you are looking for trouble, it is usually not hard to find. Likewise, if you are not looking for it, you are less likely to find it. Most of us are not looking for trouble, so we tend to give people a fair amount of grace. This may be the reason that we rarely stop to question the merits of the economic system that our leaders have chosen for us. Instead, we grant them our grace and trust in them to do the right thing.

Anyway, why should we question a system that has been the world's economic captain for hundreds of years now? Sure, this captain has run us a ground a few times, but so what? Besides, changing over to a different system really feels like that would be a mutiny. Does anyone really like change anyway? It is just easier to forgive and forget gracefully; at least, this is what most of us tend to believe.

However, the ever-increasing economic divide between the rich and the poor has awakened concerns about our economy. There are deep concerns about the fairness that our current system affords to the bulk of the population. The awesome difference in wages between citizens in our workforce is astounding.

It seems some people truly believe that they are worth thousands of times more than other hardworking human beings. That being said, our economic system says that there is nothing wrong with this attitude. It's fair to exalt yourself under the systems rules, that is, if you can. Most of us are comfortable with this attitude, and we just accept it; after all, we have been attached to this system since birth.

You might, however, not feel so attached to the system once you understand its numerous corruptions are mostly built-in on purpose. These built-in corruptions are there to support those people who have feelings of grandeur. In the end, these corruptions give a select set of people a great advantage over almost everyone else.

Worse yet, those taking part in these corruptions do not feel remorse; rather, they are proud of themselves. They hide under the disguise of shrewd aggressive businessmen who delightfully promote the rule of "do on to others before they do it to you." This seems to be their typical view on the price systems rules. Shamefully, most of us admire them because of their success. What is wrong with us?

From what you have read so far, I hope you agree that it is time to consider, at the very least, a review of our economic system. There really is a need to look more closely at the money system that we think so highly of. We need to look at it from a different perspective. If we look at our monetary system through the eyes of a criminal, we might gain some insight.

If you and I were criminals, what kind of an economic system would we want to design? Let's suppose we have a lot of time to build it. We would design it so that we could slowly gain as much advantage over as many people as we could, without drawing attention. It has to be a superior con capable of reaching all areas of daily life. These thoughts lead us to a system based on money as we can then create our second greatest tool, debt.

We would certainly hype it as the best economic system in the world. Our marketing department would convince everyone that there is no other way, but ours. This would be done by having our chosen and trusted political leaders present it, as if it is truly the only genuine and credible system worth looking at. We of course have to convince everyone we can that it is the best system possible.

We need to present it as fair and honest to all. Hopefully, they will not notice that those of us in charge of the money have most of it. Further, if we control the legal process, then how could anyone doubt us? This should convince anyone that our system is on the up and up; after all, we would be the law. The law makes it right, wouldn't you agree? We are counting on that.

Now, we, as the criminal masterminds that we are, choose most of the leaders. We do our best to choose bankers, lawyers, judges, senators, presidents, and everyone we can who think like us. This way, we can be assured that they will follow our orders. They will see things the way we want them to or we will do whatever we can to prevent them from getting those leadership roles.

If we can con the leaders we chose into accepting our system as fair and honest, this is all the better. Even if they just go along with us and at least not question it, they will push our hidden agendas for us. From our point of view, it's an even better con if they go along without questioning too much. We can arrange this by making sure the system pays them a handsome return for their loyalty to it and their lack of scrutiny.

We can also cut in the necessary players that have the means to disrupt the system by exposing its flaws. Key players, like the media, can really be an asset to our cause. If reports of criminal actions on our part are minimized, redirected, or not reported at all, then most people will not know what is truly going on. We can do this by using our simple axiom—when you steal, steal enough to pay off everyone you need to. This isn't a problem because we are going to steal from everyone.

We can also weaken the whistle-blower laws so that honest people will not want to come forward and report our criminal behavior. People pretty much will stop looking, after a while, at our system, because time tends to add credibility to established policies. Further, if we put enough roadblocks in the way to fixing things, those that know there are problems get tired banging their heads against the wall.

In addition, they will more easily give up if they assume their "trusted" leaders will be taking over the fight for them. We will spend the money, if necessary, to convince the general public that their leaders are on their side. However, most of those leaders will answer to us, even if they don't realize it. The general public typically will not question their so-called leaders; we count on their grace. In fact, if we tie our system to everyone's lives in a patriotic way, we will guarantee their support.

Having our own people in the right places allows us easy access to extort other people's money. The design of our money or price system will provide us the capability of stealing money from people, directly from their bank accounts, without them suspecting it. For this, we only need to control the means to lower interest rates on their savings account. We can also raise loan interest rates. Our employees at the Federal Reserve give us that capability.

What if we could steal money right out of people's wallets, so to speak, without them knowing? We do this by our control of inflation. We simply have them pay higher prices for the same goods and services. When we do this, we explain away those higher prices to shortages of supply.

We will have more control over these shortages than they will suspect. If we are smart, we will only charge what the market will bear; and people can bear a lot. Of course, when people complain, we can justify our raids on their money by telling them we are trying to control inflation or help others who are less fortunate. We might also blame it on the weather, the wars we instigate, or whatever fits our purpose.

By wrapping all of our activities up in this price system, which is based on supply and demand, then we would have full control. We merely have to cut our production or increase it when it is advantageous to us. This can be done in many ways. Incidentally, some of those ways we do not even have to manipulate ourselves; we let Mother Nature do that for us. By encouraging wars and the migrations of populations, we can create growth. Through those same encouragements, we can also create shortages.

For us criminals, this system of ours is indeed a sweet system. We will encourage millions of small businesses to operate under our rules without them knowing what we are. It really works to our favor, because then we can hide quite well. The price system is the perfect vehicle for crimes of all sorts. Somehow, as criminals, we just need to keep it going as long as we can and hope that the people don't figure this out.

The only bad thing is that we criminals do get greedy; a system based on money is prone to this. Some of us might get too bold and take nearly everything; if that were to happen, our sweet system could fall apart. However, even if this happens, that unsuspecting public is likely to let us start up the same con all over again. Let's hope that the targets of our scheme don't wake up and start looking into things.

These few activities, which were just mentioned above, are just the tip of a giant iceberg of corruptions that the price system allows. Most of them we actually know about. Oddly enough, we accept them as something we just have to put up with. Perhaps because things have always been done this way, we see many of those actions as being legitimate or at least fair. It is all proper, especially if you have a suit on; somehow, this makes it more justified. Speaking of suits, I would like to take an even closer look at governments, as none of this would be possible without the support of our governments.

We are severely impacted through our government's use of the price system. Not only our nation but also the nations of the world have been witnessing the destruction of humanity, by a huge system of usury. No matter what the national system is, the people of the world have all been tainted by the price system. Be it communism, socialism, or capitalism, the price system has crept in to cause economic and moral failures.

These government's moral failures all seem to be generated through their economies, I might add corrupt economies. It would be nice to stop repeating the same mistakes over and over again, if that is possible. We are long overdue to find a new form of economics and a new form of government that works to represent the bulk of the citizens much more fairly.

If possible, we need to wean ourselves off the old price system. It is time to improve our economic and governmental systems. When we do, many more of us will have a greater chance of succeeding in an honest fashion.

Hopefully, we, as noncriminal common citizens, will design much more balance in our systems. These would be systems that would provide more justice and equality for us. This will only be possible if we do not "design in" weaknesses to be exploited by the criminally minded minority.

In the past, we have always been steered into certain kinds of fixes for the problems we have with the price system. We are told that they, these fixes, worked well before, at least at some point in our history. We have had some short-lived successes, but as noted above, corruptions always seem to find their way back in. Those fixes always seem to allow the old ways to return. Still, we all too often feel that if we return to those suggested ideas, we can restore our economic health.

In reality, this hopeful thinking has, more often than not, only set us up to repeat the same up and down economic cycles again and again. The main reason for this is that we continually allow corrupt people to reinstitute the same price system pitfalls again and again. If we decide to reuse old ideas, we should understand that generally, those governmental regulations will contain purposely built-in failures.

If we are truthful to ourselves, we will admit that we don't currently live under a single form of government or economic system anyway. You might think that we live under capitalism. However, we have morphed into a mixture of capitalism, oligarchy, socialism, theocracy, dictatorship, democracy, communism, and a republic—all at once and each to various degrees. Of course, we are told that we have capitalism, but it looks more like corporatism with a good case of oligarchy. Oh, that's a new definition for us - "corporatism": The Oxford Dictionary defines it as - "the control of a state or organization by large interest groups."

There have been times when we have witnessed mild forms of dictatorships. One example here is when most of the nation did not want our military to go into Iraq, but we went anyway. This was mostly at the behest of an executive office gone wild, surrounding the tragic 911 event. By 2015, our government had already spent more than 1.5 trillion dollars on Iraq; and those costs are still growing. We, common citizens, have very little to show for such a great expense; however, globalists have made excessive gains.

In addition to the above expense, our government spent about 10 billion dollars a month in Afghanistan, well into 2014. Costs for Afghanistan still continue, even to this day, as we still maintain troops there. Again, globalists have gained, but how much better off is the common citizen from this activity? How much more in debt are we?

We now have more veterans that are homeless, and we are less able to help them, because of that huge debt we have. We no longer have legitimate money to spend on that. That is because a great deal of our taxes go into paying the interest on the debt we owe. Yes, we could try to borrow it and add it to the existing debt or we could just print it; but that isn't really legitimate.

On the other side of our problem here, who is the recipient of the interest on that debt we owe? If you guessed that it's that small percentage group I spoke about earlier, you are correct. That group champions globalism and runs the price system. There should be no wonder why they have so greatly benefited from all of this.

After the housing bubble burst and the economy broke in 2008, once again, certain banks and large corporations benefited. Biting the hand that fed them, which was us, they gave themselves bonuses in the aftermath of our bailouts. They shored up their bank vaults and bolstered their company's profits via the use of those bailouts and then gave themselves raises.

Before, during, and after the 2008 economic bailout, those banks did not press for any real financial control measures to be placed on them. *They* didn't want any controls at all. The measures, which were imposed, did not go far enough to protect us.

During the Trump administration, controls were reduced again. It seems those really in charge are looking forward to having it all happen again. The saying, easy come easy go, does have merit here, especially since it is your hard work, represented in the form of money, that they are so loose with.

All of these things should have raised a flag in our minds to consider the need for a new system. That new system should be one that serves more than just 10% of the people. Do we really want a system that puts us all in debt and our children as well? We are slaves to debt. We have to work to pay that off, and our leaders don't seem to want to reduce our burden.

Our leaders would however tell us that socialism not capitalism puts burdens on its people. The truth is that both "ism" here, as we have seen, are capable of taking advantage of their citizens. Is there a way to mediate the effects of both "ism" on us?

Perhaps, you didn't realize it, but we already have some forms of socialism here in the United States. Take, for example, our Medicare system; don't we all pay into it while we work? This is a socialistic concept.

Incidentally, the price system doesn't like that socialistic idea. They want more control over Medicare. There is money to be made there for that select group, of course at our expense.

Medicare consequently gets a lot of negative advertising from the price system leaders. It is constantly blasted as a socialistic entitlement that should be cut or eliminated. However, there is not as much written about the tax breaks to corporations and loopholes for wealthy citizens at the expense of the common citizens.

Those corporate and privatized entitlements are even worse of an idea as they really are a form of communism. There is not much talk of that in the media. The media would avoid at all cost calling those corporate payouts entitlements. Those in charge of the price system wouldn't like that, so the press conveniently ignores those suggestions.

Socialism can be misused, so care has to be taken. For example, both our departments of defense and education were also designed as socialistic in nature. Today, both of these departments have been pushed into sharing some of the traits of communism. They are no longer as socialistic as they used to be when they were originally established.

From the vantage point of the common citizen, for those who care to look, our current form of government is even walking toward communism. When only a few people make determinations as to which banks, businesses, or organizations get bail outs or tax breaks, we can see communism's evil reflection. When national leaders are chosen from banks, businesses, or organizations that ultimately received bailouts, we should be concerned.

Here are some additional concerns. It is a concern when fewer and fewer people set the curriculum for our educational system. It is a concern when our governments set our labor standards up on an international level so as to favor big business. It is a concern when our government makes trade agreements that give up our national sovereignty.

Perhaps, the biggest concerns lay with our military contracts. It is a concern when our executive and legislative branches are not given full access to some defense programs. While the need to know rules should be followed here, those same rules allow for corruptions beyond reason.

Programs that are able to hide costs in the name of national defense allow for private companies to skim off profits. The paper trail for billions of dollars each year often goes unaccounted for. Unaccounted for, that is, in any real professional manor.

So much money has been lost that it really is unbelievable. The Pentagon has not been able to account for trillions of dollars that were given to them and their skill at tracking their expenses is still a cause for concern. Their dark projects have the potential to hide direct theft schemes, and this is only part of the problem.

Certain military complexes will not even allow our president to tour their facilities. I get the need to know theory, but isn't there a need to know that the money is being spent wisely? Somehow, someone needs to check the checkers. This is necessary if there is ever going to be a valid verification process.

The current highly restricted oversight protocol appears to be ripe with the potential for a bottomless pit of corruptions to take place. Dark money caught in a black hole can easily disappear over this event horizon. Why? This is because all of the money cannot be fully audited. We should be asking serious questions. Just who really does have control—the government, the military industrial complex, or a shadow system? If the price system did not have any involvement here, I would of course feel more comfortable, but that is not the case.

The Federal Reserve's activities are also cloaked in secrecy; and again, they conveniently, albeit legitimately, claim that this is for our economic security. That legitimate claim is an awful conundrum for us, for because of it, the Federal Reserve has never been fully audited, ever. Do you really think they aren't doing any mischief behind their closed doors?

One only needs to note that the 2008 economic disaster occurred largely under the watchful eye and control of the banks themselves, who later claimed that they didn't see that coming. Banks, as you know, make up the Federal Reserve; so, it seems, the bailout was a foregone conclusion. Their mischief was done right out in the open, in full view of the Federal Reserve authorities. Strangely, there still has been no full audit of the Federal Reserve.

It is obvious that our leaders also do not question the worldview that we have all been taught. This view was developed by those in charge of the price system. Our leaders, in general, don't question it, because, more often than not, they are closer to these corruptions than they care to admit. They accept that there is a higher power that rules from a distance and wishes to remain unseen. For them, that higher power is not God, but those "controllers" that we have been talking about.

I have presented a rather evil face for the price system. In actuality, the price system has millions of evil faces, too numerous to pinpoint one specific head. Yet their huge numbers work in unity. Their uniform methods of shared but hidden operations tie them together for one purpose—greed. However, even this medusa-like group could be conquered if you had the resources of the National Security Agency (NSA) on your side.

Unfortunately, even the NSA, like all of us, seems tied on a personal level into the price system. Remember that criminal network I talked about earlier? If you were a criminal, you would have a definite advantage if you had control over the NSA. Those top officials there are in positions of knowing who the players really are, that is, if they are as good at their job as we believe they are.

If the NSA were controlled by criminal elements, they most likely would never give up their patrons. This is because the patrons would already know who they can trust. In the NSA's defense, nearly all of their members would likely be die-hard believers in the price system, because they are taught to be. Their loyalty to the system has to be even greater than ours or they would not be accepted into the agency. That loyalty would likely prevent them from investigating that "dark side angle" as that would be unpatriotic. I could be wrong here; however, isn't it strange that many seemingly obvious wrongdoings are never fully explored in Washington DC?

At this point, I wouldn't blame you if you're thinking the following. This sounds preposterous it's too much cloak and dagger to be real. True, why should you believe me, after all you know nothing about me? I could be crazy. However, what if a U.S. president also made reference to these controllers I speak of?

In fact, two U.S. presidents, Eisenhower and Kennedy, made reference to these behind-the-scene powers. Eisenhower referred to them as the military-industrial complex.[1] Kennedy also was clearly talking about the same organization in his speech to the press when he described their powers and activities, which were well beyond legal limits.[2] For all intents and purposes, here in this book, this same organization is both behind and part of the price system we use today. The behind-the-scene players here have helped to shape our current worldview in support of the price system.

I have been calling those who are trying to control us "controllers." They have also been called the military industrial complex. Some people call them the central bankers and their cohorts.

Remember that while they only represent a small percentage of our population, nevertheless, there are millions of these people, and they fit into a great number of occupations. We cannot point a finger at only one group. To simplify things here, I will try to limit myself to these names mentioned above when I refer to those basic overlords or controllers. There are of course a number of other names that encompass the gist of this organization. People using those names are generally written off as quacks by the mainstream press.

The point of all of the above is to point out that those controllers have arranged to give us the worldview that most of us have bought into. It is a view that benefits their agenda. It is a story that benefits them royally, but not so much anyone outside of their circle.

For now, however, let's go back to our new plan. If we decide to continue using old ideas, like socialism and capitalism, we need to consider being more honest about it and combining them for balance and control. Our control can be aided by setting limits. We don't want socialism or capitalism to get out of control as both can be devastating. When out of control, each of them seems to end up in the hands of a small elite group of controllers. We need to avoid that.

Most importantly, we need to change our worldview away from the current one, which was set by those price system leaders. If we wake up to see the world as it really is, we should be able to vote much more wisely on the final plan. Now, being awaken means that those price system controllers will not be able to sell us their old plan again. This means that we would have a better chance of gaining control over our own lives.

One could argue that the United States had at one time the rudiments of a balanced hybrid system of both capitalism and socialism within the republic. The balance, though fragile, actually helped to extend its longevity. Over time, the balance was upset several times. Typically, this happened when the capitalism side got out of control so much that they wanted nearly everything to be privatized.

When excessive privatization occurred, the controllers could make more of a profit off their system. Private control of banks, prisons, mercenary armies, and even the elections often reeked with corruptions. This happens because the poor price system values encourage it.

Consider just the election process where billions of dollars are given to private companies just to elect a president. This enormous expenditure of time, money, and effort only makes sense under the price system's worldview. The whole process is very nonproductive in nature; it lacks common sense because of its excessiveness. Its aim is to support a controlled pseudo-power struggle. The real powers behind the struggle are the price system controllers. They end up retaining their price system and a strong likelihood of continued wealth and real power.

We need to be honest about our early Founding Father's achievements. While they did a good job under the circumstances, their early documents were far from perfect. That perfection that they sought, is it really possible in this world? Their original, seemingly honest, approach to fair government dissipated markedly, as corruptions began to spread within this new government's core.

These corruptions began very early on. However, due to the extent of the abundant land resources available here in North America, these corruptions went on mostly unhampered. The huge resources here paid off a lot of dissenters of the price system; as such, the system easily perpetuated itself. Even today, our resources have caused many people to turn a blind eye to the mischief of the controllers.

Today, the resources have been reduced substantially as the population has grown. That being said, there are still a lot of resources left. However, we need to manage them better, if we expect future generations to enjoy a favorable lifestyle.

Because of the diminishing resources, even the price system has had to modify its tactics a bit. They have shifted away, just a bit, from using our national land resources and more toward using people as resources to make money. This has resulted in an even greater divide between the rich and the poor.

Money in these hard times is now being extracted from the main body of the citizens as well as the remaining land resources. The masses are just beginning to see the face of the flawed economic system that they have been a part of. They have begun to feel the pinch of it, and the need for a new economic system is becoming a little more apparent, at least to some.

Just a side note here, recent improvement in automation such as self-driving vehicles and in artificial intelligent machines will allow the hard-hearted price system controllers to cut jobs at an alarming rate. The 90% group that had been used for cheap labor will no longer be necessary.

Unfortunately, in the price system's business plan, people are expendable. That is because without a job, you cannot buy anything anymore. The price system's plan is purely business; they are not going to send people home with pay for the rest of their lives. Their business plan allows for a much larger cut in population than would be necessary if we employed a balanced approach now.

The following discussion is partly based on a Mother Jones article titled *It's the Inequality, Stupid* in February 2011.[3] Statistics in 2007 indicated that 90% of our nation's population was forced to share about 27% of the nation's wealth. By 2015, 90% of the nation had roughly 15% of the nation's wealth. If nothing is done, this percentage will be much worse by the time you read this book. Considering that our nation hasn't fallen to the great economic depths of a third-world nation, quite yet, we are lucky. So far, the leftover resources are still enough to make life tolerable for the common citizen; however, the controllers want those resources as well.

Currently, as I am writing this, the national debt is approaching twenty trillion dollars. That debt adds a layer of additional risk on the dices now being rolled by governmental authorities. Just how long the luck of the common U.S. citizen will last, if we continue under a globalist price system view, is not easy to answer.

Consider again those reports noted above that said that in 2007, 270 million people or 90% had only about 27% of the wealth, while 30 million people or 10% had about 73% of the wealth. If we break this top 10% down further, we find that the top three million people or 1% enjoyed a 35% share of all the money in the top 10% bracket. This left 38% to be split by the remaining 29,970,000 people or 9% in that group.

While this distribution of wealth seems bad, it gets worse. If we take that top three million people, or 1%, and break it up into one hundred pieces, we find that the top 1% of this group again received the bulk of this group's wealth or about 85%. This means that most of the wealth of this nation in 2007 was in the hands of about 30,000 people. This 1/100th of 1% at the very top is so incredibly rich they make the balance of the top 1% look poor; still, that poorer group lives a lifestyle that most of us can only dream of. Their lavish lifestyles help to make them firm supporters of the current process of economics, and most see no need for change nor want any change. Again, if nothing changes, those figures above will only get worse for those in the 90% group and extremely better for those in the 1% group.

However, regarding the question of how long our luck will last. In 2011, we found that the distribution of wealth had continued its aggressive march into the already full pockets of the top 1% of our population. Again, this top 1% segment represents a little more than three million people. They were said, by some, to control about 49%

of the nation's wealth. The remaining 9% of the top 10% were said to control another 49%, for a total of 98% of the country's wealth.

An Associated Press article released in July 2011 reported a different set of statistics in which the disparity wasn't as high.[4] They said that the top 10% had 56% of the nation's wealth in 2009. Those figures, while better, still represent a huge inequality and a terrible injustice for those people who fall outside of the top 10%. Why? This is because it means 90% of the population had to share 44% of the nation's wealth. That is still a terrible imbalance.

Here, again, we should question the news we receive. Why is there a different set of statistics being offered? Psychologically, the added confusion of multiple results lessens our concern, because it suggests that more research is necessary. We think this even though both sets of statistics report a very lopsided distribution of wealth and a need to fix it. Conflicting reports are a subtle way of taming the negative news. Somehow, mentally, we are less concerned by that lower number; be honest, aren't you?

However, it should be a great concern to us that within this top 1% group, one 1/100th of them or approximately 30,000 people are now said to control an even greater bulk of this nation's wealth. Why the concern? It is because this evidence supports the idea that the hands of the controllers are working their magic. In other words, with this information, we can more easily believe that this small group might very well be manipulating things. We can, at the very least, believe that the economic trends are pushing the money into their pockets.

Note that we are now starting to look a little more like a third-world nation. Our population is gaining an ever-increasing amount of third-world citizens. It is rather obvious that the price system's globalist view is the main reason behind this population shift. Their open-door policies have helped to add wealth to the top 1% while diminishing the wealth of nearly everyone else.

At the very least, about 90% of the nation has been negatively impacted by the current price system practices. Those wealthy people in the top 10% of our population, some 30+ million, are also feeling the pinch of those in the upper 1%. Their wealth has also begun to diminish as the wealth of our nation gets concentrated further into the top one hundredth of 1% of our economic pyramid. Yes, even their wealth has begun to fall into the hands of the top 1%. Still, they are a long way off from being in the same boat as those in the 90% majority.

What will be the final number of elites? Again, the current system basically has concentrated the bulk of the wealth into less than 1% of the nation's population. This is far from the ideals of the America that I grew up with. I grew up being told that this was the land of opportunity for all, not just 10% of us. I sure thought that more of us would share in that wealth. Instead, the existing plan tends to reduce the number of citizens who can even experience the basic American dream, as it was imagined even just fifty years ago. It reduces it in favor of giving the top tier and even greater share of an already excessive allotment.

Should not the intent of any country be to honestly increase the standard of living for as many people as they can? We are told that we are a nation of sharing, a nation of helping one another, and a nation of building up one another so that we all prosper. Clearly, this seems to only apply to the top 10% of our population. For the rest of us, those noble ideas are drifting away; in fact, we are mostly here only to add to the wealth of those in the top tier.

Tragically, that 10% group isn't just an American group—it is a worldwide group. Other nations have been drained of their wealth more aggressively than ours. So far, we have been one of the lucky ones who still enjoy a standard above that of a third-world nation. However, the price system's plan is working for them, and that means it's only a matter of time for us.

Perhaps, a clearer understanding of how that price system really works will generate support for a new system. If done right, our new economic system will bring some greatly needed reforms. The reforms required are not only in economics but also in other areas of our lives. These would be reforms in our systems of justice, politics, and even the tax system, to name a few.

Metaphorically, if *their* existing economic system where a sheet of glass, it would be filled with numerous deep scratches. Each scratch would represent one of the many existing corruptions that have severely weakened it. That glass will eventually be broken. One thing helping to hold it together has been the lopsided global trade agreements. These agreements do add weight to the glass; however, at the same time, they act like tape across its surface, adding some temporary strength. Tape isn't the kind of fix we need.

The controllers have pushed though these trade agreements against the best interest of the bulk of the people. Each new trade deal added some life to the system. However, each of those trade deals also added additional burdens to the glass, cracking it more. The not-so-funny thing here is that with each new piece of tape, the rewards to the top-tier players have gone up. This is occurring, while at the same time, the weight of the remaining population has been adding an increased risk of damage or brakeage to the system itself. Those players, at the top, are willing to take that risk because they plan to be bailed out again should that glass brake.

Pres. Donald Trump has indicated that those trade deals are problematic. He has plans to make corrections so as to make those deals more favorable to the U.S. citizens. The globalist will certainly have something to say about this. Hopefully, the globalist will take the hit, for now, on these deals; this remains to be seen. They might recuperate their loss in some other manner from some other victim. Even if Pres. Trump does make progress on this one issue here, he just represents one country, and the globalists are worldwide.

It will take a worldwide effort to oust the price system completely. If at some point, the United States or some major country could initiate an alternative plan, then perhaps others would follow. Ultimately the price system will bring about its own end because of the inherent corruptions that exists in far too many of us.

This then is the reason for this book, as it presents ideas for a new system. Hopefully, our new system will allow more citizens to participate in a new more widespread American dream. It also would address some reforms that would improve the general public's way of life. If the citizens decide to undertake these ideas, the real work will fall to that part of our population that we might today call the young and the hopeless.

That is, they would be called the young and the hopeless if we were to continue on with a system like the one currently in place. They don't have to remain the young and the hopeless, but perhaps, they really could become the free and the brave. However, to do this, they, this next generation, will need to have a new view of the world.

Their new view should not support the idea that there should be excessively super wealthy individuals. Their new view also would not support keeping those behind the scenes faceless manipulators, of our marketplace, in power. Nor would this view support those schemes that leave loopholes for criminal activities to occur.

Their new view needs to be more inclusive. Economically, they need to include the highest percentage of the American public that they possibly can. The goal is to give as many people as possible a chance to pursue happiness by working in a field that they have a talent for and enjoy. This can only occur if the bulk of us can purge out the criminals and establish a new economic/government plan.

The new plan needs to reward all those that want to really work for it. This is preferred over those who would set up a system that puts their "select lot" in the most favorable place. The new plan shouldn't have freeloaders at the top or the bottom.

Their new system should try to enrich the earth and its inhabitants both now and in the future. Money in this new system should not be championed above all else. Truthfully, it is very likely that this new system would have to contain a system of money. However, that monetary system needs to be relocated to a secondary status, somehow.

The importance of money needs to be diminished. I should remind everyone that money does not necessarily make people happy. Happiness can come from more than just having "things." It will come from our efforts to see both the world and its inhabitants improve instead of degrade.

Said another way, happiness and riches are not always presented to us in the form of money. Since most of our current mental manipulations have driven us to love money, it is hard for us to get off that train. We have often been brainwashed into useless consumerism and fast-talked into purchases we really don't need. Our purchases sometimes only keep us interested briefly, and then, they are often discarded. We are thus often sold various forms of short-term addictions.

We have also, all too often, been fast-talked into wars and private bailouts. Such wastefulness depletes the wealth of the nation's common citizen. However, that wastefulness fills the pockets of that top 10% of our population. We, as a people, need to push past this human fault of wasteful spending. If we do, our new system will likely reward us with improved national economic wealth. Hopefully, we will use this wealth in more positive ways. We will not be victims at this point, but will enjoy the blessings of acting responsibly.

America was founded on capitalism, and the way it was initially set up, it worked pretty well, granted it did have an abundance of resources to work with, which made that early system work better. It had the resources of animal hides and bird feathers, lumber, gold, coal, iron, copper, and vast amounts of land, to name just a few. These were all basically untapped resources so they were there for the taking.

The checks and balances to this early system were not as tight as they should have been. Consequently, there were many corrupt schemes that have been documented in our history. Today, the checks and balances in terms of regulations have tried to rein in those corruptions. However, those regulations all too often become meaningless statements of intent, because other legal procedures can be used to allow the seemingly prohibited actions to occur.

The writers of the Declaration of Independence saw firsthand the corruption of the central banking system in Europe. This central banking system "fed" off the capitalistic dealings of any government that it could convert over to its process. In this sense, the Federal Reserve's nickname of the FED is appropriate. This is how the bankers and their cohorts made their fortunes and still do today.

Our country's early beginnings were free of this system of banking, and while it was not easy to adopt a new system of economics, our early leaders did just that. I am sorry I cannot tell you that it all went well as you know, they had a rough start. They of course had to fight against those bankers who took every opportunity to worm their way back into control over our money supply.

While the banker's actions impaired our early progress, the sheer size of the resources available to our early settlers allowed this country's common person to share in that growth despite the banking system's hindrances. Several times in our history, the central banking system caused the common person to suffer. The new globalization changes that they made during the 1970s and 1980s have brought about detrimental conditions to the general public; however, those actions have worked well for those in the top 10%.

A deeper study of our American history will indicate that our progress as a nation was generally, though briefly, improved when we were free of the influences of the world's central bankers. However, those people who stood to lose their excessive wealth worked behind the scenes to bring back the central bankers. This is not to say that during the central bank's control that our country didn't have economic growth because it does and did. That growth occurred because our resources were phenomenally extensive then. It has taken those pillagers a long time to deplete them. Today, of course, they are still in control, and of course, our natural resources have dwindled, but we still have a lot left.

Unfortunately, several of our nation's resources have been removed from our full control. During the last few decades, the globalists have worked to distribute many of our resources into foreign ownership. I don't mean foreign nation ownership exclusively, but ownership into the hands of private foreign people who are loyal to the world's globalist central banking system, that is, the price system. These are the people who run that very system—to be more clear, those that perpetuate the price system intentionally.

This is how globalization is pushed. It is supported by major corporations in such countries as the Kingdom of the Netherlands, the United Kingdom, Germany, Japan, and various other foreign international, but privately owned corporations. They together control a huge chunk of our remaining resources. One example here is our Great Lakes watershed, the foreign bottling of water, beer, and various canned goods uses a great deal of our water resources.

In addition, various military corporations also have business roots extensively planted out of our country. Even corporations that are considered American are really deeply planted in foreign lands and hands. We truly need to view them as independent of the United States of America, as their allegiance is to the business globalization movement.

Mainstream historical records have politely divulged that the existing economic system has sucked the life out of many nations repeatedly. Even the United States suffered under it more than once. Most notably, we suffered during the Great Depression, but there have been several recessions that have severely hurt far too many people.

There have also been numerous historical recessions and depressions worldwide. You may be asking yourself how that system could be charged as being responsible for them. Perhaps, you're asking, have they really worked their tricks before?

If you are asking either of those questions, I think it is because we humans have very short memory spans, and to make matters worse, we have very narrow memories. We tend to remember the good things and forget the bad things. This, by the way, helps us cope with the terrible events that the current price system imposes on us; thus, it works to the controller's advantage.

The central banking system has excessive influence globally. They have even been able to influence, to a great extent, the history books that are published. Their strong influence can and is being used to alter the understanding of events. Generally, that influence tends to minimize *their* actions and to place the blame on other people or events.

They also control the world through their distribution of wealth scheme. Controlling a person's paycheck has more often than not produced compliance. All of their control mechanisms have, in the past, been able to drag many a nation to ruin. The aftermath can often lead people to fight with each other as in revolt. If the ruin is excessive, sometimes they are left to flounder around on their own in a lawless environment.

Following their ruinous actions, and over some period of time, the people are convinced by the paid-for historians and media that the "current controllers" had little to do with it. Perhaps, the blame is put on some long-dead member who is made to look like he was a rogue agent. Then, if new natural or human resources are found in those countries, the bankers start the whole process all over again. Those that know the truth are either eliminated, ignored, or made to look crazy.

The above basic scenario happens over and over again all over the world. Their economic system, which unfortunately today we are using, always fails the common person. The longevity of their banking scheme is normally determined by the amount of resources the country has and the resolution of the people of that country to fight back. One thing for sure, their system always rises and falls or comes close to failure; it's the part of their design that helps to glean the wealth of any nation under its influence.

This means we have a chance, be it small, to change things when our economy does fail. We might rebuild by using a new economic system that is not constructed on their banking system deceits. These are deceits that always end in monetary failure and human suffering. That is, suffering for the common citizen, but not for the top layer of elites who work the process.

If given a chance, we can design a new system. This system, even if free of just some of the bloodsuckers, would still be a better system. It would be more like the one our nation's founders initially wanted to put in place for us. Ben Franklin once warned us, and I paraphrase, "You have a republic, if you can keep it."[5] This advice is just as sound today. We need to remain vigilant in our efforts to establish and to maintain the new system, whatever that might be.

In my opinion, this new system should consider some of the ideas our early founders had, capitalism, for example. Unfortunately, capitalism under the price system was taken to extremes. There is a large place for the kind of capitalism based on people who work hard. However, there is little room for the kind of capitalism that uses the hard work of others to excessively profit a select few.

Under the price system, the hard work of the common person is excessively redirected to those running the system. Those in charge justified their actions by claiming they are shrewd businessmen. They truly believe they are superior to others who do not think as they do. They lack guilt because of this attitude. Guilt, in their definition of business, doesn't exist. They also see no problem with being greedy. The result has been the wasting of both natural and human resources for their personal benefits. With our new plan, we can put limits on capitalism so that it will not be as easy to abuse.

We will design a better form of capitalism. The design will keep it from growing and going back to those old abuses. In order to do this, we need additional systems in place to balance our design.

The founders had no problem employing socialism where it made sense. If the founders were here today, I believe they would use socialism for a couple more things, than what they did back then. They of course used it to fund our governments and our military.

As time went on, they saw a need to use it for police and fire departments and even education. Today, if they were here, I believe they would use it for health care as well. I believe they would see health care as part of our national defense; after all, in case of war, we need a healthy population to draw from.

There was a lot of wisdom in our Founding Fathers' values and their efforts. There are a number of benefits to be received from the implementation of certain socialistic structures. If we do choose to use some of these social ideas, be aware that those *controllers* will attack these ideas vigorously. However, if you understand that they have a selfish motive for doing so, that shell game of theirs should end. You wouldn't want to play.

The price system mostly seems to give the world the impression that it is a completely capitalistic system. That is not a truth. Their excessive form of capitalism has also been twisted into a perverted form of socialism. This gives the controllers power over to corporate leaders via a form of corporatism.

Corporatism here is an excessive variation of socialism, which also allows too much power in too few hands. The result of these actions has allowed the 10%, if you will, to take excessive advantage of the bulk of the citizen. The wage disparity between the 10% and the 90% affirms this reality. This bad form of socialism is something we do not want. Our hybrid system will be designed to put limits on both the socialistic and capitalistic ideas that we choose to use in our new plan.

The balance required between these two systems, capitalism and socialism, can be designed, just as the imbalances were designed. Because of their individual styles, these two systems can also work to limit each other's influence. Through the limiting of the power that each of them has, we can balance their negative natures. This provides us with a positive influence, not only on those potential negative natures but also on our total economic/governmental plan.

This division of power should actually work to improve the quality of our government's operation substantially. It should reduce the partisanship behaviors that, under the price system, worked to destroy the effectiveness of the support for the common citizen. This is again evident in the wage gap between the 10% and 90% groups. The price system is a system where, in reality, only one in ten really succeeds; the rest have to make the best of a bad situation.

Our new design would also work to limit the negative influence that excessive amounts of money in private hands tend to generate. We can roughly say that one in ten people will tend to use that extra money to their own political advantage. This is done through the following acts.

Money is used for the buying of elections. This is accomplished through the use of constant advertising. Even a lie if said often enough will be used to sway voters to see things their way. Money has also been use to buy congressional support.

In the courts, as you know, money is sometimes used to buy teams of lawyers to argue support for what should be considered criminal undertakings. These are things such as the lifting of rules or guidelines meant to protect consumers. Here, I am suggesting to you that the housing bubble did not happen by chance. Criminal actions led to the 2008 financial collapse.

All of these negative actions would be substantially reduced under our new design. Why? It is because money just wouldn't have the same amount of power. That is, if we plan it correctly, in a balanced way.

This decline, in the power of money, will actually work to the advantage of those who don't have it. Money, under our new system, will be important, but not absolutely necessary. Remember that we will institute procedures that will reduce the influence that money has on us. This reduction in the importance of money should bring about the following positives.

We should have less crime, less homelessness, and even better mental health. Our new plan would allow those who work hard to have more money. This should encourage the bulk of the population to be more productive on their own.

With proper government, their basic needs can be delivered without the need for money. Again, those needs will be sufficient but rather minimal to start and only increased if the system allows. This helps because most family arguments revolve around the lack of sufficient money. Under our new system, they will have less cause for arguments, which should improve family life. Improved family life means better mental health and less homelessness as well.

There have been reports that the world's central banking system and its associates, a.k.a. controllers, have over the years spent trillions of dollars worldwide to alter our thinking. The money was spent to develop in our minds the idea that socialism is really communism. They have paid talking heads, news readers, to read these ideas to us. A variation of this thought perversion is that socialism always leads to communism. You should note that this meaning, or forgone conclusion on their part, isn't actually represented in those earlier definitions in chapter 1.

Their warped ideas may not be in the original definitions, but that doesn't stop those controllers from saying things like that. I have heard these bent definitions being taught to us on both broadcast and cable television networks. Generally, they are coming from the multitude of pundits, but often, they come from the anchors themselves. Remember that it's the job of the mainstream media to convince you to stay with the current system. They are experts at telling you half-truths.

If you think about socialism from a banker's mind-set, you'll discover that socialism bites into the excessive money-making schemes that the controllers or central bankers have, so it's bad for them. You wouldn't hear them say that; instead, we are told socialism is bad for us because it can turn into communism. That is the half-truth we are told. A more factual statement would be if left unchecked, socialism can turn into communism. It might also be said that if left unchecked, capitalism can turn into communism. I have read that roughly 10% of the people in communist nations are in the party, and they have the majority of the wealth. This is something to think about, as we have an elite party of 10% in our country that has 90% of the wealth.

Being a predominately Christian Judaic country, we understand that freedom of religion is paramount. It has also been said by many people that communism doesn't work well for citizens who believe in God. In its pure form, communism would not allow religion. So far, there hasn't been a pure form of communism that has been able to eliminate religion completely.

Today, diluted forms of communism work with and for the central banking system, just as the capitalistic systems works with and for them. Even China is being used by these banking leaders to manipulate the bank's worldwide activities. Note here that these bankers have no problem working with communism. I have heard it said that true communism would put a stop to those central banks in a hurry, but again, pure communism doesn't really seem to exist anywhere.

In fact, the world's central banking system is working to strengthen its control over all forms of government. Communism, socialism, and capitalism are integrated in a system they call globalization. Since the central banks control them, they have no fear of allowing any of these systems to exist.

However, for the common citizens of the world, communism, of any sort, is a bad idea. It is not something we would want. We need to note that the fear of communism, which the central bankers and their cohorts have taught us, is not something they themselves hold to. This should tell us something about their characters.

Their character should give us cause to reexamine the conditioned attitudes they have given us toward socialism. It may be that those stories were designed to further the ends of the central banker's corrupt system. *They* used the fear of socialism to drive up the profits of the military industrial complex.

For those who feel uncomfortable about these positive views on socialism, I say to you that it is unlikely you would agree with these views. This is especially true if you haven't had any of these ideas presented to you before. After all, my presentation, thus far, cannot compare to the years of indoctrination that we all receive by simply living within the price system.

The alternative views suggested so far in this book have to compete with years of media teachings, telling you the exact opposite. We have all too often been taught that all socialism is evil. I ask those of you who may feel that way, to indulge me for now. Shelf your fears for the moment, and let's explore the options first, as there are options to the government we choose.

Remember that we are trying to design a new and better system and an open mind is necessary for that to happen. Our country's success hangs on us working together; if we fragment ourselves, the existing leaders will come back to take control and reestablish their same old system again. This will mean more pain and suffering again and again or until the resources are completely gone, and we are all gone.

In my view, the intent of the ideas in our new plan should not go against God or our country's best benefit. If you think our current system also holds this view, why do they make lopsided trade deals with evil-willed nations and countries that would seek to eliminate God, communist? These deals have worked to make our potential enemies stronger. We only have to look at the military buildup that China has accomplished, since our leaders opened the doors of trade with them.

The lopsided trade deals have also created an ever-growing disparity in the distribution of wealth between the super rich and the general population. These excessive economic extremes are not something to be proud of or something we should want to continue.

They are making the common citizen poorer and the world more dangerous.

I believe that during the first century of our country's existence, a number of good ideas came along. Many of them worked well, even though they were not generated or supported by the price system controllers. The price system's authorities, of course, had to launch media campaigns to control those good ideas.

Those good ideas might otherwise have spoiled price system schemes. Many of these ideas were attacked as being socialistic or communistic. We have to remember that extreme capitalism can also lead to that perverted form of communism. That is the form we see the world's central banks are working toward. With this in mind, we should revisit what might have worked in the past, but was shot down, and try to incorporate those ideas into our new economy, if they pan out.

I believe that we have to look at the available systems of economics, both old and new, and piece together from them a new economy. Consider the engineers who combined the state-of-the-art telephone, monitor screen, computer, and software programs, to come up with the iPhone. We also need to piece together our state-of-the-art economic and governmental plan, from what is available to us at this time.

This can be done by taking the best ideas surrounding economics and government and putting them together to find a fair and balance system—hopefully, a system that has greater defenses against corruption from the excessive end of the private sector influences. We will need to build a system with safeguards that will keep out those evil influences of the get rich quick crowd. That crowd tends to get their wealth mischievously via unmerited favor and at everyone else's expense.

Several governments in our world at this time are headed for self-destruction. We are not the only country in trouble. Through the world banking systems, we are conveniently linked together in these failures—convenient for the banks, but not for us.

When the economy collapses, it will do so on its own. It is unlikely the common citizen will knowingly do anything to hasten its downfall. This is because the perpetrators of this economic downfall are the central bankers and their cohorts themselves. It is in essence their baby. These private enterprises, through their own self-serving actions, within their own system, have been slowly causing their own system to crack.

In part, the design of their system slowly works itself toward failure; so this is their plan. Normally, this failure is not allowed to get too extreme, but just enough so that recovery is possible. However, a complete breakdown of their system can be caused when some insiders get too excessive in their greed.

Routinely in the past, the controllers have slowly drained the power and money off into their hands, while the countries that they brutalize are told it is simply market conditions that caused the problems. This brutality is harder for them to hide when those greedy players take too much too fast.

When it works well, their actions could be compared to a good slow cooker. When things get to hot, they add in a cooling agent to keep it from burning. When things get better, they begin to drain more money off, careful to not do it too fast so that no one notices that the stew is too watery. This process goes on and on, each time they extend the life of their corrupt system so that they can exploit their victims again and again.

However, since their system is basically a form of a chain letter scam, it will eventually fall apart. Think of it as a kind of like Bernie Madoff's *Ponzi* scam, except here the main central bankers plan to get away unscathed.[6] They are hoping we, as a group, don't put it all together, for they are the real criminals.

We have seen financial collapse here in America before, and yes, this same price system was behind it. They were also behind the financial collapses in many other countries. You may ask, why have I never heard that they were to blame for all of these things? The answer, in part, is simply because they control the mainstream media, they rewrite the history, and they have subtle control over key positions in law enforcement all the way up to the federal levels.

If you need more proof of their actions, there are several books that were written about it. However, those books were not widely promoted in the media. There is also an abundance of blogs and dot-coms that address these awful truths in great depths. I will list a few of these resources in the reference section of this book to help you in your personal study.

For now, it is just important to point out what our economy will look like at the point of collapse, so if you look at the central banker's previous work, you will get the picture. Our leaders will be running around like chickens with their heads cut off trying to save the banks. From the leaders' point of view, those banks are extremely important to save. However, for the common man, those banks have not acted in a very favorable way. Still, like it or not, we are all tied to this corrupt system, and their demise will cause us even more pain.

In the past, this pain and suffering threat has caused us to save them. Yes, we have saved the very people who take excessive advantage of us. Such was the case in our 2008 bailout. We wrote them a big check—sorry, make that checks, plural. They did a good job of scaring us so we did a second and even a third round of check writing.

The banks know that eventually, even these bailout actions will fail and the whole system will collapse. They will have to wean themselves off this bailout money or the system will fail faster. We are told that just as we do not want a system failure; they also do not want it. If it fails faster, it will be because of their excessive greed. They will however try to keep it going as long as possible as it generally is to their advantage to do so.

I have to briefly expand on the word excessive, that is, as to what it means to me. I hope you agree with me that capitalism works well in a free market. That, at least, is what I believe. The problems I see with this existing system is that those people with excessive capital use it to manipulate the market. In doing this, the market isn't free anymore.

In short, the free market doesn't work when we allow truly excessive behaviors to exist. People with multimillion-dollar incomes all too often use their excessive money to manipulate markets. This manipulation allows them to gain even more wealth. Through their manipulations, they obtain fuel, money, to finance the furnace of corruptions in Washington DC and around the world. When people have excessive money, like the ones I am talking about, they all too often tend to use it to influence people to back their views.

Spending a few million dollars on lobbyist in return for billions of dollars in profits is, to them, just business. To me, it represents our sons and daughters marching off to wars that those with excessive money all too often instigate. It represents the laws that are altered so that they can gain unfair advantage over their smaller competitors. It represents the thousands of families that had lost their homes and then had to live in tent cities due to the mortgage scandals that this system created. With only a small part of their excessive monetary gains, they corrupt the free market system. Through the perverted use of their price system they corrupt our economy. The general pitfalls of this price system are also explained by the North American technocracy project.[7]

It is unlikely that enough people will believe this negative description of the price system to put an end to it before its collapse. Some people have to see it firsthand in order to believe. Will enough of us come to our senses, as a group, before the economic failure? Based on past history, that is very doubtful. Regretfully and painfully, our only hope is that the next economic collapse will be enough to wake people up.

That economic failure of course will hurt us, but it will also give us an opportunity to prevent it from happening again. If the economy fails, then this is where we need to jump in, if we can, and try a new approach. Make no mistake, those central banks or controllers will try to keep their place and pretend they had nothing to do with what happened. This is where your knowledge of what they really did is so important. I believe your knowledge will be put to the test. It is likely that their excessive greed will eventually give you this opportunity to be tested.

At the collapse, the controllers will want to call all the shots and make recommendation that will be designed to cause the whole cycle to begin again. This cycle is where they repeat history and drain off more of our wealth again over an extended time. We should not listen to them, but instead develop a new economy to rid ourselves of the overpowering central bankers and their price system. These controllers, after all, have supported other excessive behaviors within our society. They represent a level of greed and power that should be distasteful to all of us.

CHAPTER 3

———◆◆◆———

The Influence of the Price System on Different Economic Groups in the United States

I really do not like placing people in groups. Why? It is because there are usually some people that get pushed into these groups by mistake. However, in an attempt to simplify and shorten this discussion, I will make an exception. So, view these groupings as rough approximations and by no means completely accurate. To keep it very simple, I will only use two groups.

The following is based on those 2007 distribution of wealth figures we discussed earlier in chapter 2. Since 2007, the disparities in wealth have gotten worse. However, there is no need for an update because even these milder 2007 figures get the point across.

Here in the United States:

A. About thirty thousand people or about 1/100 of 1% of our population had average incomes of over $27 million a year.
B. About three hundred thousand people or 9/100 of 1% had average incomes of over $3 million a year.
C. About two million seven hundred thousand people or 90/100 of 1% of the population had average incomes of over $1 million a year.

D. About thirty million people or 9% of the population had average incomes of over $164,000 a year. The people identified in A through D represent group 1. They are roughly only 10% of the population.

E. That left about two hundred and seventy million people in group 2 or about 90% of the population. This group had average incomes of $31,000 a year.

This means that, back in 2007, the top 10% of the people had over 73% of the wealth of the nation, leaving the bottom 90% to split 27% of the wealth.[1] This division of wealth is much worse today.

The Top 10%

Those listed above in A, B, C, and D are group 1. This group, in general, contains the greatest number of people who lack compassion for the masses. Their respect or concern for people typically diminishes as they climb closer to the top 1/100 of 1% in this group. It is true that not everyone in this group is evil or corrupted. However, as a whole, most of them have been, at the very least, corrupt in their belief in the system. They of course would not see themselves that way. If they did, they would not be using their positions to promote the system as it is.

It is a system where group 1 feeds on group 2 excessively. That very top section of people in group 1 contains people who are, sad to say, totally corrupted. For the most part *they* only care about themselves. Many of them do not even care about their own families. Their stockpiling of excessive wealth seems to be designed to afford their families protection. However, the shear excessiveness of their reserves makes the world that their children live in a worse place to exist. To me, that vast amount of horded money implies either extreme greed or extreme fear.

If it is fear, the question becomes, what are they afraid of that requires so much wealth to protect against? I believe that because of their controlling roles in the system, they are closer to understanding the real financial problems that the world has. They see the coming economic pains and social disorders that will result from their price system's economic collapse.

Those at the top level of corruption are said to have collaborated to build huge underground bunkers. They have been building those fortresses to ward off all those people that they have forsaken on their climb to the top. That top level has had to step on a lot of people to get where they are today. Consequently, their protection includes private security forces, police, military, and even agencies within the government.

This expensive contingency plan has a problem however. The neighborhoods and support services they are trying to create will be populated by people just like themselves, for the most part. What does this mean to their lives? It means they will be surrounded by manipulating, self-serving, and self-absorbed people. Their children, if they are not already infected with those tendencies, will soon be indoctrinated into them.

Their children will have to live with people like this. Compassion is not the strong suit for this group. If it was, they would not be taking such excessive advantage of the general population. These troubled people make some of the people on *The Jerry Springer Show* look like saints, and that is no exaggeration. We typically don't see these flaws because they can hire people to clean up their messes.

Their infighting is generally not out in the open, but it is much more severe. Sure, they are cleaned clothe and appear to be proper ladies and gentleman, but inside, they have no real substance, no real character. It is very likely that many of them might suffer from a form of mental illness, but it is a form that allows them to function without being tagged as ill. This is because they have been able to control the narrative of what greed is.

Their underlying dysfunction, which is their lack of compassion for human beings, causes them to inflict pain and suffering on more people than Jack the Ripper could have ever dreamed of. They are responsible for most of the pain and suffering surrounding drugs, human trafficking, and wars. It is their system that makes these things flourish.

Privately, their sociopathic tendencies are subtly displayed without regrets. They condone their actions by using their own self-analysis methods. This self-analysis allows them to claim, of course, that they are normal.

One might say I am being too tough on these people, but am I? Look where the world is today. The enormous progress that could have been achieved by mankind was thwarted by this group.

It is true that this group did do some good, but the net effect of their behaviors created a huge loss for the world. Their obstructive behaviors stifled potential achievements that went counter to this group's total control. Group 1's control measures assured that less than 1% of the world's population would have the bulk of the wealth.

The untold dreams and aspirations of billions of people were directly affected by this small group's behavior. That behavior was designed to forcibly remove the pathway for most of those dreams, unless those dreams could be used to ultimately profit that small control group. You see, the control group wrote the rules, which mostly favored themselves.

Those rules create progress-impeding mechanisms, which channeled almost all things through their selfish and sticky hands—mechanisms that push otherwise good ideas and people aside so that this group could make more profit. For example, the world's pollution problems should be attributed to them. The world's financial problems are also their works. Let's not forget about their wars. Several of them were instigated so that they, their small lot, would live in affluence beyond an appropriate level.

Their level of affluence should be considered as an example of some mental illnesses. One illness that comes to mind is the illness of hording. As poor as some people are, they understand the idea of excess. However, these wealthy people seem to know no limit.

Hording—this is a mental abnormality that afflicts some people causing them to fill their homes with material things. These things can be items even as simple as napkins with notes on them, rusty bolts, or whatever they deem important. Doctors say that these people have a condition that causes them to put excessive emotional importance or value on almost anything they come across.

I am suggesting that perhaps the wealthy have put excess emotional importance or their lifestyles. While their rooms are not filled with junk, perhaps this is only because their rooms are large enough to hold those objects without notice. What's more, they can afford to get the best junk, so it all looks neat and clean. Tell me how many cars do you really need? How much "bling" is enough?

In my view, those who excessively crave wealth really do suffer from an organized version of the hording condition. That would be a version that doctors haven't acknowledged yet. While the world is under the control of those in group 1, there is little chance that the rich will be condemned for their behavior.

To some extent, we are conditioned to accept this excessiveness, by the programs presented to us on television.[2] Those programs rarely tell the whole story behind the rich and the famous. They don't tell who gets hurt in order for them to have that wealth. Excessive wealth is mostly portrayed as perfectly normal.

The 10% at the top are not all mentally ill, in the hording sense. Some are criminally ill, at least those that look for every means to take advantage of others. However, to be fair, a few are rather normal; their only issue is that they happen to have just too much money—more money than is reasonably healthy. Now, great wealth happens to be part of the original American dream that I, from my childhood, was taught to aspire to, someday. The price system, diabolically, allows that dream to be as excessive as you want.

My version of the American dream wasn't the same as those that live to excess. I didn't imagine having to drive around in a bullet proof limousine. Where from it, I would have to pass through slums or homeless tent cities to get to my private jet. Nor did I imagine traveling along past malnourished children playing in neighborhoods that aren't much better than garbage dumps. I didn't imagine not giving a damn about their problems.

I rather envisioned an America where most of us enjoyed a healthy standard of living. Yes, my vision is one where great wealth still does have a place. That level, however, doesn't reach to the excessive limits that we see today. It is a vision that requires prudence and discipline. One reason we don't want excessive levels of wealth is simply this—we do not want to condone mental illness.

We in society, as adults, know enough to teach our children to look both ways before crossing the street. We teach them early on so that when they cross the street, on their own, they will know what to do. We are justified in teaching them, because their actions, in life, have consequences. They could hurt not only themselves but also other people in our society. Should we disregard our own wisdom and allow children and adults to do whatever they want regardless of the consequences?

Children or adults who disregard the wisdoms of society put society at risk. When adults indulge in excessiveness, sooner or later, someone gets hurt. It may not always be obvious who that someone is. Eventually, however, their victims' resulting pain and suffering comes forward. This is a process that may take years. The sooner we learn to discipline ourselves in regard to excess, the sooner our world will become better.

As for the criminally ill, it would be great if the existing criminals would turn themselves in, ask for mercy, and try to make restitution; but that is not likely to happen. Still, I hope that perhaps, something in this book might cause someone with criminal intentions to turn themselves around and start doing the right thing.

Perhaps if they did turn themselves around, they would be able to open the world's window of opportunity a little wider. This would be our window to establish a new economic system here in this country. Someone inside this inner circle would surely be a great force to have working for us against the world's central bankers and their price system. One can only hope.

For those in the top 10%, group 1, who are wealthy in excess, but are otherwise of sound mind, little needs to be said. Chances are that they wouldn't mind giving up some of their wealth if it meant building a better America. I am not suggesting that they give up their money just to give it to the opposite end of the spectrum. That is, those who want a free ride in life.

We wouldn't want to give it to those who can work, but don't want to. This lazy bunch is every bit as much a leech on society as the elites who have been sucking out the wealth from our country. While those elites in the top 1% have been more successful at this, the lower-income leeches come in a close second. We don't want to penalize our hardworking citizens with a new economy that isn't fair.

In fact, we need to find a way in which a relatively large degree of wealth can still be secured by the hard work of citizens in our society, to keep our new healthy view of an American dream alive. This wealth however, as I said, should not be excessive. This however doesn't mean it cannot be rather large.

Now, we will have to define what excessive is, in terms of money. Whenever incomes are asked to be controlled, the claim is made that this is a socialistic idea. However, there are other reasons to control incomes.

Is it socialism, or is it just a matter of basic psychology that determines excessiveness? That is, what mentality is healthy in terms of excessiveness? Again, is it socialism defining wealth, or is it just a matter of common sense. Since money corrupts, it would not be wise to establish a threshold too high.

If we change the way we perceive money by drastically reducing the role of the price system, then we could lower the problems that excessive material things bring. People with extremely large amounts of money tend to use it to make more.

Unfortunately for us, people at that top level in the price system usually resort to market manipulations to make things happen. This would be the bribery, the payoffs, and the lobbyist activities that occur today. Those who want more money want it because to them, it means power. We do not want to feed self-serving power. On the other hand, since money does have an effect to motivate, the threshold cannot be set to low. We need to find a balance.

For the vast majority of us, winning a million-dollar lottery once in our lifetime is our dream. However, the reality under today's economy is that this might be too low of a threshold for us to shoot for. Of course, our American dream ideals will have to be based on the value of the economic system that we design. For example, if our new system was to have a value comparable to the dollar value of today, it may be possible and allowable for some people to earn the equivalent of a million dollars a year.

If our top scientists are used to determine our economic paths, as part of our new leadership, they will have to determine what is appropriate. With a strong economic system, inflation would not have a detrimental influence on our incomes. So our private incomes, along with our public certificates, would go a lot further. This would be because our basic resources would be shared by all. That sharing in itself would be a great economic benefit.

Perhaps, we will establish a Department of Innovation. The scientist there will be working to improve our existing resources and to create new forms of resources. As these resources become available, we might have a distribution matrix that allows for our basic standards of living to improve still further. Remember that our long-term goals would be to not deplete the existing resources too severely so as not to put future generations in jeopardy. If we can create renewable resources, then we can improve our lives and those lives in the future as well.

The new economic system should include a strong role for our scientist in decision-making. This idea comes from the North American technocracy plan and is explained better in their study course. I have touched on some of their duties, but for other possible details or ideas, I recommend that you investigate technocracy for yourself.

Keep in mind that we can pick and choose the ideas that benefit our plan the most. We should use good ideas wherever we find them. Ideas can come from sources we might not always agree with. However just because we may not like the source, that should not be grounds for discarding useful ideas.

In our hybrid system, however, the scientist would likely share their control and establish protocols for governmental duties. I personally lean toward giving greater weight to the general scientific community in decision-making matters. They might form various tiered councils. The first tier might form various specialized second tier councils. Then, those councils might form third tier councils for research. Reports from the various councils would work their way back to a first tier council. This first tier council might ultimately report to a national council, but only if the matter warranted this oversight. All of these ideas are just suggestions for an ultimate plan that we need to decide on.

I have said a lot of bad things about some of the elites. Why am I being so hard on them? I happen to believe in life after death. This means that they will have to face their creator someday. God will be harder on them than any of us could ever be, as he can deny them entrance to the afterlife. If in life all things are ultimately possible, why should a spiritual idea be the exception?

Some of you might not agree with my belief in an afterlife, but even if you don't, you should agree with me that you are alive today. This fact begs the question, how do you wish to be treated in your life? Should you be treated as a material thing under the controls of supply and demand?

How do you want to be treated while you are living? Remember many of those economic elites knowingly became parasites on the general population. You as a living person are part of that population.

If you view yourself as a realist, you should admit that many of those economic elites will kill to stay at that excessive level of wealth—that wealth, by the way, they have craftily stolen from most of us. They do not feel bad because their crafty behavior is simply their worldview. That view is that other people are there to be exploited because God doesn't exist.

You might not believe in life after death. However, I'm sure you believe that sickness, pain, suffering, and death are realities that exist. These events should generate a sense of compassion in you. If you can feel that compassion, then you are likely to know good from evil or right from wrong. While this is not the same as a belief in God, it is enough for us to agree that we should help each other.

This shared idea of compassion can provide us with unity. One attribute of this kind of unity is that we will be less inclined to take excessive advantage of each other. Very few in the 1% group believe in compassion, unless there is a business motive behind it.

We should understand that even when their corrupt system fails, they will still want to maintain their control over events. The system is their power structure. Power is something we haven't talked about much as yet. It is another layer of control.

Their power has led us, several times over, into economic downturns. Once immense wealth is secured by them, it in turn helps to fund their power structure. It is a cycle that needs to be broken in order for a healthy system to develop.

Power is being able to have control over things that humans need. It is natural for us to have healthy hopes and desires, as a spirit can be found in them. That spirit leads many of us to our faith in God. However, in order to truly control all of us, the controllers have to have power over God. Why? It is because the spirit of God stands against the uncompassionate style of the price system.

They want and need to diminish his power. This is done through their use of money and power, both of which help to undermine God. Our controllers use these tools to maintain the status quo of the price system. The very idea of God is a threat to the price system.

Some of you might be saying now, "Why is this guy bringing God into this?" "What does God have to do with our economy?" Well, you might recall some of the early documents that founded our country stated that we had God-given rights. Remember those life, liberty, and the pursuit of happiness ideas, for starters?

These ideas threaten those in power today. They have spent vast amounts of money to convince our general populations that God doesn't exist, and therefore, there is no such thing as good or evil. I do not know about you, but I have an easier time believing in God, rather than believing that they, the 1%, are not evil.

In their minds, without "good and evil," there is no "correct or incorrect"; so in a way, "right and wrong" doesn't apply. This is how God gets removed from the process. Instead of God-given rights, you now would have "man-given" rights only. Of course, they, those controllers, would be the "man" giving you those rights. It is a lot easier to take away your basic human rights, if God didn't exist. If God didn't exist, then he couldn't have given those rights to you in the first place, so they can take them away.

The price system doesn't really want to be held liable to those standards or rights, which God gave us. They will do what they think serves them best, and without God in their way, they will not have anything to restrict them. Life, liberty, and the pursuit of happiness—are they important to you?

I offer one final thought regarding those elites who may be mentality or criminally ill. If we succeed in getting our new economic system, we need to be sure that we set up a proper medical system for our use. That system should include care for both physical and mental illnesses.

Mental health care, under our new system, should be provided to everyone. In fact, it should be part of the controller's conciliatory acts of restitution to us. They should be mandated to undergo treatment to assure us that they can return to reality. We need to provide the service so that effected elites can get the help they need to overcome their illness. Many of them you see would find it hard to live on less than twenty-three million dollars a year; living on a million dollars a year (if that did become the final number) would require some good hard therapy in order for them to cope.

The Next 90%

This is our population, group 2. If we do get the opportunity to create a new system, we need to balance it so a larger amount of people can enjoy more of the fruits of their labors. Remember that less than 10% of our population controls the bulk of the wealth of the nation. This then allows them to control the nation's resources. That control prevents any kind of an equitable balance to be made between the rich and the poor.

The corporations haven't demonstrated any desire to share their wealth with the public. What if this corporate wealth was shared in a balanced way? If that happened, then groups 1 and 2 wouldn't exist as they do today. This is because the economic sharing also means power sharing. This is the kind of balance we should strive for. The nation's resources have to be returned to the public at large in order to get this balance.

Sure, the people are said to own these resources already; however, this is in name only. Those resources are almost always put into the hands of private corporations. They in reality control those resources. With that private control, there is little chance of an appropriate balance of wealth being made.

However, if the people via nationally owned corporations were allowed to control the resources, then a more equitable balance is possible. Publically owned corporations could be set up to ensure that the people fully participate and reap the rewards of our capitalism. This would assure that the corporate profits are more evenly and more wisely shared. Every person in the country would share ownership in these public resource corporations, as part of their citizenship.

If this becomes part of the plan, it could become a major pathway for improvements to our national standard of living. However, in order for this standard of living to be high, we as business owners will have to contribute. We can do this by contributing our labor to our business. Most people, I believe, would work harder if they owned part of the company.

Ideas such as these are not new; they tend to get shot down by the very wealthy price system crowd. Those in that 10% group get very angry when someone tries to take their gift horse away. They will spare no expense at getting their talking heads out in force.

Those media experts will no doubt rally to put the mark of death on any idea that opposes their beloved price system. Money is no object for them to spend on this kind of campaign. Remember that they have anywhere from 75% to 90% of the nation's wealth, depending on which report you go by.

All of the above new plan ideas should give us a sense of meaning and purpose for our lives. The final plan may be a mixture of socialism, capitalism, or other systems—anything is possible. Whatever mixture we choose, the plan we create hopefully will provide ample time for us to enjoy our lives. I believe it is possible that the number of hours we work per week in our public sector jobs will give us time to pursue our other interests.

We might use that time to follow our own personal capitalistic ventures for extra income. We could study to better ourselves.

We may choose to improve our artistic skills. We might want to do research or just spend more time enjoying family and friends. The new economic plan should allow for more life-enriching choices. This would then allow more people to fulfill their own personal version of the American dream.

That dream doesn't have to be only great wealth. The American dream can be whatever your passion is. Just as long as your dream is not excessive, then it should be possible. There are a lot of ideas out here in our field of dreams, and we should start considering them.

We need to even the playing field so that we no longer suppress individuals from sharing in a better lifestyle. After all 10% isn't much of a chance for success. That is why the old 10% versus the 90% line of thinking has to go.

Still, we do not want to pretend that everyone is the same. We know that there are differences in people. We know some people work harder than others, or even simply try harder than others. It is natural to reward those deserving people more. Those who will not work need to be discouraged from taking advantage of others. We will find ways to do these things appropriately, in a humane way.

There should be a larger middle class. Our experience has been that where a healthy middle class exists, living conditions improve for the whole society. This is because they are better able to support the economic system. We could enlarge the middle class simply by changing the levels of disparity between these existing groups, the 10% and the 90%. Further support for building the middle class would come from the efficiencies of scale, which our new system would bring.

Today, some people, in that 10% group, think that they are so much better than everyone else. In fact, they reward themselves hundreds of times more than their average worker. Psychology indentifies people like this as having feelings of grandeur. They are not really psychologically healthy. They exist under a rule of "might makes right." Since they make the rules, they get away with it. This however, in reality, doesn't make them better. This is an example of their selfishness. No one person should consider themselves hundreds of times more valuable than the next.

What then is the real difference between people? Can a person's value really be measured without either prejudice or bias? These are difficult questions to answer. I am not sure I do have an answer; however, I can say this.

Suppose you compare the average common person to the average millionaire. The commonalities between these humans are greater than their differences. They really are a lot closer in comparison, than we are led to believe. Of course, most of those millionaires wouldn't care to admit that, because than they can't justify their hefty pay.

The main way a person becomes a millionaire is to use the price system rules to benefit themselves. This is not something to necessarily be proud of, once you understand how those rules work. Not everyone is comfortable working under those business codes, but that doesn't make them less of a person.

It is common that once a person gets wealthy, they often think everyone can. This is a half-truth or perhaps a 10% truth. The price system doesn't allow everyone in, as then it wouldn't work to create the excessiveness that the controllers designed into it. If you are in, you are in the lucky 10%, and the controllers count on your support.

Every business person should understand the following point. The negative effects of too much competition will put you out of business or make you part of the 90% group again. Therefore, while you might say everyone can do it, the reality is that they better not or you will be back in the 90% group again. These are the price system rules. Still, generally, only those in business are the ones that tend to get into the 10% group. This is something to think about, isn't it?

Returning to our question of what the real difference is between people. Can we put a value on those differences? Is one person really excessively more important than another? We really should approach this issue by using our reasoning skills. What real good comes from giving someone hundreds of times more than they really need?

If anything, it only goes to corrupt their mental state of mind. In other words, it isn't really healthy for them. I think you will find that psychology supports what I am suggesting here. However, so far psychology, as a whole, has not wanted to apply this diagnosis to group 1.

What then is a healthy spread of wealth for our new system? I would like to think of this spread as being geared to our individual aspirations. Think of this as a drive to do something. We all start out with a clean slate at birth. As we grow, our personal aspirations are, in part, defined by the environment. However, we also have different mental or physical abilities that affect our lives. These conditions, in which we live, help or hurt our abilities to grow our natural individual gifts or talents.

So our gifts are supported both by our environment and by our physical and mental abilities. These things help to determine what our personal drive or aspiration could be. Note that no person grows up alone without other humans around to influence his or her life.

We should not tune out the level of help or hurt that our environment brings to our individual growth. Therefore, as individuals, we need to strive to make our environment healthy. This is required so it can affectively support the humans within it. There is a cycle here where each one feeds the other, and this cycle needs to be perpetuated. This attitude will secure our future.

Now, our individual aspirations will be different; as each of us are different. Environmentally, a person who aspires to help sick people is not any less valuable, as a cog in this system, than a person who aspires to be a public leader. Our environment has need of the gifts and services of a multitude of individuals.

We need people who have the ability to do things many of us would not want to do, because of our own personal aspirations. Why should we punish people who are doing the things we do not wish to do? The answer of course is that we shouldn't. Things like this have to be considered in order for us to narrow the gulf between the rich and the poor.

Now, realistically, we know that there will always be people who will want to take advantage of others. They will exist no matter how much we improve their environment. We have to own up to the fact that we live in an imperfect world.

These advantage seekers are the reason we will need to set levels of value on individual efforts. We will have to be careful that these values will not be twisted around and used against us. The value system needs to be as fair and balanced as we can get it. If we establish new values for how work ethics are measured, we can improve the economic balance that has been upset.

If we can physically or mentally work, but choose not to, well, we become a strain on our communities. This is because our communities will be providing for us. There is no way around this result. However, this doesn't mean these people will be allowed to enjoy the full benefits of the system either.

There will be those who do not want to admit that they are relying on working people to pay their way. Should a person who chooses not to work expect to be supported at the same level as a person who is contributing? That would not be economically feasible under our current environment and shouldn't be expected under our new plan.

We should consider the possibility that people who could work but choose not to may be experiencing a mental health issue. In our new system, we should help them overcome that condition. Hopefully, we will find a way to correct that condition.

Those of us that choose to work will be contributing toward everyone's basic needs in both sickness and health. Now, as I said, some people, no matter how easy their job is, will not want to work. This is where we need to draw the line as to how much support we will give to these individuals.

This then forces us to set a value on services rendered. These values will wash through our total communities. They will affect our environment in major ways if they are not established in a fair and balanced way. Yet I believe we can make good decisions here and minimize the negative effects.

Frankly, I believe most people will be happy to have a job. Better yet, it will likely be in a field that they will enjoy working in. I say this because many hands make for light work.

Citizens will have multiple job opportunities in the public sector. Our work days should be shorter and thus less stressful. We will also be able to improve our lives by working our way up in the job position structures that we create in the public sector. Those structures will add extra economic, personal, or social incentives for us.

Our individual feelings here could have negative effects on our environment. So, we need to develop a fair and just job value system—one that nearly all of us can understand. I say "nearly all" because selfish people will never agree. The values that we put on the various jobs should limit the negative effect that standards like these sometimes can have on our total environment.

I have to mention this because it is normal to feel slighted when value decisions are made about you and they do not match your view. We will mitigate this issue with a second-tier or even third-tier review system. For a healthy environment, these things have to be taken seriously.

This value system should be based on our understanding of humanity. Not everyone is the same, so we don't all aspire at the same time in life and in the same direction. We also, as a whole, do not have the same exact levels of aspiration. Some of us choose simple lives with seemingly less responsibilities, while others seek challenges for themselves.

We should not believe that those who have high levels of aspiration are necessarily better than those with lower levels. It is unfortunate that we described aspiration in terms of levels as this tends to paint some people better than others; it shouldn't. The reality is that high aspirations do not always determine success.

Unfortunately, excessive levels of aspiration can be detrimental to our world. These would be those that are excessively high and those that are excessively low. Again, excess is a problem, so we need to define it. This is something we can do as a group.

We need to establish levels of job value within our new economic plan. Perhaps, a system with five to ten levels is all that might be required. This could end up being ten to twenty levels; who knows at this point? Psychologists will help us to determine what healthy degrees of variation are.

Human nature is, of course, part of the process in making up these levels. There are at least two main reasons why people would want to move up in their job experiences. The first being their personal sense of self-worth or need for achievement. The second being their desire to have more material things or their personal level of need. It is normal to have needs, and material things can help to make life more enjoyable.

Let's face it—we all have some greed in us. We are better off acknowledging it rather than pretending that we don't. However, we don't want that greed to get too excessive; remember that isn't healthy. It's not healthy for us, for society, or for the planet.

Because we know that our world is not perfect, we know that not everyone will want to participate in our plan. We also know that some people will not be able to participate. These issues along with a few others will quickly cause us to understand that our new system will never be perfect.

Just because we know we will never have a perfect system doesn't mean we shouldn't try. We should look at it this way. If our new system is only a little better than the old one, we will have succeeded. This shouldn't be hard to do as that old system left a lot of room for improvement.

So a continuation of the good old boys' club is not what we need. That old system was a system strongly built on clicks and connections. If you were in the click or knew someone, you got the job much easier, even if there were better people available. Hard work often didn't contribute as much as we were let on to believe.

Our new system will not be giving those free rides as much as the old one did. Golden spoons in the form of excessive family riches or in the form of welfare fraud will be things of the past. This is not to say that families will not be able to help each other enrich themselves; only that the excesses of the past will not be permitted. The new system should have a better chance at raising the living standard for more people and in so doing providing them with the pathway to achieve their educational goals or life roles.

In the price system, there can only be a limited amount of doctors, school teachers, firemen, engineers, chemists, dentists, artists, and on and on. In our system, those career choices will be able to hold a lot more professionals than ever before. Our system will not be built on the need to create shortages to maximize profits. Therefore, people will have a better chance at reaching their career goals.

In the technocracy system, there is a plan where the machines of production are owned by the citizens, not by private people. If we own them, we can run them twenty-four hours a day, seven days a week. This would help to increase our levels of employment. Machines, owned by the citizens, would provide jobs in all of our public resource industries. This would be the food, clothing, shelter, and security industries. We would now own and labor in these industries. Many hands would now make our work much easier. Instead of three shifts, we could have six shifts in every resource industry, making the basic needs of the nation.

A typical public sector work week suggested for the average employee in technocracy would consist of four four-hour workdays a week. This schedule would allow each of us lots of free time. We would have time during each work day plus we would have three full days off to invest anyway we wanted. Every capable person would work in these public jobs.

I would like to say right here that I think this four-hour and four-day objective might be optimistic. I believe we should realistically consider that we might have to work more hours per week at first until we get more in tune to the new system. If our population exceeds our resource base our work hours would have to be extended initially.

These work schedules would need to be determined by the number of machines we have. Another factor is the number of industries that we run as citizens. In addition, it would be easier for us to achieve these optimistic work goals if our expectations for what we should get in return are not unreasonable.

By running both the machines and our public services twenty-four hours a day we provide a means to produce products and services at substantial savings. This provides a means to utilize the machinery, and our labor pool, in the most cost-effective way. If we the people owned the machines and the resources, economic gains for the vast majority can be obtained. These machines would then truly offer all of society an easier lifestyle, which of course was industrialization's original intent.

Labor and machines both become real tools in the toolbox of the economic health of our nation. These public sector jobs provide a way for each of us to pay our own way in this world with our labor. However, that limited work week means that job benefits from the citizen-owned businesses will correspondently be lower.

Remember that we will only be getting our basic living needs from the public sector. These include basic food, clothing, shelter, and security. On the plus side, all able-bodied citizens should be able to find a public job and still have time to pursue other opportunities. Those opportunities should fill the aspiration of a whole lot more citizens than the price system ever could have.

Citizens could find a private capitalistic venture to work for. They could even start their own business. If they want more in life, they will have to do these things. This is because their public sector job will not provide them with all the bells and whistles in life. Right now, most people want more—those constant commercials have convinced us of that. So our system should have compassion and allow those extra work options to be available to them.

Most likely, we will not be able to implement the full technocracy plan. Their plans did not require extensive trading with countries outside of their regional area. We would have to modify their system to accommodate our potential trade deals with other countries. Still, there are a number of technocracy ideas that we could adapt rather easily.

For example, their plan has interesting ideas on building interstate waterways. This provided a means for shipping goods cheaply between the states. Their plan also provides for the public sector machines and the labor force to make it happen.

Interlaced in their plan was a means to offer education to workers/students, both high school and college, who might be working in these traveling jobs. Imagine young people travelling the nation while being employed and being educated all at the same time. These ideas should be studied to see if we could make them fit in our new system, if given the chance.

We need to reform ourselves. We have been inundated with more wasteful consumer consumption ideas than any population that ever existed on the planet. There is a lot of brainwashing for us to overcome. The millions of hours of commercials, which taught us to consume, have created problems for us. However, knowing about it is the first step in the right direction.

Under the price system rules, unless there is economic growth, there will always be unemployment. However, their growth plans purposely encourage additional populations to grow in our nation. This then nullifies the new job opportunities that would have otherwise been available. This further perpetuates their never-ending call for growth and never-ending lack of jobs.

Consider the current jobless situation that was built on a false need for population growth. That growth was really required to create a cheap labor force for the private industries. This kind of growth has had ill effects on our country's total economic health. It is part of the reason we have such a huge debt.

In our new system, there should be no need for anyone who can work, to be without a job. Unless of course, our population becomes so excessive that our resources give out. However, armed with the facts, citizens will be better equipped to make sounder decisions for their families.

I believe it is possible to manage full employment, even with our current population. However, the scientists will have to determine what our standard of living will be at this higher-population level. Our new plan should make all citizens aware of how our population levels, along with our resources, contribute to our standard of living.

Each citizen will receive a minimum level of support automatically. This will provide them with minimum food, clothing, shelter, and security. It likely would not be much, as incentives to work need to be established. Note that as little as this might be, no one would be homeless, starving, or without basic healthcare or clothing.

Those of us who want more 'things' will have the opportunity to work more. I believe most of us would appreciate having more job opportunities, especially if we have a number of occupations to pick from. These jobs will provide additional compensation so that luxuries can be purchased.

In order to have fairness, our basic standard of living needs to be determined. To this end, we determine how are resources can be divided among our total population. This then will determine what basic standard of living we should have.

This is no different than what a normal family of today might do. If a father and mother have two children and forty dollars a day to live on, that's $10 a piece. If a father and mother have six children and forty dollars a day to live on, that's $5 a piece.

This is basic economics, not a hard-line socialistic evil. If we chose a system or plan, where we as citizens own the resource corporations, we shouldn't expect to be excessively poor or excessively wealthy. We should strive, at first, to provide the basic needs to our citizens.

The benefits that we would offer would of course only be in the industries that we operate. Excess monies made by our corporations would be fed back into the social system. This would add additional funds to help support city, state, and federal systems of government. By the way, both public and private job opportunities here would work to enhance our system.

Our needs here would be initially set at the basic living mark and only improved if conditions warranted. Other economic systems, namely, capitalism, will work together with this public plan to determine a person's total standard of living. Remember that there should be ample time during the public sector work week for workers to pursue other avenues of lifestyle improvements, if they so desire.

I should tone down my optimistic picture of this new system here only because I do not know how far we will fall in our economic collapse. I would rather be honest and say, "I don't know." However, I truly believe that our new system would be less painful on us than a restart back into that old system. I believe the level of pain there would be a whole lot worse.

Our new economic system should be designed to allow as much individual freedoms as possible. Those extremes or excessive behaviors however have to be stopped or we will fall back to the same principles that the price system holds. When some people hold excessive freedoms, they take away freedoms from others, by hook or by crook.

Just as we teach our children that they cannot always have everything they want, we adults will have to learn that we cannot always have everything we want either. Our system should not be a system based on debt, especially if that debt would prop up or support countries that could likely become our future enemies. Debt should be drastically reduced, if we allow it at all.

If debt is used in our new system, it should be used cautiously and only used in dire circumstances. Since debt is a pathway back to the old system, we should avoid it, if at all possible. As responsible adults, we sometimes have to put aside ideas, goals, and dreams until they are financially affordable. We need to start being better adults.

If we are smart, we will give our citizens the tools they need to fix the problems in our world. It is important to remember that these are problems that, very likely, the old price system put into play. That legacy is something we will have to face, and for a while, it will hold us back from doing everything we might otherwise do. We shouldn't pout about it, as it does no good. Besides, our new system should produce positive results once it is up and running. However, this is a huge country, so it will take some time.

All in all, our citizens should begin to live an improved lifestyle, and this should grow with time. The efficiencies of our factories and machines will play an important part on our lifestyles. The skill of our workers will also help determine our standard of living. They will of course have to contribute by working four to six hours a day and perhaps four to five days a week at public jobs.

The public sector employees again would be compensated for their service. Their salary will be appropriate for the work they do. The compensation provided here should help to further improve a person's lifestyle, even for those who only want to work in the lesser demanding professions. No tax would be collected on these public sector jobs, as your service sufficiently covers that particular responsibility.

It is likely that most people will want to aspire to higher-paying positions. So, a strategy will be established to provide those opportunities for career enhancement. Our economic design will have measures that will help make these things possible.

Efficiencies of scale, for one thing, should help to support this system. The common ownership of basic resources will help to reduce the excessive pricing practices that we faced under the pricing system. The lower cost of food, clothing, shelter, and security should enhance our lifestyles as well. The security resources will include health care for all citizens. You might be a public worker in this industry if you aspire to that calling.

By allowing a private capitalistic system to exist as an adjunct to our publicly owned capitalistic system, we will provide additional opportunities for our citizens. There will be opportunities to add extra income to further improve their living standards, should they desire. This private capitalistic system will also have to have restraints on it. Without restraints, it would return to the monster that caused our current financial woes. We would tax this system, and the proceeds here would be used to purchase resources to further support the public system.

I should clarify that tax on income mentioned above. This time we would establish, by vote, a flat rate tax, with no loopholes, on all private income. Our new government would square this so that it conforms to our Constitution.

We will limit capitalism's negative attributes by controlling the size of the private individual companies. The positive side to this action is that it will increase the number of competing companies. This works to enhance a free market atmosphere. The result is that capitalism is forced to function as it was meant to.

A truly free market is good for employment. It also works well to control the excesses of wealth which are proven to bring in corruptions. These would be corruptions such as buying off the local politicians at the expense of the general public. Additional corruptions that can be curtailed are the excessive waste of natural resources, the destruction of our environment, and the many negative impacts on future generations; debt is just one.

Today's 90% group also contains a small segment of people at the very bottom of this economic pile. Their percentage grows as the economy worsens. It is likely that a good part of them do not want to be freeloaders, but they have little to no choice under the price system. Unfortunately, some of them have become freeloaders intentionally, because they have given up.

However, we all know that some human beings will end up as leeches no matter what system is in place. So, there is a need to be a little harsh on economic leeches in any sector of our economy. There are freeloaders in both the top 10% group and the bottom 90% group.

In our new system, even with the planned improvements to reduce the burdens of life, there will still be freeloaders. Yet, with our new system, freeloaders are more likely to be those in need of our mental health services. I say this because any healthy person would want to be active and work toward self-improvement.

In our new system, there should only be a few freeloaders. However, if that segment grows, it could cause a lot of harm. We will work to improve our system so that the citizens will be happy with it. This will happen if we are fair and balanced in our treatment of each other.

Those economic freeloaders who will not work at all, but are capable of working, should face economic consequences for their actions. However, in our new system, these people will no longer have the excuse that they could not find a job. This is because we will have jobs for them. Jobs in the public sector will be so numerous that finding work will not be hard.

Freeloaders in the top group will also be addressed under our new system. Since everyone should work to support each other, they will no longer be exempt from it. A few hours of work in the public sector, just like everyone else, is fair and just—no more golden spoons. Don't worry, a little work will not hurt them.

Those people in the top sector now should expect their incomes to be reduced. However, it is likely they will still remain at the top of the heap. Yet, without the huge incomes to insulate or protect them from work, they will have to participate in their civic duties just like everyone else.

Excessively wealthy freeloaders, after all, would look for ways to take advantage of others. Perhaps, they can redeem themselves, in part, by giving rather than by taking under this new system. Who knows, they just might like their new job better. In any event, we should not feel guilty for making them work the same as everyone else.

Now, there are a great number of people who truly cannot work. This could be due to their diagnosed mental or physical conditions. People with medical conditions, whatever their status, are in need of our help, and our system should find a way to address their needs.

In addition, our retired senior population would not be required to work. They could however apply for work in the public sector, if they wished. There would be numerous light work activities that would be available.

Now, those people who seek to take advantage of others will have to face the same medical and criminal screenings that we all would. The goal of these screenings is to provide either medical or civic help, and if need be - prison hardships. Those hardships would be required to discourage corrupted behaviors.

It should be our hope that all citizens will begin to think of themselves at the very least as owners/employees of the new economic system. If they do, they will be welcomed as part of the workforce, perhaps starting at the bottom level. However, they do not have to remain at the bottom. All of us working together will be able to contribute to our American culture in a positive way.

Drugs

Today, many people in both upper- and lower-income groups have fallen victim to drugs and crime patterns associated with our current price system. The new system should be designed to offer assistance for the addictions that exist in all segments of society. Its motif will place it in a better position to help people with these problems.

It will be more likely to help, because its nature is that of an inclusive design. The design provides mental health care to all. This alone is something the price system avoided, as in their view, it would not make them money. Hospitals often discharged patients early for economic reasons. Our new citizen workforce will allow cost savings that will improve recovery plans.

All people that wish to participate in the new system will be welcomed, and they will receive the opportunities that are available. Money will become secondary in this new process; so the old system will be less likely to creep back in. However, we should not let our guard down, as we do not want a repeat.

It is true that a system that would mix public labor certificates with a money system leaves the door open for crime. The use of money always has this potential. There are, however, other ways to close the door on crimes, for example - how should we view drug crimes?

Drugs are, as most of us know, a means to exploit the citizens. Lower economic groups have tended to suffer the most when drugs are involved. We can design a system that will give them a better chance at relief. We all have to learn to use self-control—this much we know. Those with addictions will hopefully be given a better chance at doing this, under our new system of economics. Here are a few reasons for this, which I think you will agree will help.

First, we should revisit our policies on drugs. We should have an easier time controlling this problem if we can set limits on how much property and wealth a person can have. In a sense, this is a limit on greed. Greedy people have no problem taking advantage of people so they can live in excess. By setting limits on wealth, we will have some control over those excessive behaviors.

Drug pushers want extreme wealth as they desire excessive life-styles. To obtain their lifestyle, they will use anyone they can. With their excessive money, they find ways to advance their drug trade. A limit on material wealth will stop a lot of criminal activity, as we will be able to see the abuses very easily.

Under our new system, it will be harder to hide their excessive wealth. Our design should set limits to prevent excessive lifestyles. Their home would have to be more modest than they would desire. Homes beyond their economic limit would stick out and be easily noticed. If a million dollars a year is our cap, then they are going to have a hard time explaining were all the extras came from.

Our plans should include this cap on income. However, there is a need for a certain degree of allowable wealth. Why? This is because it is part of the American dream. Excessive wealth, however, provides incentives for greedy individuals to take advantage of others. We will find a balance by experimentation.

There are many things we can do to reduce the appeal of criminal acts. For example, there are plans to allow marijuana to be sold in as much the same way as whiskey, beer, and cigarettes are today. On first thought, you might say this doesn't make sense, as would any prudent person. However, our world doesn't make sense if it did no one would take drugs, right? We need the wisdom to know the difference as to when we can help and when we are just making things worse.

It may be easy for children to buy whiskey, beer, and cigarettes these days. However, that being said, it is far easier for them to by marijuana. The market for this is so lucrative, and the people involved mostly get involved because other job opportunities are not available. Our system needs to take away the drug workers and the drug marketplace as well. There are things we can do here.

The public corporations will provide those employment opportunities, in our system. It will afford jobs to nearly everyone who wants one. These opportunities alone will help to reduce the drug trade. When fewer people are there to illegally distribute, the problem will decrease. This alone would not solve the problem, but it's a start.

Obviously, removing the prohibition on marijuana would drastically reduce the illegal marketplace for the drug. When the drug can be purchased less expensively at the store, the illegal market will shrink. Customers would also prefer a quality-monitored prepackaged form as well, which also would shrink the illegal market. Even just the convenience of being able to purchase the drug at specially designated locations would further reduce the illegal trade.

There would be at least seven immediate benefits from these actions:

1. The drug wars, which cause so many deaths at the borders and elsewhere, will be sharply reduced.

2. The cost of the drug war can be drastically reduced, as a large part of the problem is coming from marijuana dealings.

3. Taxes can be extracted from the sale of this product. This will help improve our deficits.

4. This new source of business will employ more people; this can be a new farm product.

5. We will be better able to keep this substance out of the hands of our children.

6. Our national forest will not be misused for growing marijuana, so those parks will be safer to enjoy.

7. By allowing marijuana as a product, we would also be able to increase the use of hemp to be grown. Hemp could open up several new industries, from clothes to building materials, as well as other business ventures. Hemp could become a new cash crop to support our farming industry.

This approach requires us to adjust to a new paradigm, a new way of thinking. It requires us to stop thinking that we can win a war on marijuana. Obviously, the huge financial resources we spend are clearly not enough to do the job. Adding more economic resources to the current attempt will only hasten our economic collapse.

The war on marijuana has to be seen for what it is. That war is a plan that has caused more harm than good. This can be measured by the number of deaths it has caused. That being the deaths of innocent workers and by-standers during the process of enforcement.

Further, we act hypocritically in allowing alcohol, a substance that is just as bad if not worse. With alcohol, we witnessed the same violence during prohibition, and we learned that it was ultimately more humane and economic to allow it. Despite all of its miserable downsides, it made sense to allow people access to alcohol.

We could use the money we save, from the drug war, to educate people instead. This education would be on the harmful effects of any drug on our bodies. We will teach people to use extreme caution when considering drugs. We can use the power of advertising to assist us; this time in a positive manner.

Remember that the current war on drugs provides the price system with a multitude of ways for money to be extorted.[3] Those in charge of the price system could care less who gets hurt in the process of the drug trade. They make money in both fighting the war and selling the products. People using the price system use its corruptible design to make excessive amounts of money.

That is how the price system was designed to work. This means the system itself supports not only illegal drug trade but also all other illegal activities. Just simply changing the price system should drastically reduce a number of our problems.

The New System versus the Price System, Continued

The 90% group at the bottom, under a new economic system, should be able to improve their lot. Still, we know that some people will choose not to participate in any system. We will need to allow our system the flexibility of grace toward people who choose to drop out as we know some will.

People want and need personal liberties. Our task should allow for people to wander the street if they desire. In return, however, they will have to agree to not impose on the good nature of others. They must agree to not sleep on public or private property unless it is allocated for that use.

Their rights should not trample other people's rights. In order to achieve a balance here, every city should be required to set up temporary shelters or areas designed to accommodate transient system dropouts. Street people will have to sleep at these locations or undergo mental health testing to determine if their condition warrants treatment at a mental health facility. Individual freedoms do not supersede social freedoms in order of importance. This means we will have rule of law.

Yes, we need to provide a mental health-care program again. It should be top-quality care using state-of-the-art techniques. We should no longer throw troubled people in jail because of their mental problem, nor allow them to wander the streets.

There actually is some cost-effectiveness in using proper care facilities. There will be savings to local police departments, who are often called out to care for these problems. Those call outs will be reduced. The cities will also benefit as less crime will improve the business climate. The commercial atmosphere will be healthier and less stressful for everyone.

The price system encourages the idea of excessive wealth or *bling*. That instills poor values, a trait in our society that instigates most of the problems we face. For example, it promotes the borrowing beyond our incomes, which causes us to have the financial problems we face.

Further, in order to keep their terrible system going, creative criminal actions are necessary and have to be preformed. Those doing these things all too often get away with it, because they are in control of the system. They make the rules, so many of these criminal behaviors are not even considered crimes. You may be asking yourself, what is he talking about?

You've likely heard that old expression of "you can't see the forest for the trees." The price system is the forest and *they* populate it with those trees. Because of this we tend to see what they want us to see. We are indoctrinated to believe that private ownership or government taxation of the sun, wind, water, and land resources are perfectly normal things.

We are told that there is no problem with a few people having most of the money. They tell us that it is our fault that their system is in such bad shape. They borrow heavily in our name in order to maintain their financial system. We are then told that we need to buy our goods from their overseas businesses.

Our purchases have helped to make several countries wealthy. Some of those countries have used our money to build up their military. Those military forces are now ready to be turned against us. The price system has even gone so far as to borrow money from our potential enemies. The results of these actions have now exposed not only our armies to harm's way but also our very heartland. This is the system that those that benefit royally want.

Income Disparity: Entitlements

Another needless dilemma that the price system gives us centers on incomes. Around the time of the 2008 economic breakdown, many communities came face to face with declining tax revenues. Many local governments had to cut jobs and lower wages or benefits. These cuts were mostly in the support-level government positions. Upper-level positions didn't always face the same threats. The cuts hurt city workers, teachers, and even the police and fire departments.

There was and is a strong feeling that these workers had previously negotiated unreasonably excessive income and benefit packages. This then was the reason given for the economic hardships that the cities faced. Those workers were however just using price system practices to receive those excessive benefits. In the end, those lower-level workers were not always allowed to keep all of those excessive benefits.

To be clear, I am not trying to defend the excessive wages and benefits of some public employees. In my mind, public employees should never have had excessive wages and benefits to begin with. We need to stop thinking that some people are excessively better than others. People in general are pretty much the same.

From the perspective of the price system elites, it is fine for them to make as much money as they possibly can. They seldom if ever have to return the money; instead, they have us repay it for them in the form of bailouts. Their leadership roles insulate them from returning their excessive incomes, because in their minds, they deserve it. We however do not deserve to be treated fairly, especially when it comes to income.

By the way, the elites here include our federal congressional representatives and their upper-level staff. These elites have also carved out excessive benefits for themselves. However, we should not limit the swamps to Washington DC only. They exist all across the nation.

They cry that we common people have too many entitlements. They fail to see the entitlements they have set up for themselves far exceed those that we have. They have far better health care, better pensions, and better incomes than the majority of the citizens. Their entitlements truly are excessive, but no, we are not to look at that. Don't look behind the curtain because they are the great and powerful leaders of the free world.

You on the other hand should be trembling, because you are not their equal. I may be going a little overboard here, on my criticism. My frustration with these overlords causes this. I will admit that there are still some sincere and honest people in government; unfortunately, the price system overwhelms them easily.

How Do We Value a Person's Worth?

It is true that we all have special skills, talents, abilities, and gifts. Individually, some of these gifts may seem inconsequential. However, in the broader scope of things, sometimes these seemingly lesser gifts equal out. Gifts that seem unimportant sometimes really are important. Some on close inspection can rival the gifts of geniuses, perhaps more than one would like to admit.

For example, the gift of patience, being able to put up with boring work operations, should not be taken for granted. Nor should it be taken as something that just is. How long would some self-proclaimed elites last if they had to do the same redundant task or a dirty job over and over again all day?

Today, in the general job market, people said to have the gift of intelligence are generally rewarded above those whose skills are of the physical nature. Yet, intellectual jobs are often easier in many ways. Menial work on the other hand, more often than not, requires patience over a vast amount of time.

We should consider that patience may be a different type of mental ability. Menial workers typically do not end up with better working conditions. By the way, even these jobs require some training, and a lot of people do not make the cut. Yet these jobs are typically relegated to a vastly lower value. Our new system should take things like this into account when setting job values.

I am not saying that intelligence should not be rewarded or that menial jobs should be rewarded above all others. I am just trying to point out that our God-given gifts need to be reassessed. If we did not have all of these numerous gifts, we as a body of citizens would be in deep trouble. We as a society are a team. Now, a team functions better if we keep all members properly rewarded and healthy.

The price system's approach to valuing jobs is distorted in a false reality. For example, the job of picking crops can be just as hard as the job of helping to design the next new rocket engine, only in a vastly different way. Given the chance, who would not want to work in a comfortable environment? Who really wants to work hard bending over in the heat picking crops all day? Guess which job in the price system is valued more? You got it, the comfortable one.

The rationale is that one person has more schooling than the other. True to the price system's demands, schooling costs you money, so in order to get that comfortable job, you have to spend money. This is, after all, their system. Yet even if you get that education, you may only have a 25% chance of getting a design job under the price system. That means, you could be educated and still be picking crops.

Field laborers could help to feed our military, and rocket engines could possibly be used in our defense system. Both jobs can support the same customer. Based on their possible uses, each job has value beyond their initial face value.

Even working in the janitorial industry can be as important to our well-being as work in the health industry. It is because germs anywhere can cause disease and death, unless someone eliminates them. Today, we allow our vanities to get in the way of honoring those who do the dirty work, and the price system encourages our vanities. Why we humans honor glamour and glitz instead of substance is something we all need to work on.

We make many occupations out to be less important or less respectable, but are they really? Would our elites like doing that dirty job? Of course, they wouldn't want to do it; but instead of honoring those who have the gift that allows them to do that work, the elites far too often make those workers into inferior people.

The price system all too often does not acknowledge various gifts. Their economic occupation-valuing scheme is designed to skim off profits from these workers. What unacknowledged gifts might those be, tolerance, patients, grit, perseverance, kindness, caring, or even simply a drive to help?

The price system has to reduce the value of many occupations. This happens because the controllers would not be able to slice off part of the wages from those employees if they honored them properly. In other words, the controllers would not be able to keep their lion's share of the profits.

Viewing their system this way allows one to see how and where certain people get their wealth. In some cases, their employees lost potential income so that others in the company could make excessively more than they deserved. We the people were led to believe that the price system is the only economic plan that is possible. Further, they want us to believe that it is an honest system. Do you really believe that either is true?

The Price Systems and the Olympics

The price system compelled Athens, Greece, in 2004 to hold the Olympics. This was supposed to help their economy, yet today, they are in very rough shape. This Olympic venture was just one example of how the price system's private industry ended up winners while the government, the citizens of Greece, were asked to pick up the tab.

South Korea announced that it would spend twenty-seven billion dollars to expand Pyeongchang for the 2018 Winter Olympics. This investment is expected to produce 230,000 jobs for the private sector. The potential return is said to be sixty billion dollars in consumption. It remains to be seen just how much of that money the public sector will actually see.

I say this because Greece was told similar things when it hosted the Olympics. Those things didn't happen. Deals like these usually end up enriching the private sector at the public sector's expense; while they don't normally bankrupt the country, they generally benefit wealthy private contractors—contractors using the price system to increase their bottom line.

In the end, "the price system" divides up the money in an unequal portion. The 10% group, at the top, gets an excessive share and the 90% group gets the leftovers. It has always been done this way. Don't you think it's time to try something new, something that doesn't create such a huge disparity between rich and poor?

CHAPTER 4

—◆—

Influences on Government by the Price System

What good are the Declaration of Independence, the Constitution, and the Bill of Rights if they can be violated by offsetting laws, confounded by mountains of legal requirements, or simply ignored? For that matter, what good is any new economy if the same treatment can be expected to be applied to it?

While I have great admiration and respect for our original founding documents, I still know, as those who wrote them, that they are not perfect. They knew that parts of those documents had to be changed in order to get the necessary support from the various colonies. Concessions were made to businesses mostly. The price system was behind those changes.

In making some of those changes, the documents became flawed. For example, there were changes that led them to allow slavery, create imbalances in taxation, and others that promoted the fragmentation of ideals. While those original major documents were something to be proud of, for many reasons, those side-panel concessions were not. In fact, those deals are the reasons these documents cause us pain and suffering even to this day.

This pain and suffering predominately comes from those compromises that were made by the price system politics of their day. Those document changes mostly had a monetary, price system, cause to them. Any system powerful enough to allow slavery is a system that warrants our caution. Still, even with the flaws, the documents had many other ideas that were good.

Using the basic framework from these old documents, we find great examples of an attempt at fairness, justice, freedom, and most importantly simplicity. We should explore the idea of possibly renewing or reviving their essence in a new form. The trick is to do all this with an eye on giving these new documents some further safeguards that our Founding Fathers were not able to achieve.

Basically, the originals were relatively sound documents in design, but their substance was at times perverted by the politics at that time. Again, those politics were instigated by the price system itself. We need to design a governmental system with document safeguards.

The safeguards would be required to prevent the wicked few from seeking special favors over the general population. Even to this day, those favors are secured by provisions, that is, loopholes, for the price system—favors designed to benefit a chosen few. Our new documents will need to present severe impediments for the cunning politics that always want to creep in.

This would mean changing our systems of justice, business, and money. The system of taxing has to be changed as well. Most importantly will be our changes to our system of politics.

The price system's control over our government ends up causing most of the problems we face. One aspect of this is the way in which we elect our representatives. The method is painfully short of fairness in opportunity.

I for one would like to see a change in the way we choose our executive officers. However, any new process that we come up with would need to have armor. Its skin would need protection from the potential attacks of unscrupulous corruptions.

If the price system falls, we might have an opportunity to reduce the political process to a simpler and more representative form. The new system should bring about a constantly changing leadership hierarchy of highly qualified people. There should be a much stronger role for scientists of every discipline to be involved.

There should actually be schools designed to educate potential leaders for the government roles they might aspire to. Our leaders would thus be tested, and their skills would be predetermined so as to assure a high standard. People shouldn't be sent into any job without some training, experience, or guidance from a peer. Schools also provide standards, and this is preferred over the anything goes approach.

Our leadership structure should consist of both scientists and diplomats. That power structure is something we would have to work out. Our goal would be to limit the ability of outside forces to corrupt our government and to simplify the governmental process.

Various chapters in this book offer ideas on possible changes to our systems of justice (courts), business (corporations), and money (banking). These systems have all intertwined mischievously with politics to create the chaos that the bulk of our population is feeling today. Changes in these systems would help to cement our new plan together.

Politics: Two Parties and a President

"A house divided against itself cannot stand."[1] Today, I might add to this statement by saying, "Hence the reason for the Democrat and Republican parties." Yes, I am implying that these two parties are giving us many of the problems we suffer.

I am saying that they are actually tearing down our house. You may not agree just yet. However, this book should at least give you some reason for concern. If you do not agree, here are some thoughts that hopefully will influence your current line of reason.

Nearly all of us have witnessed how poorly the two party-system works, at one time or another. The partisan voting and arguments have damaged the economy and prosperity of the common citizen of the United States of America. For example, when one of these two parties controls the majority of seats in congress and the president happens to be in the minority party, then our government is said to be a lame duck.

We are told then that the majority party has less reason to work with the president in order to improve our countries condition. The idea is that if they do help him or her, then the president might end up taking credit for their support. Thus, they would actually be helping the president's party to be reelected in the next election. This lame duck condition is only one reason that a two-party system is a poor design for the general public.

More recently, this obstructionist behavior occurs even when one party is the dominant party. So, in actuality, the idea of any one party helping the president of the opposite party is really a full-term problem. This problem is called partisan voting.

Why would anyone want to tolerate a system that allows these severe impediments to government functions? Yet that is what we do. Just a side comment here, President Lincoln's house divided comment was also expressed in the Bible by Jesus.[1]

Yes, the two-party system doesn't work well for the general public, but it works perfectly for the price system itself. The people running the price system count on this division so that they can continue to have extreme influence over governmental affairs.

The price system supports the efforts of the two parties to squeeze out any other perceived rival or threatening political groups. The two parties do this by severely limiting participation of minor parties into the debating process. The Democrats and Republicans have often joined forces to accomplish this.

In the various states of our country, they have both worked to impede the access to the ballot box, that is, access for any independent party that might threaten their local superiority. Nearly all, if not all, fifty states have election rules that favor the two parties over any contenders.

The two parties have clearly controlled the media networks. In doing this, they have relegated most opposition parties into obscurity. This is done through the use of ridicule. They often brand them as stupid or as threats to our way of life.

So effective are these media actions that the voice of only the two major parties is nearly always consuming the airways. Most people think that there are no other valid choices out there. This leads people to feel that they are locked into choosing one or the other of these two parties. This is exactly what the price system wants and needs.

Both parties have connived to establish a lobbying system that allows wealthy corporations and organizations to purchase favors. The lobbyists fund activities that support candidates for election or reelection. These efforts produce the money required to run the expensive campaigns. Those campaigns are required for candidates to get and stay in office.

Lobbyist money thus in the end helps to buy the votes that are required from the public. Yes, those campaign ads are truly selling something. They are selling candidates. Ultimately, those lobbying investments are later returned in the form of favors. This is actually happening up front and within sight of all of us as if there isn't anything to worry about.

These favors are purchased legally from members of congress and even the executive office up to and including the president.[2] This process has in essence created a one-party system. The effect is that these promises to lobbyists have, far too often, put both parties on the same side of these special interest issues.

That one party wouldn't necessarily be bad if that party was on the common American citizen's side. Unfortunately, both parties ultimately side with the price system. We the people end up with the short end of the stick. Worse yet, they generally use that stick to beat us.

This leads me to a quote that I heard the other day—"If you have lost faith in man's Elephant or Donkey try the *Lamb*." Sorry, I don't know the source of the quote, but it sure fits well here.

Early on in our history, our government found that lobbying was a bad idea. The government back then constantly had investigations into the shady dealings of lobbyists. They tried everything to control them. However, lobbyists always found a way to work their way back into positions of influence. Very often, their influence worked against the individual states.

Our founders wanted a small central government that would have allowed the states to retain many of their sovereign rights. The states were to maintain a great deal more power than they have today. Over the years, the federal government has expanded its roles. In so doing, they expanded the amount of money that they extracted from the individual states. More precisely, the money was extracted from the citizens of those states. The states became weaker and weaker, and the federal government grew in power.

The central government, via the price system, used the power of the printing press in three ways to secure its power position. First, they got control over the printing of a national currency. The price system allowed the printing of what is called "funny money," because they established a private fiat system.[3]

Secondly, by controlling the money supply, they indirectly secured control of the newspapers and later nearly all the other forms of media. This was done through licensing permits and other political favors. It's easy to see how lobbying may have played a role here.

By using various combinations of these two printing powers, they secured additional powers as well. These powers allowed them to exercise additional control over the states. The main power here, and the third one on my list, is the power to allocate funds.

The federal government can allocate special funds to be given to certain states. Federally funded programs are distributed, with strings attached. Those strings provide a means to achieve control over the local governmental authorities.

This is because authorities are constantly in jeopardy of losing their funding. You should see this as a testament to the idea that if you control a person's purse, you control the person. Once again, the price system's design subtly infects or corrupts our lives. This control wouldn't necessarily be bad if it benefited the common American citizen, but it rarely does.

The end result of those actions is that the federal government gets the lion's share of our tax dollars and even more power. They have bloated themselves up in size, organizationally on purpose. This helps them to provide additional political favors to donors via regulations. Let's not forget those lobbyists who want those favors as well.

The federal government's size, along with their actions, is helping to crush our economy. Our founders wanted the federal government to be limited in power and size. Somehow, we forgot those old words of wisdom, "Absolute power corrupts absolutely." This is the system we have and need to fix. It is a system that feeds off the price system and vice versa.

Our founders also championed a system of checks and balances, not to create a lame duck government, but to make it run smoother. This is why they created the three branches of government. The branches put balance into the system. It may have worked if not for the perversions that it attracted.

Somehow over the years, the executive branch grew in power. The executive branch of today now causes us reason to question just how balanced our government system is. In addition to adding to the partisanship attitudes of both the House and Senate, the executive has also increased its influence over the judicial branch. This situation has created a whole other set of problems.

The resulting effect here has caused tremendous waste in government operations. The excessive construction of laws has created a vast amount of waste. The manipulation of the courts, to render opposition rulings, has increased the need for adjudication and hence more waste.

Now, it seems to me that we are smart enough to fix these problems. We need to understand how those issues all crept into the systems. Could they all be linked to the price system? You bet.

The fix will require many solutions within each of the primary systems that effect our government. These are the systems that make our country operate. Perhaps, we need to start first with the executive office.

So I will offer a suggestion that hopes to make use of current technologies to accomplish its goals. This fix involves the way we elect our president. Based on past performance, I believe most people would prefer a new system without politicians involved in this process at all.

This next section is written in a way that would allow the current price system to adopt it. They would adopt anything if there was money to be made. Still, the ideas in this next section contain the flexibility for use by our new design or the old price system, if it could make them money.

The Executive Office, Its Role, and Capitalism

To start with, let's completely remove the executive branch of government from its economic links to the House and Senate. We could mandate that the executive office, the president and vice president, as well as their cabinets, close advisors, and staffs have no economic support from the parties. Funding for these positions would be solely by public funds.

Removing these positions from the economic control of any political party should eliminate partisan political schemes at the executive level. Those schemes typically stifle progress in government affairs. The executive leaders, as a stand-alone public entity, would then be much more inclined to do the right thing for the country.

This would be better than doing the right thing for any political party. These days, it seems neither party truly represents the public anyway. If we require that the executive branch become a completely independent body, we then increase the chances that our government will work more effectively, that is, work for the common American citizen.

Executive office holders would not be able to charge fees for speaking engagements or any other commercial activities while in office. After holding their office, there would be limits on the fees that they can charge for potential speaking, book deals, or other commercial activities. All funds above those limits would go to the federal government-to pay for public programs.

Perhaps an annual limit here would be equal to the salary they received while in office. At one point after his term in office, it was reported that President George W. Bush had racked up $15 million in speaking fees. Compensation such as this should be viewed as possible payola and should not be allowed. Things like this should, at the very least, be perceived as conflicts of interest.[4] Not to mention, it is extremely excessive.

To assure that the executive branch is filled with the most qualified persons who are not beholding to any party, I propose a new system of electing these positions. Instead of the parties picking these candidates, I support a plan where the American people themselves pick the twenty most qualified candidates in the country. I say twenty, but there could be more.

The two or three individuals with the most votes would become the candidates for president. If one of these candidates becomes president in the general election, the new president could pick one of the runner ups as the vice president. The balance of the candidates could be hired by these two, for staff and cabinet positions. They might even choose from the top candidates from previous contest.

One caution here is that term limits would and should be applied; otherwise, candidates tend to forget they are political servants and begin to consider themselves royalty. When that happens, we have problems; and it happens more times than naught. Staying around, in office, too long makes them subject to the antics of unscrupulous individuals, who want special favors at the expense of the general population.

The executive branch would, in part, be charged with generating or overseeing governmental improvements. These improvements would have to benefit the majority of the citizens of the country. Legislation that is selective in nature and benefits private companies or individuals over the majority of the citizens would not be allowed.

Perhaps a computer matrix, an actuary of some sort, could be developed to calculate just who is benefiting and just how much from any legislative bill that is being requested. The executive branch could use this tool to help render decisions as to what bills would be allowed to pass. It would also be a good tool to monitor its success.

Now, being a country that has championed capitalism, we must assure that the majority of citizens profit under it. We should consider "the United States of America" as a business owned by the citizens. Our public businesses would become the primary businesses of the land. The legislation that is passed should promote our public interests first. This means we should have a monopoly in our public sector industries.

Under the price system, monopolies were said to be discouraged. However, in practice, there are many extremely large corporations that exist. It seems the rule is really there just for show. It gives us the perception that those large companies are not taking advantage of others. This allows private elites to succeed, not the common citizen.

In an effort to reduce the power of big money interest, companies in the private sector areas should be restricted to noncorporate status. By limiting their business power, they will no longer be able to unfairly advantage themselves over other companies that they compete against. This will allow more businesses to exist in the private sector.

Why is there a need to do this? Whether you realize it or not, private corporations always work to monopolize their field of service. Control over a sector allows them to funnel excessive profits to their executives. This is only one way in which they advantage themselves over others. Under our new plan, the public corporations would now insure the profits would be evenly distributed to the whole population, not mostly to select individuals.

Capitalism, as such, would then work mostly for the common citizen's favor. Today, those profits primarily go to huge private corporations. Two simple rules for us to consider establishing are as follows: Rule one, private companies are always secondary to the corporations of the United States of America; rule two, we should only allow public sector industries the full rights of corporation.

These rules are necessary because private corporations have a tendency to downsize their employees for personal and selfish reasons. Through the reduction of jobs, they can increase their profits. Reducing hourly wages is another way in which executives guarantee their bonuses.

These are actions that excessively enrich the executives of these corporations. They are also reasons for why we the people need corporate ownership. There are a few other things private corporations do to take advantage of others, and I'll get to those later.

One main principle of our new capitalism is it should allow a lot of competition in the secondary business realms. Competition allows more people to have business opportunities so that they too can have easy access to capitalism. Today, most people do not own corporations, but corporations seem to benefit the most, under the price system.

In an attempt to balance our new system, in an area where it would do the most good, corporations should only be owned by the entire population and not by private business owners. By doing this, we stop the price system from running corporate advantages solely into the hands of a few select people.

Corporations themselves make more sense if they are owned by all the people. By allowing all the citizens to own the corporations, everyone receives the advantage of the corporation, not just a select few. Not only does this make the system fairer to the common citizens, but also it makes them active owners in the business.

The president of our country seems like the obvious choice to oversee the handling of our corporate businesses. The reason for this is that in this plan, he would not be hampered by partisan bickering. Congress would likely work for those scaled-down business interest, but their lobbying efforts would be drastically reduced. They should work for everyone, but under the price system somehow, that doesn't happen as much as it should.

Now, with an independent executive office, the House and Senate would have more reason to work together with the executive branch. Why? If, for example, the House Republicans offered a bill that proved to benefit the majority of the public, then their party would get credit for it, increasing their appeal. Likewise, the other parties would have reason to compete and so improve their party's favor within the country. But how would we pick the president, and other executives, if the parties are not involved?

This Is the American President

When you think about it here in the United States, our presidential candidates are picked out by a very small number of self-selected and self-appointed leaders. That is, the American public at large does not truly participate in the initial selection of our candidates. We think we are selecting them, but really, they were picked long before by the price system controllers. We generally don't hear about candidates until the hierarchy in some political association begins to promote them.

Prior to our awareness of these candidates, the controllers use various veiled systems to scout for and identify potential candidates. These associations then begin to spend their money on those candidates, at least initially. They have to be sure those candidates do things their way or the backing is withdrawn. The resulting support causes the candidate to acquire a debt to these groups. If you have any experience in the world of politics, you should have learned that nothing is free. That debt has to be repaid.

In reality, the process of candidate selection involves relatively a few people. These people pick out and promote their candidates to the general public. Since these self-appointed organizational groups also control, to various degrees, the five to seven mainstream media outlets, they also control, to a great degree, who and what we all talk about. It should be of no surprise that we predominately talk about their choices.

Therefore, it shouldn't shock anyone to find that we are funneled into only two choices, political party A or party B. The media doesn't really give any other choice a real chance. They do this by spending the majority of the airtime talking about these two parties and the preselected candidates. This gives those who watch the idea that there really are only two choices.

The limited scope of media coverage generally discourages any support for potential alternative individuals. Anyone who spends their time watching or listening to only the mainstream networks suffers from being fed a select version of either party A or B. This narrow view serves to further the goals of the self-appointed few who provide you with those two choices. By their design, you are given a choice of one party or the other.

The media is controlled or directed through advertisers who sponsor the various political party-talking heads. Constant redundancy of topics provides an abundance of support mostly for these two parties. This is accomplished by filling the airwaves with repeated party A or party B discussions, which occupy the bulk of time the stations are on the air. In short, this is all they are paid to talk about, so that is mostly all we hear.

The loyalty of the media doesn't come cheap. Presidential elections have been running more than a billion dollars per election cycle. Where does the bulk of that money come from? Certainly, it does not come directly from common American citizens. Under the price system, it is normally only the owners of successful businesses, who can easily afford to invest in candidates. Without such backing the common citizen is pretty much out of the selection process. Unless, of course, those that do the selecting see you as a person of interest.

If so, your ideas have to match their ideas. On top of this, you have to have the kind of oratory skills and personality that they are looking for. They might even want to have a little dirt on you so that they have a way to control you, if necessary. If you are a person that can be molded to follow their agenda, they will back you economically.

Now, you will have to sell out your fellow common citizens if you want that wealthy backing. This is the only way common citizens, those in the 90% group, can get access to run for president. Basically, then, under this system, the majority of the citizens were not in any position to choose a candidate, from the very beginning.

Even if we could pick our own candidate, we are not in a position to promote them. We do not have our own main media outlets to promote our candidate. Those main media outlets happen to be all privately owned or privately funded. The owners or funders are deeply entrenched in the price system and wouldn't want to change. They would be giving up billions of dollars in income if they lost control.

The system we currently have in place is very close to another candidate selection system that has been reported on in the press. That report involved a foreign country's process. We need to analyze that report. Perhaps by comparing our system to this other system, we can learn something.

The report roughly explained that in Iran, the Ayatollah gets a list of names from religious leaders and/or perhaps business leaders as well.[5] Then, he looks at these people and weeds out the ones he doesn't like. This then leaves about eight candidates or so that he approves of. Then, the people of Iran get to choose from this group. By the way, even the American press admits that this system is flawed.

However, our American system has a similar process in that only a handful of elites here pick the candidates for us. These elites use money, which they basically take from us, to back the candidates, and they don't want to spend this money foolishly; it wouldn't make good business sense. They want to elect someone who will help them in return. I think you can see the problem with this system. Where is the candidate that represents the common American citizen? Shouldn't there be a candidate of the people and for the people? We instead get price system candidates.

Not all elites are part of this evil system. I believe there are huge numbers of elites that are supportive of the common citizen. That is, there are elites supportive of the original intent of the Republic of the United States of America. These elites do not want to be counted as part of that corrupt group of self-selected leaders. It would be nice if some of these good elites were also business-minded enough to take a chance on supporting the unusual idea I am about to suggest.

Sometimes, ideas seem strange when you first hear them. Then, after you think about the idea, it doesn't sound so silly or strange after all. This next idea does sound very strange. Still it is a way to get the common American citizen involved in this early selection of our candidates. That is, involved in a way so that they feel they have someone that really represents them, someone that they can truly say they are sending to Washington DC.

Many of us have mixed feelings about shows like the old *American Idol* program. On the one hand, shows like these can be used to distract the citizens from the more important things in life. On the other hand, they can be a necessary diversion, of sorts, from these very same troubling, but important things. Things that, because of our lack of control, can sometimes tax are sanity.

Programs on the order of *American Idol* can be of some benefit by breaking our tensions and temporarily relieving our anxieties. Wouldn't it be a bonus to America if an *American Idol*-style television show could be made into a tool for political reform? I think with some creative retooling, it could.

Years ago, during one of the *American Idol* shows, a couple of people in the audience held up a sign. It read, "Simon for President." Simon Cowell was one of the judges at the time. I think the audience appreciated his critical objectivity, at least sometimes, and of course, this is certainly something we need in Washington DC.

Of course, Simon wasn't eligible to run. However, the people with the sign sparked the idea that the show's already established platform might have another use. It could be a great launching point for citizen candidates for president. Perhaps the show could be adapted to have contestants compete for a position as *the American Candidate*.

The structure of the show, it seems to me, lends itself to being more of a democratic means of picking a candidate from among our midst. The winner of the show would be helped to secure his or her name on the ballot in each state for the next election period. This might be assisted and secured with the help of a fan-based support system developed and established during the show. Perhaps, a possible scenario for how this would work would look like the following:

Phase 1

Each entrant would be required to fill out and submit a standard background check form. They would provide information such as family ties, friends, education, and economic status, just as any presidential candidate would do. They would also pay an entrance fee. The fee should work to avoid wasting the judge's time on insincere entrants. Their background check would be enhanced more appropriately in a latter phase of the process.

Phase 2

As a prerequisite, each entrant to the show would be required to construct a basic political platform. They will need to explain and defend each plank. Their platforms would have one common thread. This would be their sworn allegiance to serve the common American citizens, collectively, above all other special interest or private concerns. To thin the field and secure the best possible candidates, a testing process would need to be devised.

The entrants would initially be screened by having them complete a similar battery of test used on the television show called *Jeopardy*. This battery of test would hone in on the skills that a national leader should have in order to run the country. Possible skills sets would be knowledge of American history, world history, political history, business, science, economics, social systems, logic, and current events. This testing requirement should be tough enough to reduce the contestants down to say three hundred or less.

Phase 3

All remaining entrants would now be run through a more thorough background check. This is necessary to uncover any obvious character flaws of a criminal nature. We also would want to make sure they are not ringers from either of the two existing parties. We thus would check if they have any direct working affiliations with political parties, within the last few years, perhaps the last three to five years. This might narrow the field a little bit more.

Phase 4

The entrants that pass the background check and testing would then face an initial panel of twenty-four judges. Judges made up of perhaps teachers, policeman, fireman, doctors, engineers, nurses, scientists, factory workers, waitresses, college students, construction workers, and small business owners. These judges could be any mix of common citizens, not economically employed with the two major parties. They only need to have civic-minded intentions and the ability to pass an initial qualification test. This test would determine if they are able to understand their duties and perform them. They have to be smart enough to understand the platforms they would be judging. They would also have to be able to understand the scoring process.

Once confirmed, together with the other judges, they would listen to and question each of these contestants in order to score their abilities. Their primary goal would be to choose the candidates that would best represent the majority of citizens of the United States of America. We don't want a candidate who would serve a few self-interested groups.

This reduction phase of the process would require a good deal of time. It is likely then that the American public would typically not be able to view this segment in its entirety. So it could be taped and edited in advance, similar to the way of the actual *American Idol* show. Each contestant could be given twenty minutes, or more, to explain and promote their basic platform. If required, perhaps up to an additional forty minutes, or more, of questions from the judges could complete the task.

Possibly, eight or more contestants could be judged each day. Judges at this point will be looking for answers to the various categories on their scoresheet. They will not need to have complete economic details on how each contestant's plan would work. The general feasibility of the contestant's plans will be scored. The mental capabilities of the contestants will also be judged.

At this point, it is important to know basically only the following: what is it that the contestant, he or she, would like to do given the chance at being the president? Judges would also look at their temperament, patience, understanding, and other leadership strengths. These are all part of the categories that need to be scored.

The judges would fill out a score card on each contestant and give them points for their various skills and ideas expressed under each category. Points scored would be based on each contestant's ability to explain their plans, defend their platform, and display the necessary social and leadership skills required. The judges would grade each entrant, and perhaps, the top twenty entrants would advance to the next phase, although there could be more or less.

Along the way, the judges would provide some benchmark ideas to help instruct the audience as to how they scored these contestants. This would be done through a condensed video profile of the ranking process during this phase of the process. This would provide opportunity for some scoring hints, opinions, and pointers to be passed on to the audience. In essence, the audience's task in the next phase of the show would be assisted by watching how the judges performed their job during phase four.

The judge's goal, again, would be to choose the candidates that would best represent the common citizens of the United States of America, that is, the candidate that would do the most good for the most people and not just a select few. The idea here is that doing the most good for the most people would in the end be the most profitable for our country as a whole, a basic principle of capitalism. This is a truth only if we view the country as our business. The word "our" here means that we the people, not some private corporation or corporations.

Phase 5

The American public now gets directly involved in the scoring process in an expanded version of phase 4. During phase 4, the show's host would have explained the ranking process to the audience. An official Web site would also be made available to obtain ranking forms for the final twenty contestants so that the home audience can follow the process and vote. This form should be simply made up of names, scoring squares, and categories with point values.

Now, these twenty contestants will take their platform to the next level by explaining, on live TV, how each idea they have relates to their total plank. In essence, they would explain more thoroughly what they would do and why. They would tell us how they would be the kind of an American president that would improve things for the common American citizen. The public would now use the forms to track each of the final twenty contestants as they continue on to explain their platforms on multiple occasions.

A refined telephone calling process coupled with an Internet voting process could be set up. Perhaps, a variation of the process used on *American Idol* could be employed to determine the results for each contestant. Each voter could be given a virtual card to use for voting. If so, this card would work similarly to a virtual charge card. Your voting would be charged to your account.

This method would restrict the charging to one vote per card per episode during the show's course. You could get an e-statement of your vote(s) on demand. This system would allow for an outside audit of the voting process to determine if there is any vote tampering.

The audit would allow for a review panel to be able to look at your vote, with your permission, and verify it. This is to assure both your statement and what he or she found in the records match. Since this is not the final election process, the secrecy of voting should not be a major issue.

Once the number of contestants is reduced, candidates might even engage in debates and possibly offer up their ideas in a press conference kind of trial. At an appropriate point in the process, contestants would start to be dropped off until the top one emerged as the candidate who would best represent the common citizens of the United States of America.

This idea, as dumb as it may sound, is still wiser than allowing our controllers to pick our leaders for us. The idea calls for the American public to select a common citizen from their mix in a more direct way. This is necessary for the following reason: having a candidate chosen directly from the people would put that candidate beholden to serve the majority of the people.

When the majority of the people prosper, the country will prosper. This process should net a positive effect on the health and wealth of America. Citizens, common or elite, should want to see an America that has strong moral and economic wealth.

Globalization plans, under a president for the people, should be redirected to return sovereign rights to the common citizens of all nations. This would allow fair trade to be conducted by common citizens, that is, common citizens working in unity for the good of all, instead of a select few individuals working in collusion for the good of themselves.

The goal then of the common American citizen would be to support candidates who work for everyone. The top two or three finalists would be placed on the ballots in each state. They then would participate in the primary elections on a more equal footing.

The above suggestions are only a starting place. I am sure there are a number of things that others could think of to make this an even fairer, more democratic, and a more entertaining process. The point is that if this worked, America would have a candidate that would be, to a far greater degree, chosen from and by the ranks of the common American citizen.

The questions you might ask are as follows:

Would a process such as this help improve the American dream? I believe so, as now the cost of participation in presidential elections would not be such a great economic obstacle. The common citizen will not need hundreds of millions of dollars to run.

Who would sponsor this show and under what conditions? We the people would present it on public or network television or both. Even under the price system, money could be made here, and as such, they might agree to support it.

Would we really allow candidates to enter regardless of their non-mainstream views or even radical views? Yes, that is the democratic way and a long-standing constitutional belief. I understand that there is a possibility that the American public might choose a poor example of mankind. However, the chance of that happening already exists so that possibility wouldn't change anything. To guard our original goal, the candidates would have to take an oath.

What would that oath be? It would be to do the most good for the most people. In addition, they would swear to not work for the select few, but for the good of the whole body of citizens. It is more likely that the price system would not allow this kind of process to occur. If this process was to occur, it likely would be after we had established our new economic system. At this point, we would want assurances that as president, our candidate would not take us back into the old price system.

If we allowed the common citizen to pick the candidate, would the proponents of the two-party system stay completely out of the process? It is not likely, so a rules committee and security teams will investigate and monitor the process. While the price system exists, this would not be easily done. Money has a way of turning people away from the good of all to the good of *me*.

Perhaps the biggest question would be, is the American public ready for this or would the hypnotic trance of the mainstream networks disrupt the whole intent? I think enough people would watch since it has all the makings of a good reality show already. If we could add the intellectual element of a show like *Jeopardy*, then that would make it even better. I still wouldn't rule out stiff competition from network television to try and draw people away from the process, at least while the price system exists.

I will admit that the above American candidate process is a flight of fantasy at this point. Dreams are not always things that make complete sense. However, there could be elements in them that others might be able to build upon.

Politics Part 2

If you have Internet access, you may have gotten an e-mail from a friend that contained the story of the five monkeys; that is how I received it.[6] The story provides us with some interesting food for thought. On the outside chance that you are not familiar with it, I would also like to share this short story with you as it was sent to me:

> If you start with a cage containing five monkeys and inside the cage, hang a banana on a string from the top and then you place a set of stairs under the banana, before long a monkey will go to the stairs and climb toward the banana. As soon as he touches the stairs, you spray all the

other monkeys with cold water. After a while another monkey makes an attempt with the same result; all the other monkeys are sprayed with cold water. Pretty soon when another monkey tries to climb the stairs, the other monkeys will try to prevent it. Now, put the cold water away.

Remove one monkey from the cage and replace it with a new one. The new monkey sees the banana and attempts to climb the stairs. To his shock, all of the other monkeys beat the stuffing out of him. After another attempt and attack, he knows that if he tries to climb the stairs he will be assaulted. Next, remove another of the original five monkeys, replacing it with a new one. The newcomer goes to the stairs and is attacked. The previous newcomer takes part in the punishment . . . with enthusiasm.

Then, replace a third original monkey with a new one, followed by a fourth, then the fifth. Every time the newest monkey takes to the stairs he is attacked. Most of the monkeys that are beating him up have no idea why they were not permitted to climb the stairs. Neither do they know why they are participating in the beating of the newest monkey. Finally, having replaced all of the original monkeys, none of the remaining monkeys will have ever been sprayed with cold water. Nevertheless, none of the monkeys will try to climb the stairway for the banana. Why, you ask? Because in their minds . . . that is the way it has always been! This, my friends, is how Congress operates. (Robbie Cooper)

Perhaps, this insightful story is more than just a silly thought. We should look a little closer at how congress itself works or doesn't work, as the latter might be a better choice of words. Below, I have listed five issues that our new economic/governmental system should fix, if given the opportunity. I am convinced that the reason the current system doesn't fix them is that they would not have the ability to commit the corruptions that they currently do. Anyway, they are the following:

Multiple issues: First, they tend to write their bills to include multiple issues. This provides opportunities for those unscrupulous individuals to add in their self-serving plans. For example, a bill might be titled "Medical relief for PTSD military families."

The main part of the bill contains the issue that everyone would be inclined to say is absolutely necessary, so you would want to vote "Yes." However, within the body of this bill would also be a provision to perhaps "Allow gambling at all gasoline stations." This would be something you might not want your kids to be exposed to, so you would want to vote "No," but how can you? That provision is linked to the other so a "No" vote would shoot down the whole bill. These are the dilemmas that congress constantly presents and purposely might I add. They create bad bills at our expense.

Excessively large bills: Another tactic is to produce bills that are hundreds of pages long and then rush them through so that the representatives do not have ample time to read or study them before voting on the bill.[7] True, they may have their staff of congressional workers divide the bill up to read it. However, with each member reading a part and then reporting back to the representative, the full context understanding is lost.

In addition, this relegating of duty puts the representative's responsibilities on unelected people and that should not be allowed. This process also leads to hidden issues slipping through without being seen. We have to remember that today, many bills are actually written by the lobbyist lawyers, and again, they were not elected to do this for us. Would you think they might add in sentences that would benefit them or their clients, instead of the best interest of the country? You bet they would.

Poorly worded: At times, the bills are written purposely to confuse the issue. This is where sometimes voting "Yes" actually means you're against the issue instead of for it. This is often found in amendments to the bills themselves. The amendment process is in itself another means of confusion and manipulation, not to mention a terrible waste of time and money.

If the bills were written to only contain one issue at a time, fewer amendments would be needed. This would lessen the confusion and save time. Hopefully, single-issue bills will provide clearer and more meaningful legislation.

Extraneous congressional actions that are not appropriate for the forum: The work of congress is often riddled with extraneous issues that would be better handled in other places and times. These duties, compared to the task they should be dealing with, are often an inefficient use of taxpayers' money. I am referring to the issues or actions for honoring a person or organization or commemorating an event. These important issues should be delegated to congressional staffs and addressed outside the chambers, in a manner more appropriate to those being honored.

However, the naming of buildings after political individuals should be few and far between, if at all. Buildings belong to the people and should hold municipal titles. Name changes on buildings often hold a political motive for political parties. These motives can lead to frequent name changes at the taxpayers' expense.

In addition, there is a certain factor of confusion that the citizens have to incur when name changes occur. There is also an expenditure of time and money involved in these congressional actions. That time could be used for other more important purposes. You might be saying, "What is the big deal? These things don't take much time." However, the reason this wasted time is so important is apparent in the next congressional pitfall.

Time limits during debates: Congress very often only allows people to speak for only five minutes or less. I have to question how effective this is. Suppose we applied this technique to other areas of our lives. In talking to your child's teacher, your doctor, or even your spouse would you really want to say, "Sorry your five minutes are up." If you're trying to find solutions to our nation's problems with restraints on you like this, well perhaps that is why all those problems exist.

Now, all of the above problems are pretty obvious to anyone who watches them on television. I would bet they are also obvious to new members of congress. Perhaps, their actions here are all lessons learned from the five monkeys.

Wouldn't you think they would get together to fix these things? They could, but then how would all of those under-the-table deals and political payoffs for the price system get accomplished? Without the cover of the confusions listed above, they would have a harder time creating those loopholes.

The primary way to prevent most if not all of the above atrocities from occurring is to change the way lobbying is done today. Closing the door on lobbying abuses would be very easy if we change the system we have in congress. Once we understand that the corruptions that enter into congress come from the political deals being made outside their chambers, it is easier to fix.

First, let's go back to our new main purpose of the president of the United States. Remember that is to put the interest of the common American citizen ahead of any private interest. Perhaps, that matrix of "who benefits," I spoke of earlier, could be developed and used here—used by both the president and congress to determine any issue's actual value to the common citizen. A matrix such as that could be very useful. We then could begin to prevent corruptions from occurring. To further assist in this, a law would be passed to forbid private interest from directly writing legislative bills.

Lobbyist access to representatives and their staffs should be restricted, but perhaps allowed under controlled conditions. The staffs of the representatives should also hold to the prime directives, the same as the president. We can establish an improved code of conduct, a system of guidance and controls for ethics. Part of these ethics requires a protection and reward system for any whistle-blowers who are patriotic enough to report violators. Perhaps then, management would be more loyal to the nation, instead of loyal to corrupt private individuals.

The corrupted politics of government need to be challenged head on, as the abuses can be minimized if we institute common already-known procedures. These problems are easily attacked by the same laws we common citizens face every day. We just need to make sure our congress and our executive branches face those same laws. As you know, they have a tendency to want to exempt themselves from those laws; we can't let that happen.

If our leaders had lived under term limits from the beginning, it is likely they would not have exempted themselves from our laws. This is because the level of temptation to do so would have been greatly reduced. They also would have been less likely to grant their replacements with those exemptions. This is because they understand the abuses that result.

Of course, other people will have more ideas to improve these controls, and as long as they strengthen the prime directive, they should be considered. The prime goal incidentally should be practiced to some degree by all of our citizens. That directive again is to serve the common American citizens, as a collective whole, above all other special interest groups.

Now, doubtlessly, someone will take exception to this saying that they would want to put God first, family second, and then country. This line of thinking is perfectly normal and acceptable. In fact, this order is actually beneficial to our primary goal. This view fits in perfectly because doing the best we can for all ultimately benefits our families. In addition, God gave us our rights, and we are all God's children, his family. That leaves us with his golden rule and its nature is our primary goal.

I would recommend we retain the same separation of church and state that we had at our founding, that is to say our government should assure us that any religion in our country must approve of our bill of rights. If they don't, then they would not be welcomed. They would not be welcomed because they truthfully could not pledge allegiance to our constitution. Those religions who can pledge to our constitution should also pledge to not try to establish themselves as our government.

Hopefully, our new government will follow the same Judeo-Christian standards that were brought here from Europe by the bulk of our Founding Fathers. After all, we are talking about our individual rights. Only with those individual rights can we the people control government. We want government to protect our religious and personal rights according to our Constitution.

When either religious or personal rights become excessive or infringe on others, then we should look to government to modify them. We the people, as a whole, will have to determine just what we mean by excessive. This task can be accomplished by simple common sense and basic reasoning skills. It should be voted on by all and not left up to a few privileged people to decide.

CHAPTER 5

Why Our Governments Always Run Amuck

The Government is a body of people noticeably ungoverned.[1]

The simple answer to the above suggestion is this—every form of government can be evil if it goes too far. Capitalism, communism, socialism, monarchies, and dictatorships are the principal ones that the world has experimented with. Each one of these can turn itself into evil monsters if left to run out of control.

If we are honest, all forms of government are inherently evil at their extremes. History tells us that if we don't put restrictions on them, they eventually go to extremes all by themselves. Our government is well on its way into that extreme.

Yes, capitalism is no exception; it has corruptions that can turn men and women into slaves. Our government led by the price system can and has turned one government against another. Through the pitting of, for example, one state against another, the price system gets what they want. Obvious examples of this built in corruption are those tax breaks given to corporations in the form of tax abatements or even tax exemptions. This happens when states compete against each other. It may be legal, but is it right?

They might call it friendly competition, but really, that is a whitewash. The process is not fair to the citizens who have to pay their taxes, while the large businesses get a break. That however is how the price system was designed to work; it's only one of many conundrums.

Sometimes, these incentives accumulate to include various local, state, and federal taxes or even fees as well. We are brainwashed into believing that those negotiations are made for the citizen's benefit. Private businesses are not stupid—they get what they want, and the tax payers pick up a large share of their tab.

In the first place, the price system put these governments into those poor bargaining positions. Over time, their practices have worked to negatively affect our national economy. Yes, their system has had time to engineer this diabolical scheme, and so many more.

Individuals, like you and I, are unlikely to get tax breaks if they threaten to move to another state. Corporations on the other hand frequently receive them. These businesses, by playing one state off against another, can generally get an even bigger break. This works because many states are desperate for jobs of any kind; the price system players have seen to that.

What about bailouts? Do governments bail out everyone? Again, the answer is no. For example, certain banks were bailed out during the 2008 crisis, but not all the banks. We also bailed out only some businesses, not all the businesses. This process, which gave an excessive unfair advantage to a few while ignoring others, was a corrupt process.

These corrupt practices, while legal, perpetuate the price system, which itself is a corrupt system. The essence of these tax breaks damage the very economic system that the price system is said to support. That would be free market capitalism.

Those tax break awards have a negative effect on free market capitalism. Corrupted corporate agents have meddled in the free market so much that it can be said that we do not have one anymore. The government however carries on as if we do.

How can the market truly be a free market if our leaders allow the price system to pick and choose who gets the extra help and who doesn't? The good old boys' private network is first in line for the handouts. This is an inconsistency that we are asked to politely ignore and to not begrudge them.

However, those receiving the windfalls, from the 2008 bailouts, certainly didn't waste any time giving themselves healthy bonuses. Bonuses, in part, accredited to the support of our taxpayer bailouts. This makes it hard for any sane person not to begrudge them.

Added to these problems, capitalism, at its extremes, causes many people to work for less than a living wage. This condition could be argued to be worse than slavery, in one respect, because even slaves were given room and board in sufficient amounts to survive at a basic level. Today, many people are homeless, finding lodging under viaducts, in parks, or if they are lucky in their cars. Even wages at the minimum level are not sufficient enough to obtain an apartment in most areas.

These truths are aggravated even more so, because generally, minimum-wage workers are given less than forty hours of employment per week. This provides businesses a way out of paying full-time benefits. The price system's capitalistic structure promotes doing everything possible to eke out the maximum profits; this generally hurts employees.

I should note that many small businesses really cannot afford to pay full-time benefits. Those larger businesses are however further advantaged here if small businesses try and fail. This is because those larger businesses end up with less competition to contend with. Processes like this make it hard for small businesses to be fair with their employees.

Capitalism done right provides some freedoms. However, the price system's capitalistic design uses low-paying jobs that offer less than a living wage. In fact, the very nature of this kind of capitalism inclines it to lower wages by whatever means possible.

The price system's designed main objective is to provide the biggest return to the owners, by whatever means. In so doing, it plays people off against one another until that less than living wage exists.[2] Earlier, we had states pitted against each other; here, we have individuals doing the same thing. This negative quality of capitalism works against the common citizen's pursuit of happiness.

Sure, these kind of capitalistic cost reduction measures make the owners happy, but those that have to work for less are not so enthused. Under a less brutal form of capitalism, we are not typically as miserable, that is, not as miserable as we would likely be under an excessive form of socialism. However, when capitalism goes wild, this comparison doesn't hold true anymore.

Whenever excessive capitalism conditions are created, they are just as bad if not worse than excessive socialism. The Great Depression was a very obvious example of capitalism at its worst. Today, those examples are not as obvious, because the pain seldom is as sudden as that depression was. We have gotten used to working for less through a series of recessions and other manipulations. This is that five monkey indoctrination reworked into another form of that mental conditioning.

Consider this, if we were to employ a new plan using both a controlled capitalism and socialism platform, nearly all, if not all, people would work for one of several publically owned corporations. They would work for a corporation that they have a vested interest in. Their labor here would provide for their basic living needs.

All of the citizens will vote on just what those basic needs will be. This will in part determine what their work schedule would be like. We take the number of citizens, the resources we have, and the basic needs we require and then figure out what we can actually allocate to each individual.

Initially, we should not set our basic needs goals to high. We need capitalism to balance our system, so we need a shorter public sector work week to do this. Now, this shorter work day/week could provide individuals more choices.

They would have time to work other opportunities in the capitalistic sector. Shorter hours would thus allow people a chance to enhance their standard of living, above that which the public sector would provide. Balance between these sectors would have to be maintained so that both systems can flourish equally.

Earlier, it was suggested that four, 4 hour work days a week should be ample enough to provide a basic living standard for our population. If those basic items are produced well within that time frame above, well that is all the better. That would allow the possibility for improvements to our basic system, which in balance would also help to enhance the capitalism sector.

Those improvements would be an option that worker could decide on. With our population, there should be sufficient workforce to supply the hours required to have that short work day. Employees for now would be limited to those work hours.

Perhaps, they may elect to use their spare time in the private capitalism marketplace, to add to their lifestyle. If social needs create a demand, they might find additional employment in the public sector with extra credits applied for their labor. This flexibility might even be a way to help balance the systems even more.

With the public ownership of our resource industries, there is no need to pit one person or one state off against another, as we would have no need to take advantage of them anyway. We, as owners, now have no need, nor would we want, to take advantage of ourselves. Our socialized capitalism here would work to advantage the public. This is because there is no need for us to abuse each other or ourselves. This public ownership makes us all better off for that.

In excessive socialism, we the people could end up directly paying for everything, while overlords bask in luxuries. In excessive capitalism, the same thing happens, though more subtle. This happens because eventually, any increase in the cost of the products gets passed along to the consumers of the product itself. Private corporations have thus set us up to pay their share.

Sometimes in capitalism, these price increases are also passed along to everyone, mostly in the form of subsidies to private companies, paid for by all citizens, not just the consumers.[3] This sounds a little like privatized socialism, don't you think?

Socialism has no exemption from being able to go to its extremes; it also can turn men and women into slaves. It can steal away all of their individuality and personal freedoms, if left to run wild. Socialism and capitalism can be bad, but monarchies, dictatorships, and communisms can be even worse. Many of their histories demonstrate that their evil manipulations are sometimes even more horrific.

Basically, capitalism and socialism are the two best-known options we have trialed. Somehow, we need to find a way to combine these two, with perhaps a couple of other forms of governments. The goal would be to create a hybrid balanced system that includes the publically owned corporation system explained earlier.

We need to defang the less offensive forms of governmental systems. Balance is the tool we can use to do this. History has shown us that governmental failures occurred when these systems, either individually or in combination, were taken to their extremes.

What if we molded a new system of economy and government using the best parts of these older systems? By not giving supreme control to any of them individually, we might be able to restrict them from growing too powerful and then going out of control. If we take the state-of-the-art parts from the many different systems available, could we fashion a better system?

We might achieve a balanced system by using two or three of the systems already talked about. Of course, we would have to limit the powers that any one system could achieve. Since absolute power corrupts, we can avoid giving absolute power to any one system by dividing the power between the systems we choose.

In a real sense, the governmental systems draw their powers from four principal components. Absolute power actually rests in being able to control the four major dynasties. These are the dynasties of education, finance, politics, and religion.[4] These dynasties can be partitioned so that no single focal point in the governmental system has absolute control of all of them.

Further, by limiting or rather leveling the power of private citizens, we can better balance the clout that any one citizen might selfishly try to exert over the systems. In addition, by dividing the monetary process between two systems, we could limit the power of money, as touched upon in chapter 1. The existence, or life, of any of these ideas depends on your answer to the following question: Do you want a better world?

What if I told you that most of us really don't and I have evidence to prove it to you? You're first reaction to this might be to deny that I am right. It is very possible that you would scoff at this, without providing a reason as to why I am wrong. Perhaps, you would just ignore my statement and avoid me altogether. After all, everyone wants a better world. That's a given, isn't it?

That is what the mainstream media has us all convinced of. They have reinforced our instructions that the current system is nothing but the best system possible. So a person suggesting trouble in paradise is someone that you don't have to listen to. Why? This is because you already know more than he or she does. After all, the media tells you everything you need to know. Anyone who suggests that we don't want a better life must be one of those people that should not be taken seriously.

I would bet that some people actually have taken that approach to my comment and are in the process of ignoring me or it right now. If so, they thus would have provided me with my first proof. Their action would suggest that at least they don't want a better world, because they don't care. Otherwise, they might have taken the time to find out my reasons for why people don't want a better world.

I should perhaps give you some idea of what a better world means to me. That way, you can compare your idea of a better world to it. Because we are individuals, we will differ in our opinions, even on very important issues. So here is a partial list of what my idea of a better world is. From it, you will see just how well you and I agree or disagree. Some of the choices below might be more likely posed to your grandchildren, but for now, I give you the chance to answer for them:

My answers are marked by the **X**'s so that you can compare them to yours.

> At a hotel, would your family want to have your own room to sleep in (**X**) or would you want to share the room with other people that you had never met before ( )?

By the way India already has this second option in place.

Given the choice, would you rather eat three meals a day (**X**) or eat one meal every other day ( )?

When you go to the beach or a park, would you want to step over a thousand people just to find a place to sit ( ) or would you prefer a beach or park where there are less people and more places to sit (**X**)?

When you want to find work, would you want to have multiple people looking to hire you (**X**) or would you want to be one of a hundred people all looking to get the same job ( )?

Given the choice, would you prefer to work mostly for yourself and be happier (**X**) or would you want to only work for someone else and be miserable ( )?

Would you want to live in a world where wars are frequent ( ) or live in a world where people seldom fight and rarely go to war (**X**)?

Given a choice, would you want people to be more honest with you (**X**) or more dishonest with you ( )?

Would you want to have a little more time to do what you want (**X**) or would it be okay for others to control most of your time ( )?

Given the choice, would you want to be able to visit the habitat of wild animals in person (**X**) or only be able to view those animals and habitats on a historical video ( )?

I think you now understand at least in part what I mean by a better world. It is a world where war is not promoted by people who want to make money. It is a world where we have more job opportunities, where food is plentiful, and where there is room for nature to occur without our intervention. Most importantly, it is a world where we don't seek to take excessive advantage of others, a world where we are respected, and where we respect others.

I am hoping that you agree with me as to what a better world is. However, I know that a good number of you will not. I will concede that individually, most of us say that we want a better world, but collectively we do not.

My proof for this duplicity comes from our connection to our society. We by our nature want to comply with society. This is because as members of society, we tend to go along with the leaders.

They tell us, in their roundabout way that we cannot have that better world. They promise worldwide improvements, but these are promises they cannot and do not intend to keep. Those promises are just meant to appease us. We know this because of the following comments they have made.

They say we need more homeland security spending. This confirms the world is not getting better. They also say we need to cut social entitlement programs. How can society get better if they cut social programs?

They say we need to offer incentives to our large businesses and curtail spending on our social programs. Does not this amount to taking money from the poor to give to those who are already better off? How is the world better for the majority of people when they do this?

They say we need to increase our military presents in Afghanistan, Iraq, or wherever. Yes, they do this all while also expressing a need to cut social security or other social programs. These actions do not make things better for anybody except those in the top 10%.

Our governmental leaders have many reasons to spend money on foreign aid, poor trade deals, and wars. Most of the time, these things do not have the common citizens' best interest at heart. Rather, those things benefit the special interest groups they serve.

It is no secret that government benefactors are, for the most part, corporations. The millions of dollars in campaign contributions given to our leaders end up becoming the debt of the common citizens. This happens when those corporations seek, government contracts, reduced regulations, and even incite wars. Remember that their system runs on debt.

Many times, corporate payback has resulted in actions that have reduced funding to our social programs. More often than not, those corporate benefits come in the form of reduced taxes. With less tax, the social programs lose their financial support.

We allow all of this to happen. What is more, we have allowed this to occur for decades. Why? This is because we believe them, despite the years of empty promises. So my question is, if we allow them to do these things, do we really want a better world?

We humans have many flaws; we are far from perfect. Our physical bodies can have ailments, we can get sick, and sometimes we hurt ourselves while doing senseless things. Examples might be drinking and driving, climbing dangerous mountains, and surfing in no surfing areas; and I am sure you can carry this list on and on. Why do we do these things?

I believe we do them because we have a split in our way of thinking. In a sense, there is an "us" as a body with common sense and then there is an "us" as a body without common sense. It is like we are two different people in one body. Somehow, at times, we disassociate ourselves from our common sense.

Sometimes, we are smart and other times not so much. Our bodies are not exempt from helping to cause us to do most of those negative things. In fact, our flesh bodies often put us up to it, not that you didn't already know that. Could our minds be part of the problem? What other weaknesses might we hold in our heads?

There is one other remarkable flaw about our brains. Our brains can be controlled by others rather easily. Now, this is something most of us will want to argue, as few of us will want to admit it. It is a weakness that we as a group tend to ignore for pride's sake. Vanity is, in a sense, our downfall here.

Some people will want to call it mind control or brainwashing, but perhaps, those words are too harsh for many people to accept. Even if we use a softer term such as conditioning, they still find it hard to accept. They think admitting that their mind could possibly be controlled is like admitting they are weak. Nobody likes to think they are weak-minded, well at least nobody I know.

Most everyone thinks they are strong and cannot be manipulated. In denying to ourselves that this could happen, we unknowingly open the door to make it even more likely that it will happen. Because of our vanity, we expose ourselves to the danger that someone or some group could possibly manipulate us.

Now, I am not talking about the stories where strange women or men take advantage of little children. Most of us make sure we tell our children about these people. Those dreadful manipulators are just the easier ones to spot, and we all know they exist.

There are also the snake oil salesmen or low-level con men, which we meet and recognize rather easily. No, these people are not of who I speak. Rather, there are people out there who are not so easily detected, because they are very clever. They mask their evil deeds beneath many layers of deception. They are not openly devious and certainly not as direct as some con men who we might have met.

They take the long way around to getting what they want. Their subtle manipulation can be years in the making so that on its surface, it looks benign. Their tactics are planned out on a global scale, and they command multiple forces. They do all of this so as to secure their fortunes and power. Their well-hidden deceptions bleed our livelihoods through their deceitful manipulations. Normally, they do not suck us dry, but they skim off enough to deprive us of much more than we realize.

I recently read a short article by Eddie Brown titled *They're Watching.*[5] It was about how children mimic and learn from their parents. He talked about seeing a program once where hidden cameras recorded the actions of children playing.

Some of the scenes were of children imitating their parents. Some children did things such as scold and manhandle other children while using foul language. Others pretended to smoke and drink.

On a more positive note, some acted like teachers and some even preached good behavior. His point was that the children watch adults and that is how they learn. I would add to this the idea that children are conditioned by the environment they grow up in, even if it is simply by watching how others do things. Sometimes, they learn bad things, but sometimes, they see and learn good things.

It is pretty well accepted that we never stop learning. We are constantly exposed to conditioning. Our minds are forever being subjected to new information or ideas that sometimes challenge our opinions.

Daily, we are forced to revisit how we feel, believe, and then think. This process always leaves the door open to strangers or at least strange ideas. I hope that you will consider my warning about our potential to be mentally manipulated.

You might have noticed that our social values have been changing. You might not have noticed how that has been occurring. Everyone, even adults, can be conditioned. and just knowing that this is possible helps us to keep our guard up.

There will inevitably be some people who will not believe the above ideas. Even while all around them, they see people being manipulated and controlled. Still. they continue to deny that this could happen to them.

They are somehow smarter than the rest of us. This is vain thinking. Those advertisers, political directors, and special interest advocates have free reign over people like these. Yes. even I am trying to influence you, but I hope it is in a positive manner.

Most of us, at least on the surface, want a better world under terms similar to the ones I laid out in those questions earlier. However, a few among us don't want exactly the same kind of world we do. They want a world where they are in charge and in control.

It's a world where they enjoy the lion's share of everything on earth. They have achieved this through their control over us, via the price system. Unfortunately, there are many of us who are too vain to admit that we are being excessively manipulated. This high number of unbelievers makes it easy for those who want to control to manage things.

What I just suggested is that a small percentage of our human population has found out about our mental weaknesses. In addition, they have studied those weaknesses in order to exploit them and us. There is another reason for saying that most of us do not want a better world. It's that most of us continue to ignore the thought that we are being influenced by a small percentage of people, people who are exploiting us.

Through our acts of denial of this weakness, we have allowed ourselves to be corrupted. Have you given control over yourself to people who enjoy being in control at your expense? It is hard to prove something like this as it requires me, or anyone trying to do so, to ask you to admit your weaknesses. Who wants to believe that they could be controlled negatively by others without knowing about it? A good video for your research here is called *The Century of the Self.*[6] This video may still be available on YouTube.

On July 11, 2011, Bloomberg News channel reported that Shell Oil signed a $12 billion contract with Iraq. Well this is sure good news for that Dutch company. We sent our children in harm's way and spent our money to protect the oil fields for a foreign corporation to now come in and profit. Doesn't that make you feel a little used?

The price system tells us that we are all one big happy family, so it doesn't matter who runs the oil fields. If that were true, I would not have a bad feeling about it, but it isn't true. If you also had a sickening feeling deep down inside at this news, then perhaps there is a crack in your training or conditioning as well. Perhaps, you're not buying what they are trying to sell you either.

Another example of foreign corporations profiting at our, the common citizen's, expense comes from Afghanistan. China was awarded a contract to mine copper there. Their Mes Aynak mine site in Logar Province is expected to produce $1 billion annually.[7] Our diplomats portray this as simply "international donors" just helping to bring economic wealth back to that country. They say that Afghanistan doesn't have the equipment or know-how to mine the copper themselves.

The Afghan people have intelligent individuals the same as any other country has. There is said to be trillions of dollars' worth of minerals in Afghanistan. In an honest world, the Afghans could easily get a loan using the proven mineral wealth as collateral. They then could train and hire the necessary people and do this all themselves.

But no, the conditioning of our controllers tells us that only members of their system are capable of knowing how to do anything.

Our news media portrays the U.S. public as generous benefactors. Donating billions of dollars to help the Afghan people and not wanting anything in return. In reality, those controllers are using our, citizens', money to manipulate things. This money works behind the scenes to influence people. The money works not so much for the common America citizen, but mostly for those selfish controllers.

The World Bank has had questionable dealings in several countries, which suggest the misuse of funds. These reports are not covered very extensively in the news. Perhaps, publically backed funds are not something you would be interested in. Evidently, the news thinks you don't need to consider those events, except only very lightly.

While helping people is a noble idea in our minds, our controllers use it for their purposes. Those purposes have more to do with helping themselves. Foreign aid or monetary loans are dangled as a carrot to unscrupulous world leaders, and this money very often ends up being used for mischief.

The media does report these things although you have to take the time to consider what they are saying. Surface reading of these articles will make you feel proud, and who doesn't want that? Everything sounds like they are doing the right thing; however, there are darker deals not covered.

We are so well controlled that it really is amazing. Our government tells us that they are giving all this money away to foreign countries. Then, almost in the same breath, we are told that we cannot afford our social programs.

Isn't giving money to other countries a social program? We give money to our government services and military posts in over seven hundred locations worldwide, at any given time. There are 196 countries in the world. The money spent in those foreign countries, while not considered aid, is in essence aid; even the wars themselves are a form of foreign aid.

This shell game with foreign aid and home social programs is worked on us again and again, and we fall for it. After all of this, we continue to believe that our minds cannot be controlled. We continue to believe that we cannot be made to see things a different way, even when the truth is staring us directly in the face.

For the sake of explanation here, concerning mind control, I offer the following thought. I will go out on a limb here to present a very light story about a very simplistic view of the world. In this view, there are basically three types of people.

To make this view of the world even simpler, I will divide the world up by percentage. Let's say that 20% of the people are compelled to do good things. Another 20% are compelled to do bad things. Finally, 60% are somewhere in the middle. In this example, as in real life, there will always be exceptions within the groups.

The 20% groups at the extremes are basically the people we see who rise to power in those two extremes. Those that want to do good try to influence the masses by asking them to reflect on their spiritual nature. They may even influence you by some other form of moral compass.

The 20% that are compelled to do bad things do not have much of a moral compass. This makes it easy for them to control people. Through their control, they can make themselves very wealthy and powerful at other people's expense.

The 60% in the middle are basically just interested in ordinary pursuits, depending on their personal interest. They have the standard social interests in sports, education, the arts and sciences, and all the other things that are important to them. They however are not inclined to want to control the masses. They just want to live their own lives and not have to deal with other people's problems.

Throughout all these groups, there are degrees in ambitions. People in all groups can be corrupted and manipulated. However, in the 20% of the people who are compelled to do bad things, it is also possible for their degrees of ambition to be excessively high. When people like these get into power, there is a real chance that most everyone will suffer eventually. It is the desire for wealth, power, and fame that causes them to do terrible things in order to achieve their desires.

These people will work their ways into those occupations where they can get what they want. Their success at the extremes very often requires corrupt actions on their parts. These actions require the manipulations of people, markets, and laws. These would be actions such as creating shortages, changing the laws to allow corruptions in various industries, and even creating wars. They don't care as long as the action increases their power and wealth.

Since the 60% in the middle are not devoting their full attention to world events and matters of state, those who want to do wrong have a very easy time of it. To make matters worse, the 60% in the middle are convinced that they cannot be manipulated, so they don't stop to consider that the news they depend on is rigged. The news is often rigged on the side of those who want to achieve their goals by any means necessary. This happens simply because a small percentage of them are paying for the news to be broadcast. They sponsor the networks.

The 60%, not having the time or the desire to study in depth the political issues, depend on the news to give them a short condensed report to explain everything. Their lives are too busy to be that actively involved in anything other than short news reviews. Since they believe they cannot be fooled, they pick popular news programs on major networks and tend to believe most everything that is being reported. That is, they believe what makes sense for the view of the world that they have been encouraged to hold.

The networks are limited to presenting two basic views so as to create the impression there is a controversy in government in which citizens can take a side. Those in the 60% group do not understand the controls that have been imposed on the owners of those news networks and newspapers. These news organizations are controlled by the powerful people in banking, in defense, in commerce, and in political positions.

In other words, they are controlled by the bad group who wants to control things. These people have stronger economic desires than the majority of us. They again exist in the 20% who are much more selfish than most people.

Of course, they will tell you that they are simply more driven and work much harder than everyone else. I hope this book dispels that opinion by the time you're through reading it. Some of them do work as hard as many of us; however, that effort is focused on lying, steeling, cheating, or whatever is necessary for their success.

Since they already understand how the price system works and they embrace it, they tarnish their credibility. It is tarnished because as we have seen, the price system is a corrupt system. Yet they have elected to use that system to take advantage of everyone they can, excessively.

But enough of that, we need to return to the role of the 60%. By accepting these network news programs, the 60% in the middle become confounded. They then are manipulated into thinking they are on a team. Team #1 is the Democrats, and team #2 is the Republicans. Each day, the volleys of remarks are scored as we watch the promotional programming push one side off against the other.

Now, what little time the 60% in the middle has is occupied by useless information. The information is useless, because to the 20% who want to do bad or selfish things, it really does not matter who wins. Why? It is because they have already corrupted both parties. So they could hardly care less who wins, as they own them both. Their only goal was to keep your minds off those candidates or issues that they didn't want covered. Those would be the ones poorly covered in the news.

I know that a number of the readers here are thinking that I am anti-American, because the two party systems is a principal American construct. They are thinking, how can anyone attack America like that? We have been told that there should only be two parties. In addition, those other parties are irrelevant and not worth considering.

If you did take offense, you should question yourself as to why you might have done so. Are those restrictive social norms really being taught to us? Are we taught to jump to the conclusion that anyone who criticizes our system is automatically against us?

After all, in America, we are supposed to have freedom of speech, right? So if something inside of you sparked anger, when I told you that you should question that two-party construct, perhaps you were thinking that I am trying to pervert our country. If you had those thoughts, perhaps you had a glimpse of your controlled training coming to the front. It took me a while to question things also.

Remember that you have the moral obligation to question things, and this is only one of your freedoms.

I understand why, in this scenario, the 60% group does what it does, as I was one of them, at least for a time. I still have to point out that their acceptance of all these things without checking them out qualifies as my proof that most people do not care if we have a better world or not.

It is sad to say, but most people are content not knowing how things really work. That is basically how the 60% group thinks. This is why they are so easy to manipulate. It is their nature to not get heavily involved in the price system's processes.

I think you can see why our Founding Fathers tried to put roadblocks in the way of those controllers. They knew certain people would tend to corrupt things. The founders understood that humans could be manipulated.

That is why they designed a government were the elected officers were supposed to come and serve for two to four years and then return to their homes. The system was not complicated then, and ordinary citizens were to serve in those public positions. They were to serve short terms in office and not make careers of these jobs. "Politicians are like diapers; they need to be changed often and for the same reason."[8]

Short terms helped to reduce the temptations of office. Those would be the temptations of starting to feel like royalty and wanting to be treated as such. There are also the temptations of being corrupted by their own power and by the powers above them.

Unfortunately, the corruptions began to build as our corrupt group found ways around those roadblocks. In order to prevent ordinary people from serving their country, those selfish few have, over the years, built a maze. They have complicated the system unnecessarily in their efforts to stay in power.

They have redesigned the system to make it a government of confusion. Unfortunately, it is our human nature to believe them when they say that things have to be extremely complicated. Our acceptance of this lie has made us even easier to control.

I hope you will take the time to look into these allegations concerning the use of mind control. Start by considering how much of your life is spent just watching commercials; that should alarm you. Don't allow your vanity to step in front of our reality and keep you from seeing what is obvious. Things are not being run to favor the majority of people; they are being run to favor the controllers who are compelled to fix the rules to favor themselves.

We need to adjust our new economic system taking into consideration our human frailties. Our designs should put limits on our human excessive behaviors, namely, greed. We need to compensate for our tendency to sink into corruptions. If we do these things, then we stand a better chance at success. Is this possible? Can we design such a system?

One thing for sure, there are selfish people who will surely want to prevent our changes. They would do whatever possible to limit our corrective actions over their system. They would resist changes in the systems of education, finance, politics, and even religion. The evil influences that exist in their system come from their ability to overpower each and every one of these dynasties.

We can certainly do better in our design than what exists today. This is because we can study designs from the past. Those attempts from the past will show us how they fell apart when price system corruptions rolled in. We need to build a design that severely limits the advance of those corruptions. Then, we need to build in an alarm system when someone starts to tamper with the design.

We need a system that allows personal freedoms, however one in which personal freedoms do not trample the people, as a whole. Political corruptions occur when individuals convince us that their rights are far more important than certain collective individual rights. Our system should then limit the excessive involvement of any wealthy person.

Wealthy people, after all, would be in a position to champion their own personal changes selfishly. Changes in our society should not be allowed if they do not benefit the majority of the citizens. The design should be simple and easy to understand. Its implementation will not be easy, as those with extreme power and wealth will fight to maintain their ill-gotten advantages.

I believe however that their existing evil system will fall apart as it has in the past. Its demise will not be our doing, at least not directly. Their own downfall will be mostly due to the crimes of those who are compelled to do wrong. They will bring about their own ruin.

This is not to say that we don't have some fault to shoulder, in their crimes. If we face our responsibilities and our limits honestly, we stand a chance to succeed in building a better system. However, I will be the first to admit that it will not be perfect. We will have to settle for better, not perfect.

When the price system falls we need to be ready to jump in with a new design. This design should level each individual's involvement in our government to that of their fellow citizen. This equals the playing field. This will mean that people will have to be more involved in our economic design.

Our design should provide the time and the means for them to be involved. Currently, the lives of many people are fixated simply on existing, with little time to spend on governmental education. We should work to fix this.

Even if there is an economic collapse, our chances of success will not be easy, as those with the money and influence will focus their efforts to retain power. They will try hard to be the builders of the new economy, the new government. Honestly, they have a perfect track record of doing this over and over again. So it will not be easy for us to jump in and stop them.

If they succeed in gaining control over the design, we will be in trouble again. They will start slowly with a government plan that will provide the common citizen some relief; to do otherwise would cause major riots. Their system of economics will be reintroduced in a slightly varied form.

Eventually, we would return to a system of debt. A debt-based system will allow over time the extraction of wealth and power from the people. That power gets transferred to the individuals who run and enforce the new government. This then is just the same system that we have today—the price system.

What if, however, we came up with a plan that prevented them from regaining control? This plan would have to freeze their ability to wage war on those working to implement our new design. This plan would have to level the playing field so that those who are compelled to do "bad" will not be given unfair access in building the new system.

Part of this process might very well be that we remove from them any excessive wealth that they had procured under their old system. They would likely still be wealthy, just not excessively wealthy. Since that wealth was originally secured under unscrupulous price system measures, we shouldn't feel guilt for doing so.

Not all wealthy people will have been involved in destroying the economy. However, those that were ring leaders, their names should be held in distain. Why? It is because it was their price system that collapsed our economy. They should not be given any voice in our new system.

They should not be considered as viable representatives under whatever new system is put into place. The new system should consider their previous tour of duty in government as fulfilled and their services no longer required. New people should be given a chance.

Today, there exists a power that has grown to have control over the four dynasties. Because of its strong ties to the military, it has been dubbed the military industrial complex.[9] Their political control has few if any limits.

Our new system should be designed to limit political power. By doing this, we can begin to pull our military forces out from the political control exerted by private industry. We will have to purge the rank and file to eliminate those easily turned to corruption.

Those loyal to the military industrial complex need to be relieved of their duties. Those loyal to the United States of America need to be retained. Lobbyists will be eliminated here because the public would now own the military industries.

This part of the process will not be easy as doing anything against these private industries is highly difficult. Things would really have to be bad to get this done. I am just saying that to do it right, that needs to be done. When it is done, private greed will be less likely to send our children off to wars.

Military contracts would be given only to public corporations. This means that nationalizing the existing military industry would be in our nation's national security interest. Remember that many of these industries have used the price system to unscrupulously secure the excessive wealth that they have.

We should not feel sorry for those private interests. They likely will still be the wealthiest people in our society, just not excessively so. The public needs to be fairly compensated for their loss of life, liberty, and wealth. The loss of this private power platform will protect our nation and the world from corrupt war activities.

If appropriate, these private businesses will be fairly reimbursed based on the policies set up under our new system. Their previous corporate leaders will be held to secrecy commitments and released; some might even be hired by the public corporation to run the facilities. These public corporations will have income-level restrictions appropriate for their job values.

Power restrictions are necessary to assure the military remains protectors of our freedoms instead of our potential prison guards. Dark projects that would be used against the citizens of our nation will be terminated. We need to be assured that proper oversight exists on all projects.

Secrecy will be maintained where necessary; perhaps, a council of citizens will have basic access to all secret expenses. Dark projects will have to become more accountable to a greater number of the new leaders of our country. These leaders will include a greater number of scientists.

Our new government will change the patent system so as to favor the public more than private industry. This means that government project patents will no longer be controlled by individual private businesses. Individual patents will also favor the inventor rather than the corporation.

In order to control the military complex, we need to control their means to make trouble—their desire to have war. Our original

Founding Fathers did not call for a standing army in time of peace. It would have been considered uneconomic.

Today, it may not even be possible to unwind military operations, due to price system conditions in the world today. In time, it might become possible. With an eye on the world's problems, we should take back control of our military.

If our economy collapses, this could provide a desire for our military to help fix their dark side problems. After all, they are likely to have had a large part in the breakdown due to the excessive corruptions there. This again will not be an easy task.

Under our new system, the military purchases that we will need should be scrutinized by military scientist. These requests should be studied by more than just one group. Perhaps, a public-spending budget committee, a supreme council, and the associated department requesting the funding should jointly oversee the need.

While more people would understand the need for the expense, we could still compartmentalize the details of the complete project. This allows for the accounting of the money spent in an auditable fashion. This process will help to avoid the trillions of dollars that were lost by the Pentagon. This alone will make our military stronger.

The budget committee might also, in its turn, operate under close supervision by a government review board. In addition, the government review board could be investigated by the new Consumer Protection Agency as part of their general duties. These ideas, issues, and designs can be studied. If they work, they would help our efforts to build our new economic system. Our success in building the system will be depended on this one question. Do you want a better world?

CHAPTER 6

Ideas for Reforms in Justice, Corporate Laws, Lawsuits, and Medical Care

Therefore all things whatsoever you would, that men should do to you, do you even so to them. 1 (Matthew 7:12)

Originally, I wrote many of the following ideas with the thought that perhaps they might somehow be applied even under the price system's self-serving control. These ideas, however, really would work better under a new economic and governmental system. I will try to represent them here with the intent of using them under our new system.

I offer these ideas here only as a means of starting the discussion on how reforms might be addressed. They are not meant to be final solutions. Our new system will have to figure out what works and what doesn't.

Justice in America: New System

Why do we need a new system? The current system is far too complicated for the individual citizen. It is my observation that the extent of the legal complexities are often even beyond the comprehension of the students currently graduating with basic law degrees.[2]

This is not because they are poor students. It has more to do with the overabundance of legal materials that need to be studied. The volumes of the law are too numerous and extensive, so much so that students, for a long time now, have needed to specialize in various branches of the law.

Much like doctors specialize in order to be more proficient, so do lawyers. This complexity compels those who want the best legal defense to hire teams of lawyers. Very often now, one lawyer is just not enough.

The sheer size of the existing legal libraries creates a real question. What is the likelihood of a just defense, that is, of it being given to a defendant who only has one lawyer?

If multiple lawyers are needed to interpret the laws, then not only is there a problem of complexity, but also there is a problem of expense that enters in. The expense here is in costs for both the accused and the government.

Remember that we are the government, at least when it comes to paying the bills. In order to make our government work better, we must reform the legal system. If laws are to be obeyed, they must first be understood. If ordinary citizens cannot read the law and understand it, they have little ability to protect themselves in advance.

This last statement regarding our ability to protect ourselves points to the terrible side effect of too many laws. When the laws become so numerous that some begin to have a detrimental nature to them, the public suffers. Many of those laws actually put us at risk instead of protecting us.

The U.S. Patriot Act is one example of a law system gone wild.[3] Laws such as this actually reduce our rights instead of protecting the ones we have. While we understand that there is a need at times for these kinds of laws, they at the same time conflict with our idea of justice. These laws add burdens, which are often disparaging, to the citizens who are not breaking any laws.

To add to our imposition and disdain for these laws, we had to pay, with our own money, for teams of lawyers to create them. The lawyers who crafted those laws surely didn't make minimum wage. It is understandable why some people say it is like paying someone to slap you in the face. However, many of our laws were out of control long before the Patriot Act.

Laws such as these tend to make lawyers wealthy. First they are paid to write them, then they are paid again and again through a perpetual stream of court cases that those laws generate. These kinds of laws are just one example of how the price system diabolically connects to our system of justice. This does not happen by chance, it's *their* design.

Unscrupulous lawyers have filled the law books with an abundance of laws designed to protect their dubious clients. The subjects of these laws often provide the loopholes for those clients. Those laws use a legal form of fussy logic that allows most of the deceptions against society to take place.

Did any deceptive actions spring to mind when you read that? How about the mortgage fraud that helped to create the 2008 financial breakdown? Does the word "derivatives" come to mind? These kinds of things are only legal because those in charge say they are. They are examples of the might makes right principle. We need to rid ourselves of this misuse of our legal system.

To exacerbate the problem of complexity further, very often our governmental representatives can't read and understand the bills that they are asked to pass into law.[4] This is mostly due to time constraints, but their legal knowledge is also a problem.

When this happens, we are put even more thoroughly in jeopardy. This intentionally built-in price system aggravator of confusion negates the intent of our democratic system of government. The intent was to allow for common citizens to serve in various governmental positions. With a simple system, this was possible. Over the years, they have built a maze that has worked to hamper the common citizen's equal access.

My point here is, how can a common person serve if the laws are so needlessly complicated? Common citizens who serve are not always lawyers, but still they must understand the bills. These are bills that even lawyers have a hard time with. Can you see the problem?

If our representatives were and are to come from the general population to serve, how can they do this without a law degree? Yet today, that may not even be enough. It should be obvious that the system of justice that we have is far too complicated.

You might say that we have been given an overdose of laws and legal proceedings. In fact, you could say that our dose, in many cases, has been fatal. If we could educate our entire population as lawyers, this still may not be enough to help. How can we reestablish the goal of having common citizens serve in public office, as our founders envisioned?

How can we do this when, as already stated, a law degree isn't enough? There is now a need to specialize in certain aspects of law in order to understand the law. This is the tangled web they have built, and yes, they planned it on purpose. Who are they?

They are "those who practice to deceive" (my thanks to Sir Walter Scott for his great observation). There really is no short answer for who "they" are, but I hope this book begins to shine a little light on some of them. Their ranks, because of their selfishness, have been getting smaller and smaller, and this makes them much more noticeable.

Will their money and power protect them? They are counting on it. This is why many new laws have become more aggressive toward us, the common citizens. They need to protect themselves.

Let's go back to those tangled laws now. Very often, many of these laws where established to give some special interest an advantage, or they were written to pave the way for abuses. There are many laws that really have no basis in today's world, yet they are there making things more complex than they need to be. Here are some questions each of us should ask ourselves:

Does our legal system have to be that complex? I really think we could cut those laws in half perhaps more if we are smart about it.

How can people follow the law if they cannot understand it? Chances are, they cannot.

Should only lawyers be sent to serve in government? That goes against the intent of the Founding Fathers.

175

Is this complexity being used against the common citizen? It most certainly is, one only has to recall the many Wall Street abuses to understand this. Further elected officials these days are much more apt to ask the attorneys, who were not elected, as to what they can do and what they cannot do. The reason for this is that sometimes, elected officials make promises and then find out the law prevents them for keeping those promises.

If you stop to think about it, it is a lot easier to break the law than you might expect. The reason why is because there are just so many of them; it is ridiculous. It is likely that you break several laws each day just driving to work; you just don't realize it.

If you change lanes within fifty feet of an intersection or stopped to close to a tanker truck, you could get a ticket. Perhaps, you failed to read the local street traffic codes while traveling, thus making yourself vulnerable to a ticket. There is a whole host of other possible violations that make it easy for any officer to write a ticket.

Many of us are lucky that the police force does not have enough personnel to write tickets more often. We are given a break in that they have other duties that occupy most of their schedule. My point here is that traffic laws are a lot easier to understand than the main body of laws, yet many of us have a problem just dealing with them. The laws are just too abundant for our minds to keep up with. If our government happened to turn suddenly into a police state, we, citizens, would be in deep trouble.

One possible solution for us here is that we create a new simplified legal system. We then start using it as the primary system of law immediately. We start the system off with just a few laws and only grow the laws if we need to.

We establish the basic laws that we think will handle about 90% of the situations most people would encounter in their daily lives. To start with, we write a list of eight, twelve, or perhaps up to twenty-four basic laws. They would be written in English, not legalese, so that everyone can understand, short and sweet. We citizens would help by voting on these basic laws. This idea could be studied in a test community before implementing.

The judges will have an expanded version of these laws with specific examples of variations of each law. The judges will initially have more responsibility to ensure that everyone is innocent until proven guilty. The judges would also initially have more power in resolving the cases.

Once the system gets running more smoothly, we can look at taking some of the burden off the judges and on to the legal codes themselves. The public would be taught the basic laws and have access to the judges' expanded version. There could be instructions given to the public to help set the codes into the minds of the citizens.

As a sample, one of the basic laws might be, "It is unlawful to steal." The judge's manual will provide expanded examples of forms of steeling such as embezzlement, larceny, and fraud. The judges start using these expanded versions of the law to decide their cases. This should handle a good majority of the cases, but not all. The public would vote on any major changes to the basic laws. On minor variations to the basic laws, judicial panels might decide how to add or change the public documents.

Remember that the goal of this system is to avoid growing the laws back to the volumes we have now. This might seem hard to do; however, I think we can keep those excessive style corrupt laws from slipping back in for a long time if we are vigilant. Remember that the price system's legal design had a compulsion to make excessive money. Under our new system, those excessive money schemes would not be allowed. Laws wouldn't need to be as complex.

Now, when we have issues that cannot be resolved with the basic laws, we write new laws that the public votes on. This system, to add laws, should be designed to limit additional laws that muddy the waters or confuse the issues. The idea is to keep the justice system easier to understand.

Perhaps, we can use that voting systems, suggested in chapter 4, to help us here. That was a virtual charge card voting process. It could be used to present these laws to the public for voting.

The voting process itself might be verified by a general review team who would be sworn to confidentiality. This would allow a more open voting system. If so, a system of random vote checking could be adopted to verify any possible voting fraud.

Another voting system that we might consider is the system used by companies who allow stock holders voting rights over the internet. We could use our open voting method here so that the review team may contact the citizen to verify results and vice versa. These systems of voting will need some planning to prevent fraud from entering back in.

The judge's first priority would be to use the new legal system and rule using these basic laws. If the basic laws fail to identify the crime, the judge can use his or her authority to seek the use of an old law from the old system. How would this work? If he or she feels that the new laws do not apply to the case they are hearing and that they cannot rule fairly in the matter, then they might request to use the old system of laws.

They would point to the law they would wish to use and explain the general necessity for why none of the existing new laws could be applied. This action, when it occurs, would require a secondary review by a panel of local review judges. These judges will decide if the old legal system must be used by the judge to issue justice is this case. The panel would submit their request for review to the state's panel of judges. If that panel finds that the old law can be added easily to one of the newer existing basic laws, they might be granted authority to amend the basic laws without voter approval.

If, however, the basic laws cannot be amended easily and a new law is required, then it would need to be submitted to the people to vote on. State and federal judges would work to finalize these issues. They would also provide oversight of these laws so that their new legal codes are uniform. The new federal supreme court would begin to build the new legal system at the federal level. This would be done in the same way that the state and local governments would do it.

New laws might mean a rewording of an original basic law or an entirely new law itself. Whether or not the voters accept or reject this proposed new law, the old law would also be lined out from the old legal system so that this issue will not be revisited, by this process. This prevents attempts to reconstitute the old cob webbed system of the past. The legal system's first goal, and primary task, is to keep the laws simple so that each citizen can understand their rights without the need for understanding legalese.

If lawyers are truly clever, they will be able to keep things simple using our common language. Just because common citizens would now be able to understand the laws would not mean that lawyers would not be needed. Not everyone is at ease in public speaking.

There are a number of other reasons people might choose to have a lawyer. Some lawyers will have to learn that trying to make things more complicated, so that they themselves will have more value, is no longer acceptable. That kind of action will only serve to take us back to the confusions we had.

Since the voting process, to allow a new law, will take some time, the new system might allow the immediate case in question and others like it to use the old legal system to mediate a just end for the case in question, that is, if the local and state area review judges concur that the use of the old system is proper in those cases. This would only be allowed during the transition period while a new law has to be voted on. The old legal system however would have a limited life, for example, ten years, before all cases would have to be judged based on the new system.

After ten years, the old system will simply become null and void. This rids us of all the volumes of books with laws that have not been used in decades yet were there in the code making it more abundant, more complex, and less efficient. This provides a legal system where everyone has a better chance to understand what the laws are. This will not put lawyers out of business, but simply make their jobs easier. Let's face it, after ten years, the new legal codes will no doubt grow somewhat, so their speaking skills and expertise will still be required.

Of course, we could apply our new system's principles to the statues and ordinances at the various levels of government as well. Do we really need ordinances like it is illegal to spit on the sidewalk or play loud music after 10:00 p.m.? Things like this should be part of our basic manners, general upbringing, and common sense. Many issues might be covered through the town's code of conduct, only resorting to ordinances when common sense fails the defendant.

Offenders of laws, such as this, typically want to push their individual rights over the general public's rights. Writing individual laws to prevent such things takes rights away from everyone, and in the end, everyone's individual rights are lost. This concept of just how our rights are lost needs to be understood first.

With a little self-control, respect for others, and common sense, we would all be better off by not having to resort to writing excessive laws. Again, issues such as loud music after 10:00 p.m. would be better handled by public education. Knowing that some people are mentally inclined to cause trouble, a public nuisance statute might bring all of these common sense items together under one code—a code that can be easily explained to the general community. Note that if the new legal system isn't used to make some people excessive amounts of money, it likely will not be abused as much.

Business and Corporate Laws

Template contracts would be designed that would limit the number of conditions to reasonable levels, perhaps no more than five. The variety of these template contracts might be limited as well to simplify the contract process still further. By standardizing contracts, we would speed up business dealings.

The standard contracts would eliminate the unlimited number of provisions that confuse the issues and then lay the seeds for future litigation. Those complex contracts often cause corruptions to enter in. Here again, the rule should be that the common citizen should be able to understand the contracts without having to go to law school.

Elaborate disclaimers are today becoming a great concern to many. Even software programs have extensive disclaimers and contracts that frankly most people don't even read. They don't read them because first, they don't understand them and second, they are often too exhaustively long; and this causes the third reason, that is, they don't have the time.

Knowing this, is this then the kind of agreement we really want to accept as being binding? A standard contract would be easier for everyone to adhere to. This means that both the business and the consumer would have to compromise on their demands.

Instead of each individual company having their own disclaimers, they should choose from a very limited template base. They would choose the template that comes closest to their need. They might line out what doesn't apply to them, if need be. They would not be able to add conditions however.

Hopefully, the new basic laws will help to control the size of these contracts. Again, if the price system's profit motive schemes are taken out of the picture by our new system, the contracts will be less complex. Lawsuits would be less likely, because profit motives will be drastically reduced under our new economic system. Remember that since no person will be allowed to have excessive incomes, excessive lawsuit should be a thing of the past.

The general public should not be subjected to huge contracts. At the same time, companies should not be subjected to the unreasonable stupidity of their customers. Our new legal code will make people more responsible as the laws will no longer encourage frivolous lawsuits. I believe a happy medium can be reached, and with that, a lot of paper work can be eliminated. The goal is to have only a very limited amount of these blanket agreements depending on the category or nature of the products. Some of these categories might be electronics, energy, or entertainment.

For example, each industry might have one common template so that everyone who reads one for one company knows that another company in that industry has the same contract. Again, these should be written in English, not legalese. Citizens should not have to agree to things without fully understanding what they are agreeing to. Nor should people need a lawyer to interpret contracts. Is this possible? I think our laws will have a better chance of being obeyed if we design in simplicity instead of confusion.

In fact, the need for patent and copyright laws under our new economic system would, by the nature of the changes made, be drastically reduced. Patents and copyright laws are a product of the price system. Through these laws *they* can control pricing in *their* favor.

Our new system should reward individuals not private corporations. Doing this will limit the terrible excessive side effects of the current laws. Very often, the current laws primarily and excessively benefit those who are not really directly responsible for the invention or work of art.

Currently, corporations take their patent rights to excess and in so doing delay progress or further innovations and ideas. A simplified and balanced patent system would put the inventive or creative credit back where it belongs, on the inventor or artist. This should speed the progress of our economy.

The process would take the control away from individual corporations and quickly reward the inventors or artist directly. This leaves the ideas available for others to build off, within a reasonably short period of time. When more people have faster access to innovation, our society will reap more rewards, not only as a whole body but also individually.

Businesses that need to keep their employees from violating the general laws will need to give their employees training, if they are dealing in more difficult business ventures. They can do this by establishing a code of ethics. These codes of conduct can mimic the new laws. This would help to keep the business out of trouble.

Employees should understand that the same laws apply to them no matter if they are the least-paid or highest-paid employee. Individuals within the business will be held responsible for their own actions. If the illegal procedures were taught or imposed on them by other employees, those employees would also be punished for violating the laws, perhaps to a greater extent.

A New View on Who and What Corporations Are

Private corporations, under the new system, should no longer be able to operate as corporations, but should operate as small, medium, or large companies. However, individuals in these companies will be protected under our new system in ways other than incorporation. This will be explained shortly.

Now, under our new economic system, only the people, as a whole body, of the United States of America would own and operate corporations. Private corporations would not be allowed for the following reason—private corporations do not truly encompass the whole population of the United States; therefore, granting them special privilege is anti-democratic in nature.

They should never have been granted that status of a person as this stretches the idea of being human, beyond reason.[5] Granting inanimate subjects the same status as humans infringes on our God-given human rights. That was one reason why the price system set this practice up.

The size of companies owned by private individuals should be restricted so that they will never be too big to fail, as our system of capitalism must allow failure to happen, should it occur. Capitalism is supposed to encourage competition however corporations naturally seek to become monopolies. Logically, corporations should be restricted to only operate in areas where they serve the citizens of the United States as a collective whole. Public corporations therefore are the only place where monopolies make sense.

Our public corporations would serve to deliver basic resources and services, which are owned or used by all of the people. For example, the mineral and water resources of the United States would be owned by the people. In addition, services such as our military, fire, and police departments and government services and their associated buildings would be owned by the people. Now, if we bail out the corporations, we truly will be bailing out ourselves instead of some private concern.

Lawsuits

Frivolous lawsuits might be averted by a citizen's legal review panel. They would be the first review prior to court, and they would determine if the case warrants further governmental expense.

183

Their first approach would be to determine if the request for trial is proper.

They would review the prosecutor's or plaintiff's arguments to determine if indeed any of the existing laws were violated. If no laws were broken and there were no suggestions that a new law be added, the case would be dismissed. If laws were broken, the panel would then try to arbitrate the case between the parties.

If one or more parties do not want to arbitrate, the case would move into the next phase. The act of not accepting arbitration should put those involved at risk of court cost should the judge determine that their lawsuit is not relevant to the general public's concerns.

Lawsuits that are brought forward requesting actions that exceed "appropriate levels of restitution" should be highly reviewed. This is because they should seldom be necessary. This will help to keep frivolous or vindictive lawsuits from burdening the courts.

Note that under our new system, "appropriate levels of restitution" would be predetermined by our new medical programs and legal limit laws, defined in part below. These are the basic levels that would be paid out regardless of whether the case is arbitrated or goes to trial. These limits should be fair to the public and not just to the individuals. These restitution levels should greatly reduce the need for going to court as arbitration would be able to handle these predetermined solutions.

Citizens, individually, would receive the basic benefits of the new legal system in regard to lawsuits. These benefits include certain protections for their private businesses, homes, or livelihoods from excessive lawsuits. This would come automatically via a fair compensation provision in the penalty codes that judges will use to operate under. Compensation values will not overly reward any individual. This will better serve to treat people as individual members of society rather than elites.

Instead of the excessive use of monetary repayment or restitution, the punishment of crimes will focus first on punishing the individual at fault. This in part will be with jail time no matter who they are. Everyone gets the same justice, rich or poor, company owner or employee, senator or senator's aid, president, or mail room clerk.

This is not a new idea, but rather one that we should have been using. Here are two old examples of this idea found in the Bible: "But he that doeth wrong shall receive for the wrong which he hath done: and there is no respect of persons."[6] "For there is no respect of persons with God."[7]

With our system of justice today, there have often been special royalty privileges granted. More often than not, the rich have ended up having a different system than common citizens would. Could the designers of the price system have been more unjust? Yet most of us ignore this as that is just the way it is.

All jails will be of the same quality; there will be no resort jails. They will be clean and descent facilities highly monitored to prevent the sale of drugs and other abuses. There will be no private jail systems. All prison facilities should be owned and run by the people.[8]

Jail terms however will be shortened, because of the austere conditions that our new prisons will be imposing on the prisoners. No weight-lifting rooms, no advanced education programs, and no sports programs. Prisons might have an indoor walking track or tracks with limited access, a reading program, and basic moral television services.

Disruptive prisoners will be placed in a mental health prison. This is to ensure that efforts will be made to correct their behavior via medical procedures; if necessary. This facility may require longer-term incarceration.

Prisoners will lose all social security-type benefits, all welfare-type payments or any other governmental support payments while in prison. Those "checks" will just not be written by the government until those inmates are released and then only if the "checks" are still required. Frankly under our new economic system, if adopted, those "checks" would no longer be required anyway.

Prisoners will receive basic health care only. No frivolous operations or cosmetic procedures would be given. Mental health prisoners however will receive the latest approved mental health procedures.

Prisons should be more of a deterrent than a vacation. Today's prisons are sometimes looked upon by the homeless as a good place to get a roof over their heads, three meals a day, health care, education, and recreation. We should make prisons less rewarding and our new system would.

Again, the jail times will be drastically reduced for most crimes. Repeat offenders will be considered for entry into those mental health prisons where appropriate health procedures should help to reduce their anguish or belligerence. The new system would also work to eliminate homelessness as it will provide public housing for everyone. This would further reduce the prison population.

The plaintiffs in some legal proceedings will need financial support, most often for medical needs and loss of employment. Under the new system, they get these needs met under the "appropriate levels of restitution" mentioned above. In this case, these costs will be paid for via public assistance programs similar to that of social security disability and Medicare/Medicaid or some newly formed composite.

These programs can be remodeled to handle this. Note here the public is paying the primary cost instead of the individual who caused the plaintiff's problems. However, under our new system, these costs would be less expensive for the public. They actually would work for each citizen as a form of accident insurance.

While this seems strange, remember that, currently, lawsuits drive up the cost of everyone's insurance. Since insurance companies often end up paying, they then tack those costs back to the public. Additionally, the business of law, as an industry, burdens the public, because lawyers tie up our court systems with their cases. They use our facilities to make themselves a living. The more cases they have, the more money they make. So they tend to overwhelm our public court systems. Their marketing success thus often delays justice because they create a backlog of cases.

Further, the current process for an individual's lawsuit claim is far from fair and honest. It is dependent on the lawyer's successfulness and sometimes luck. The plaintiff does not always make out. In addition, the process might require publicly paid court fees, lawyer fees, and more taxpayer-supported judges and juries. These are all things the public has to pay for now, not to mention more court buildings and staff, as the legalized price system drums up business often unnecessarily.

On average, our new process would serve the general public far fairer, far better, and far faster. Of course, the defendant would suffer time in jail, if that was appropriate. Before our new plan, they might have been allowed to avoid jail, because of their station in life.

Not that we want to put people in jail, however in order to treat everyone equally, a person's status should never be considered. Any just and honorable person should and would agree not to be granted preferential treatment. We should work to decrease sentence time in cases where remorse is clear. In cases where remorse is not clear, then mental health treatment may be appropriate in a secure medical facility.

Finally, on the question of cost to the public, remember that the "appropriate levels of restitution" will never be excessive, but only what is fair to the individual and to the general population who has to pay the bills. The changes explained here are designed to lower the cost to the general population overall so that the new system will benefit society. The many changes outlined here will work together to accomplish this goal. These would be changes in justice, government, medical, and other systems.

Something More to Consider

Mediation over whose life is more valuable, in terms of money, is not something we should pretend we can answer fairly. With this new system, every human being is considered to have roughly the same value. This is fair because we do not know the future.

For example, a scientist and an unemployed drug addict both get hit by a car and become unable to care for themselves. Whose life was more important or more valuable? Since we do not know if the scientist might have, in the future, become a mass murderer, how can we truthfully determine that his life is more valuable? We would only be guessing.

Nor would we be able to determine if the drug addict would have straightened his act up to become the inventor of the next great medical wonder. So by treating every human as equal, we have a far better chance at justice being served. By setting limited mandatory sentences on jail time and by setting the limit on monetary fines, we simplify court discussions, and we reduce the load on the justice system.

We need to stop trying to get even, when accidents or violence happens, as this is primitive and costly thinking. Sure some people make out on court cases like these, mostly the lawyers. Society as a whole is suffering from these old ways.

The Plaintiff's Costs

Now, how do we pay for the extra disability and medical cost? One way is by allowing our new system to alter the Social Security System and Medicare/Medicaid programs. Another way is that we might design a new composite program. We should also build one huge hospital system owned and operated by the people. All of these programs could be operated as corporations and as such be expanded for efficiencies of scale. Now, for those of you who champion private industry, you should note that each individual worker at these corporations is a private citizen.

You might ask, how do these changes help? They help by reducing the number of families losing their homes, businesses, and jobs through court cases and medical costs. This helps to stabilize our economy as our workforce is strengthened. Our health-care system would improve, and our country will be more productive. Now with more productivity, we will be in a better position to accommodate social programs like these.

In fact, it is becoming clearer that the existing private medical industry is far too costly and corrupted. Our new system would offer savings in many different ways over the old private health-care system. There are many cost efficiencies that can be gleaned from a public system that private systems cannot offer, due to the fracturing nature of competition.

If we were to establish our own universal health-care system, we could drastically lower cost and improve services. It is common knowledge that when there are more people in the insurance program, the cost of that insurance is driven down. The actuaries exist to prove this. This would become one of our publicly owned corporations. We could hire some of the same talented people who used to run those private hospital and insurance businesses; except now, we the people own and control the corporation.

Note that our conditioning or some would say brainwashing has been that public systems don't work and only the private company can give you the best service at the lowest price. We should question if this is indeed true. If fewer and fewer people these days can afford private health care, how can it be true?

Further, fewer and fewer companies offer it to their employees and those that do have stopped offering it to their new hires in retirement. This indicates that private health care isn't doing the job they say they are. If they were, their service would be cost-effective, and it clearly is not.

Social programs can work and do work, but just like any private company, they have to be run efficiently; safeguards have to be built in to achieve this. We can do this just as easily as private industry can; in fact, in this case, we can do it better because monopolies have definite advantages over multiple private companies or even private corporations. There are many new ideas on how this could be done; one such idea is as follows.

Health-Care Reform

Note that the following was written, in part, to be executed today under our current price system. It could however be easily adapted to be used in our new economic plan. Actually the new plan would make it even more beneficial to us.

First, we need to decide just how much health care we really need. Do we need a system that will pay for all the bells and whistles that a luxury plan might provide? This would be nice, but it would be wiser to start with a plan that will cover each citizen's basic health-care issues and not in an overextended way. Logically, a basic plan would be more likely to succeed. If it is successful, more coverage could be trialed and, if again successful, added in at a later date.

How Would a Basic Plan Help?

It is my best guess that a pay-for-everything kind of health system is not economically feasible for us. That is based on the way our current government allocates our money. Our new government will also face these budgetary problems.

So we need to devise a system that will provide for the common health-care needs of our citizens without breaking the national treasury and ruining our country. A basic care system will also tend toward being fairer and more just to those people who initially might seldom use the system yet will be required to support it. Logically, however, over time, these people will on average really use the system the same as everyone else.

Now, there are mainly two views on treatment policies. It is also a known fact that some people, regardless of the odds of success, will want to continue medical treatments, no matter what the expense. This practice has often been found to be economically unsound.

On the other hand, it is a fact that some people take an opposing view. They feel that sometimes life extension procedures are cruel and inhumane. They want to cut treatments off as soon as possible to avoid prolonged suffering.

I believe that to a great extent, we can support both views to exist with our new system. However, only to a certain degree, just not to their extremes. This is because it is possible to devise such a plan.

This plan does so in moderation by covering a great part of even the worst-case medical conditions. However, it would stop short of providing perpetual life extension measures. Those measures would have us run a risk of running up the national debt even higher. There can be balances between both views that can work to afford a position that both sides can more easily accept.

How Do We Do This?

I believe a hybrid system of public corporations can accomplish this. One public corporation would exist in a basic care system paid by citizens in the same way our military is paid for today, that is, in our taxes and or in public service commitments. Since our individual labor would be used to pay a large part of these taxes, a basic care system should be possible.

Now, a separate optional public corporation could provide supplementary insurance to those interested. This would be paid for by each citizen just as it is today, from our own personal incomes. Supplemental insurance would be used to support those citizens interested in perpetuating life, in any condition.

The combined basic and supplemental systems together create favorable synergies. They cooperate to lower the cost of these catastrophic or supplemental insurance plans. The positive affect here allows people, so inclined, the ability to purchase the extra coverage that matches their convictions.

Low-cost catastrophic policies would provide citizens holding the view that life should be extended at all cost, with a means to pursue their belief. They would do so at their own expense, without forcing others to bend to their will. I will explain how shortly.

To be honest, the way we react to this extended life decision, in the end, rests within each of us. This is a difficult social issue, and to force others to go to extremes and violate their principles is not a just solution for either side. We should note that God does not force us to do things his way. It is obvious that he allows each of us to make up our own minds.

These extreme life extension issues should remain a personal choice as this is a freedom each of us needs to retain. The new basic plan would allow the supplemental insurance cost to be substantially reduced. It does so through the principle of economics known as the efficiency of scale.

Suffice to say, for now, that a great part of the medical expenses that we face today will be lowered. Since the new health-care system would be covering the major costs of medical care, the supplemental insurance plans will be able to reduce their rates. Low-cost supplemental insurance has the potential to resolve this extended life dispute as well as other issues. It does so because the extra insurance would cover the worst-case situations, which people might want to prepare for.

These supplemental insurance plans would also allow the insurance industry to reform into a new public corporation. This will help to provide the jobs required under our new system of economics. It is a system based on full employment. Our medical system will thus be our socialistic business. However, it will operate as a capitalistic venture. We the people are the capitalist here. In part, the results of our labor will determine to a degree our livelihood.

Remember that the current medical industry, as a private capitalistic venture, needs to seek ways to cut both jobs and benefits at every opportunity. This, at times required exhaustive overtime hours. We however should be able to accommodate every job position with multiple employees, because every able-bodied person will work. In fact, the workload can be distributed to reduce the stress, as it works to reduce the hours required on the job.

Our new system takes private insurance companies out of the health-care industry. It should also allow doctors and patients a little more freedom to choose their own course of treatment for care. In addition, the basic care plan would gain efficiencies of scale by assuring that all citizens are part of this basic care system. We will monitor the cost-effectiveness of the system to assure its stability.

Since even the representatives of our new government and economy would receive the same basic medical treatments as anyone else, they will quickly learn firsthand if it is adequate or not. This fact alone should help to assure that our basic care will be what we need it to be. In regards to having a private room, a TV, extraordinary life-extending procedures, or extremely vain medical treatments performed, the supplemental plans would cover this or the individuals themselves would have to pay for these things.

Our medical plan would therefore control cost through designing a system that works to provide basic care, but not excessive care. It does so by figuring out the average costs to cure people, for each individual illness, and then provides that amount of care. Its goal would be to provide care for all medical situations at the basic level, from onset to cure.

To plan, this we will have to determine what the customary treatments are and what the reasonable and customary charges should be. The individual states and the Department of Health would supervise these actions. After these cost and procedures are established, the supplemental insurance plans will be able to provide their costs for their insurance services.

Once everyone understands what the plan entails, they will decide what additional coverage they may want to purchase. Supplemental insurance will allow citizens the means to access a plan that they feel will support their personal views at a reasonably affordable price. Where the basic plan falls short in providing possible extended treatment, citizens will then be able to prepare themselves, ahead of time, economically for their value choices, through the purchase of supplemental insurance.

Other Ways of Controlling Cost in a Basic Care System

Naturally unwarranted medical procedures or test would add cost to our basic care system. Testing should only be ordered when appropriate; this basic plan will help to limit the frivolous procedures and expand the use of them when medically necessary.

The basic plan would remove any selfish incentives that doctors, hospitals, or insurance companies might have to perform unnecessary test or deny necessary test. Basic rules would be set up by the states and the national medical review boards and approved by the Department of Health to monitor those testing methods. The

Department of Health would make sure that the states provide, at minimum, the national standards for testing.

These standards are something the plan will define. Of course, the states can add features at their expense, if they so decide. The departments after setting the rules would monitor the system for necessary changes, annually.

By requiring all the medical equipment to be owned by the government instead of by doctors or hospitals, we should be able to reduce the incentives for abuse. In the past, doctors and hospitals who owned stock in certain medical equipment service companies were inclined to overuse those devices to help drive up their investments. By eliminating those conflicts of interest, we should be able to reduce unwarranted testing.

Testing can also be abused in the opposite way. This means that sometimes undertesting, not doing a test, in the end causes more medical cost to be generated. This occurs when insurance company restrictions have ended up causing more expense than if they had allowed the doctors to perform the tests to begin with.

Removing the ownership of the equipment from the private hands of doctors and hospitals and removing the control over the equipment from private insurance companies will cure these problems, saving cost. There is one other practical reason for all equipment to be owned by the public. This ownership provides a means to purchase equipment on a volume level. This should reduce equipment cost for the nation as a whole.

In order to stay current in medicine, the boards would add medical procedures or innovative ideas as they become available, that is, if the innovations are appropriate. States and local governments will retain rights to review and audit the board's decisions so that unnecessary equipment or procedures can be avoided. We shouldn't let our guard down for possible abuses here.

The states and local governments might also want to supplement or improve these rules. They should be able to do this at their own expense and with taxpayer approval. The states might also want to monitor the government's purchasing agent's contracts. One reason why taxpayers might do this is because the agents might be making some purchases from private companies and contract abuse can always rear its ugly head if it is not monitored.

Supplemental insurance will have no say in the treatment of basic care procedures. This should allow basic care procedures to remain at the basic care level. However, the medical boards should be directed to be progressive regarding medical care based on the merits of any particular treatment.

This attitude of balance is necessary so as to retain a good level of basic care. This should prevent senseless austere medical policies. Excessive austerity is something the private insurance industry sometimes directs. They weigh the cost of a lawsuit against the economic benefit from withholding a procedure or medicine.

Our plan should be austere, just not excessively austere. It should provide ample care to all who need it, up to the point in which the rules prohibit the excessive treatment procedures. Remember that affordable supplemental insurance will be available once the basic system is set up. That means, people can purchase insurance to cover their belief system.

Yes, there will be disputes with the system as there is in anything humans are involved in. So, an arbitration process will be set up. The process will allow doctors or patients and the medical review board to appoint arbitrators of their choice.

The process should not give any side unfair control over the process. Perhaps, a three-person jury of sorts selected at random out of a pool of citizens would serve short terms as arbitrators. We can work on a fair system where no one side has dominance.

This arbitration process will be a condition of treatment. This is designed to limit the legal industries excessive drive to eke out unwarranted profits off the health-care system. This will help to assure that everyone can have ample coverage.

Measures to control other legal industry excesses will also need to be addressed. Good Samaritan laws would extend to basic care services. Public training in basic health care techniques should help reduce some of the existing conflicts here.

By simplifying the basic coverage, the whole system will become easier to understand. This coupled with the fact that there would be only one system should drastically reduce confusion. This simplification of basic care will be of great value for doctors, patients, insurance, and health-care workers.

It will mean less paper, less time filling in forms, and less time trying to figure out what is covered and what is not. Doctors, hospitals, and patients will have uniform rules that apply to everyone. Confusions on the part of doctors, medical workers, and patients will be vastly reduced. This means more time can be directed at real medical procedures.

Of course, in a basic coverage plan, a private room isn't always possible, as well as phone or television service. These items are for the most part extraneous and not essential. Use of a private room under basic care will be by doctor's orders that would be reviewed by an overview panel as whether the patient's condition warrants.

There would be a limited number of hospital designs available for construction nationwide. They might predominately make use of wards and semi-private rooms. This would increase the efficiency in the construction process. These standard designs would save the taxpayer's time, money, and resources.

Typically, basic health care would use commonly accepted and medically approved procedures already being recommended by licensed physicians. New procedures will be added by the review board as medical practice evolves. Supplemental insurance would have to cover nontraditional procedures and services. That supplemental insurance could cover lower bed count accommodations if that is what a person wants.

The system would calculate the average expense for each medical problem known to us. Many of these conditions have already been calculated by the existing insurance industry. They know, for example, the average cost for a broken leg.

If the standard treatment's average cost is $5,000 and the leading alternative treatment's cost is $8,000, a solution allowing the alternative treatment might still be possible. It is important to allow the doctor and the patient to decide which method or methods they prefer to use. We can study things such as these and find solutions.

There would also be an average time calculated to cure or treat the various conditions or ailments. Conditions that go over the average times will have to be paid for by private supplemental health-care insurance. They should be paid for directly by the individual, if it is found that they are not following doctor's orders.

Procedures outside the normal practices might still be covered up to a point. We could do this by simply applying the average cost allowance for the condition and then paying it toward the new procedure. This idea and all others would have to be studied thoroughly.

Extra cost for procedures outside the standard medical practice or above and beyond basic care standards would have to be paid for by the patients themselves. This allows room then for a supplemental insurance industry to provide relief. However, it would be a publicly owned entity.

This publicly owned business would sell catastrophic or supplemental policies to anyone who wants them. Another service that they might sell would be an improved service package offering say a private room, phone service, or even television. These policies should now become much easier to afford, as now the supplemental insurance plans will know how much the basic health-care system will cover and adjust rates accordingly.

In essence, our medical system establishes a group insurance policy in which each person, and/or those responsible for them, contributes to the system. The system includes all citizens. It would be paid for by citizen's work contributions, taxes, and/or private incomes. Perhaps, its cost might require a combination of two or more of these measures. However, the costs are very likely to be a lot lower than what the rates are today.

All governmental employees including the military should be covered under this same plan. This would include all health-care workers such as doctors and nurses. It should also include all visitors or workers coming to our country on a visa. They might pay toward this health-care system as part of the visa/passport fees, prorated. All Medicare and Medicaid recipients would stop using those plans and start using this basic plan. Since all working people, in any field, would pay into this system, the cost actuaries should be beneficial to the average citizen.

As a point of reference, the basic health-care plan should compare favorably to Medicare. We should do our best to achieve that or better, if possible. This should be possible because now everyone will be using this system so the actuary cost advantage should work for us.

Our individual efforts in our public jobs could even improve this more. That could make the system even better able to afford the costs. In addition, insurance industry workers would now help to administer the new national plan. The cost savings from consolidation would also be rolled into this new system.

Again, how does all this help? This plan will have nearly every person using it, contributing toward the plan and thus making it a more viable system. Of course, there will be some unemployed citizens who might not be able to contribute. Citizens such as prison inmates, handicapped, or mentally ill persons may be sidelined. Part of their cost could possibly be covered from funds formally used for foreign aid, at least until we can find a way to do both.

Our blanket coverage concept will simplify the administration of the system. It will be easier not only for doctors and hospitals, but for the patients. This single-system plan means efficiencies in cost and less error.

The use of one system allows a better opportunity for all of us to understand our health care. That understanding is extremely important as a first step in our decision whether to purchase additional coverage or not. Will we be able to pay for supplemental insurance? That insurance should be more affordable to us.

The process to collect the physical taxes for the system might be payroll taxes or sales tax or a combination of both of them. Private employers will not have to contribute taxes toward their employee's basic health care anymore. This is because as public employees they will already receive basic health care.

The private marketplace is more likely to pay a decent wage as they now have to compete in the free market. That would make it more possible for their employees to purchase supplemental health care. That in turn would help to make this system even more solvent.

Small business may be paying a slightly higher wage. However, remember their expense should, be offset by those savings on employee health care costs. This also makes our private businesses more competitive with other countries.

It also saves the companies the expense of having to administer a health-care program. It increases efficiency so that the companies will be able to devote their workforce entirely to their main business. It simplifies their responsibilities. It means that health care is no longer a concern of private business.

Under our new economic system, all public employees would be providing a block of time to the system. Perhaps, four to six hours of work, four to five days a week might be required; this needs to be determined. This time would go toward paying part or all of their cost for the system.

It is a form of tax for the basic social needs that the government agrees to provide. If workers in the public sector work additional hours outside of this, they will be paid a marketplace wage. These wages would be taxed appropriately to help maintain our social balance. This tax would go to support government and its programs.

Our new economic plan would not provide tax credits for depended children. This credit was a price system perversion of the tax system. By eliminating the credit, the government can use that money to help to pay for our health-care system.

The elimination of the tax credit also helps to level the taxpayer's responsibilities. We need to acknowledge that not every couple or single person has children. They themselves may not have wanted any or were not able to have any. In some cases, the child tax credit might have been like adding insult to injury. It really was unfair for them to pay other citizens for having children.

In any event, this loss of a tax break makes families more responsible for their own wants and desires. Families who choose to have children will contribute their fair share toward health care. This is as it should be, since they will be using the system more. Under our new system, families would be supported in other ways.

The elimination of this tax credit would also fix a loophole that illegal workers have exploited. However, we shouldn't have illegal workers to begin with. The truth is that no country should have them. The elimination of this tax credit also simplifies the tax system, at least a little.

Our new system would eliminate tax breaks all together. This should ultimately help to regulate excessive behaviors. Perhaps, if we can correct those behaviors, we can work to eliminate them completely. That is something that doesn't seem likely under the price system.

Here Are a Few Ideas or Measures to Prevent Private Company Abuses

Now, as we all know, most corporations, given the opportunity, end up milking any governmental system more than they should. There is a long list of corporations who have been doing this to us. Capitalism can be better than the other current systems of economics. However, it still has a history of villains who repeatedly worm their way into mischief. Because of this, we need to set limits and regulations on the private sector.

By not allowing private companies to grow into corporations, we reduce their influence. Reducing their influence over both our government and our economy will help us immensely. Private corporate lobbying, as you know, has launched many corruptions in the past.

Given the chance, private companies would lobby to push off all their cost onto the government plans. That government in the end is you and me. If they were to succeed in this, then our new medical system would run a higher risk of becoming insolvent, as would all other public support systems.

The private industry should have a cap on their profit margins. This would severely limit their ability to gain excess money to lobby for special favors. Lobbying as it is done today should disappear. Additionally, we would not grant a business license to any company wanting to directly compete in the major public sectors. We likely would, however, allow microcompanies to exist as support to the major public sector corporations; this needs to be studied, however.

In any event, there will be a multitude of other industries that they can work in. We should set heavy fines for any abuse, and mandatory prison terms for those involved. The prison, by the way, would not be a white-collar prison, like those that exist under the current price system. All prisoners would be cared for in decent, but not anywhere close to a country club atmosphere.

Insurance

Will there be a need for life insurance and other kinds of insurances under our new economic government? There shouldn't be as big of a need for this kind of insurance any longer. This is because we will be self-insuring ourselves as a total population for all public sector items. These would be food, clothing, shelter, and security. Security, by the way, includes health care. For example, the reason for life insurance was normally to protect your family in case you die prematurely. Those concerns will drastically be reduced as there will be a social net to support all families. In return for that support, just to be clear, every able-bodied person would work in a public sector job for a limited period of time or longer should they desire. This means jobs for everyone in our society.

Other Issues That Affect Our Health

Cap and trade and carbon taxing ideas really do conflict with what our government tells us. Here you will find one counterintuitive story that the price system tells. It is a story that impacts our health.

If each person has a carbon foot print, it seems foolish to promote growth policies. These policies after all increase the size of our population. The price system ignores this contradiction. This allows *them* to tax us for making too much carbon. In other words *they* call for a larger customer base and then tax it for causing a problem.

Under our new system, we will not promote rapid and excessive populations. We will use common sense to determine how many people we should have in our country. We do not want our children to starve or live as slaves under a shroud of debt.

This will help to reduce potential carbon problems for them as well. We should not be encouraged to have excessively large families, so that someone can have cheap labor. That practice has driven down labor cost so that a few people can make excessive amounts of money.

Our population grows in several ways. The price system increases it by bringing in new workers under several different visa programs. They even use foreign students as workers, and of course, this adds to our population. Each person, they say, adds to our carbon footprint; so now, we need to tax ourselves to pay for this.

It was the corporations who drove that carbon footprint up, but now, they want us to pay for it. They got cheap labor, and we get the bill. Our children, under the price system, suffer because of the excessive and rapid increases in labor.

This system's contrived methods provide a select few with huge windfalls. Unfortunately the bulk of the population ends up paying for nearly all of the downside of their methods. We pay in many shaded ways, that is, there are many forms of taxes, fees, surcharges, and more that hide the true expense.

Illegal immigration is another cause for our rising carbon footprint. However, many people in our government do not seem to point a finger at this problem. Reducing that footprint, after all, would help to control our environment, our health, and even our health-care system.

We need to be more responsible as humans if we really want to improve our lot. Excessive populations only solve the money problems of the price system overlords. Excessive populations cause the rest of us to face a multitude of problems, almost too many to name.

I am not a fan of taxing the common citizen for their carbon footprint. It is obvious, based on the above, that our current government is not really serious about addressing the actual causes for our environmental problems. The issues surrounding carbon are mostly due to the price system anyway.

Getting rid of it, the price system, paves the way for reducing carbon. We can do it if we try. It is a matter of self-control and a desire to be the masters of our own destinies. That should drive us to rid ourselves of the price system.

Until then, here is one other idea on how to pay for health care, under the price system. If the government allowed us to keep more of our own wages, we would be more able to purchase our own health care. Our government would be better able to leave us with more tax dollars to spend on health care if they stopped the wars.

We are currently invested in a few, on behalf of worldwide corporations. Our leaders would say we are there, because of national interests. These wars are helping to add cost to our medical system as future veterans seek treatment for war wounds. The price system of course will not like the idea of stopping wars; there is no money in it for them.

In addition to the standard wars that the price system takes us into, we have those politically charged wars to pay for. For example, it is likely that more health-care funds could be available if they stopped the failed war on drugs. It would be far more cost-effective to use some of that money to educate everyone about the problems of substance abuse.

Another source of savings, on health, is in the justice department. If the current system of justice could just stop some of the corruptions in government, we would have more to spend on our basic health plan. That however is not part of the price system's plan. Why? It is because the price system produces these conditions so that this waste can be generated. Obviously, ridding ourselves of this system, if only we could, would produce savings.

So far, we have touched on some changes to some of the critical systems that severely affect our daily lives. Namely, we have discussed our justice system, our corporations, trade, how we handle lawsuits, population, and how medical health-care plans could work better. As this book unfolds more, I think you will see that changes like these will be easier to implement if the price system releases its control.

The deep debt they are taking us into is likely to produce a catastrophic event. This could be an opportunity where their control can be challenged. I hope the information in this book will increase your awareness here, should that time come.

CHAPTER 7

─◆─

Possible Reforms in Education, Insurance, Trade, and National Security

I would like to preface this section on education by explaining a little about how teachers could be paid in our new economy, for that matter, how everyone could get paid, in part, under our new system. The idea of the plan is to reduce the importance of the price system's ill effects. This would work to reduce costs, reduce corruption, reduce crime, and a host of other ill effects that the current price system encourages.

If we introduce a form of "public certificates" along with a smaller more controlled system of money, then we should have more stable prices. Teachers and other public corporation workers would be paid in "public credits" or certificates. They could also work for money in the private sector, if they choose.

The "public credits" would provide the basic items needed for life, food, clothing, shelter, and security. The money system would be used for those who want items above what the basic system provides. Everyone that can work will work in this system.

Education: Reforms

The major problem with socially paid for services, under our current price system, has been that lobbyists alter the services so much that we cannot afford to pay for them. We allow private industry, under the price system, to talk us into adding extraneous features to those social programs. So many extras that, guess what, yes, we run out of money to pay for the basic program.[1] The public ends up paying the private industry for items that really are not basic items.

For example, in our educational programs, there are vast differences of opinions. Each of us has our own personal likes and dislikes. Some people want music education; others want sports education. Some people want school buses; others want handicap services. Some people want expanded pensions or other benefits for teachers and staff. Some want arts education, while still others want historical heritage education, and so on and so forth. Of course, they want all of these things at taxpayer expense, granted most of them are noble causes, but this has mushroomed out of control. So much so that it is a very unfair system for the taxpayers who are held accountable.

As these things began to happen over the years, many people eventually began to complain. They had growing concerns that their taxes were becoming too high. During the recent recession they then realized that their jobs didn't pay as well, as they previously had, yet their taxes remained high. Even knowing that, some state and city leaders wanted to ask people for more taxes to pay for these social programs.

As a result of the mortgage bubble back in 2008, many of those citizens lost their homes. Community leaders found that as house values dropped, they were forced to lower taxes. Property taxes then could no longer resolve their deficit spending problems.

They thought that public servants were exempt from the downsizing activities of the private sector. The recession proved them wrong. Those in positions of power in the public sector should not have made those excessive pension and wage agreements. They held their own self-interest above common sense and so ended up hurting everyone in the process.

They no longer had the money to pay those high wages and benefits. The city, state, and federal governments are not some vague entities. Under the price system, we, the people, are the government, at least when it comes time to paying the bills.

However, we are not the government when it comes to running things. Those leaders, of ours, often run up the tab for us unnecessarily. Frankly, we just do not have the funds to pay for all the things they buy, even in good times. Perhaps, someday we will, but not under the price system, unless you are lucky enough to be in the top 10%.

Remember that the top 10% of the people have 90% of the wealth; that leaves the bottom 90% of the people trying to use 10% of the wealth to pay for nearly all of the programs. This is because currently, the top 10% have tax loopholes that allow them to sometimes pay less tax than those in the bottom 90% group. The price system helped to move that wealth into their hands, as it helped to set those tax laws up in their favor.

Basically, most of us have been duped, so this wasn't completely all our faults. However, we now have to face up to the music. If we adopt an economics of balance here, our nation will, in the end, be better off.

To achieve this balance, we need to set limits on just how much help we provide to any of our social programs. Even if the 90% group had 90% of the wealth, without balance, we would still run into problems. However, with our new plan, we will at least have hope. Why? This is because without the ill effects of the price system driving up cost, we will have an easier time making ends meet.

The issue of education, a public sector responsibility, has to be addressed in an immediate sense.[2] In order to attack those problems with education, we need to think practically and build a new system. The state and local voters should determine the level of education they want to contribute to.

The federal government should have little to do with it. We cannot afford their unfunded mandates, which are generally devised and directed to push the price system's profits. That ploy channels money into the controller's hands.

For starters, this means, we will have to find ways to pay for the services, both in times of economic prosperity or economic decline. Is it possible to set up a system that works in both economic directions? I think you already know we could find ways.

Even now, it is possible. This could be done by simply tying the payrolls of government workers to a percentage figure. We tie it to a percentage of the annual budget instead of a dollar figure.

This percentage figure could be announced at year end for the upcoming year. This would allow people to adjust their spending habits accordingly. The economy should level out under our new economic system, but for now, we could consider options such as this.

Another idea is in closing or drastically reducing the size of the Federal Department of Education. This would be a step in the right direction. The bulk of the money, in the current Department of Education's budget, could then be returned to the states and local governments.

Those governments would then use that money as they see fit. The state government would set a minimum standard for education. It would be based on limits, or standards, voted on by the public.

A new system of education could be designed at the state level and implemented at the local level. The plan could be run very austerely, if need be; or if funds where available, additional features could be added. This system might look like the following:

The Office of Education for the State of (your state):
Limited roles and responsibilities

There would be a wide variety of possible ideas here, of which the following are only suggestions:
This office would:

1. Help to establish and enforce the law regarding education. These laws would be designed around voter-approved limits and standards. They would consider the nonbinding

recommendations from federal authorities. Those recommendations would represent suggested national standards.

2. Develop and maintain a system to assure that at least every citizen between the age of five and eighteen is registered in the system.

3. Develop and maintain a series of online computer courses from, at least, K to 12 to be presented to students via the Internet at state taxpayer expense. These courses would be used as a base standard for education levels within the state. Those courses would be purchased or developed and owned by the taxpayers of (your state).

   A. These courses would set the standard minimum level of knowledge that students would need to obtain from their homeschool, private school, or public school participation.

   B. The online courses would be structured in three primary subjects. The material provided in each subject could be broken down into 15-min, 30-min, or one-hour segments. This allows segments to be combined to fit the attention span of the individual child.

The primary basic courses would be designed around the Trivium principles of grammar, logic and rhetoric.

I. Reading and Writing

This starts with the learning of basic skills, in the first year's sessions, and expands to include social studies, civics, and other topics as the years go along. These topics could be built into the course structure. For example, a reading lesson might assign reading books of literature or of history.

II. Science

Lesson segments here would begin at the appropriate place in the course design. These segments might also include appropriate history of science, biographies of scientist, or other reading material on science.

III. Math

Again, lesson segments would begin at the appropriate place in the course design. The arithmetic course here might have lessons in home budgeting, economics, finance, or others up to higher math forms.

These three subjects, above, could share lesson time and space with each other when appropriate over the K to 12 schedules of lesson. Their might even be prenatal lessons. The level of difficulty for the passing of the various courses would be set at a minimum standard. This could be determined based on current levels expected or any level the citizens approve, somewhere between 51 and 100% for a passing grade.

4. The office would determine if two different course programs could be built as online courses. These would be a college program and a vocational program. It would require a little thought on how the vocational program would work, but I believe the details could be worked out.

5. That State Office of Education would provide testing methods and procedures for the Local Offices of Education to implement. They would also do the testing for the students who are working their way through the online courses. Testing could be set up to take place every fifth day. That is, the students log four days of lessons, and then, they go for testing on the fifth day. Therefore, the system would be set up to test every fifth day throughout the course year.

   Note that the students work on the lessons at home or at private tutor locations. Another option is to use the local community structures. This would require communities to find a way to generate the income required to operate some of the buildings as lesson centers.

The state would only allocate the energy or public certificates to operate the appropriate number of local schools to be used as testing centers. The frequency of this testing program could be changed. Depending on our economic livelihood, testing could be done either more or less frequently.

These tests would mark the progress and provide feedback to the parents, students, and private or public teachers. These tests then could determine the effectiveness of the students and teachers. This would help direct changes that could be made to improve the system.

6. The State Office of Education would authorize the Local Offices of Education (the community schools) to administer these tests. Perhaps, some schools would be used for college prep testing, and others would be used for vocational programs and testing.

7. The State Office of Education would allocate the appropriate number of testing teachers for the Local Offices of Education to hire under the public certificate system. The state office would release those public certificates appropriately so that the local offices could hire the appropriate personnel.

It may be possible for the State Office of Education to pay for and provide additional online courses as supplemental studies. These courses would prove helpful for those students who aspire to go on to college programs and plan to take the tests that are the equivalent of SATs.

Likewise, the State Office of Education might pay for and provide basic programs in vocational learning. These courses might provide classroom space and tools for qualified teachers to teach those subjects with. Such courses would prove helpful for the home-schooled students, wanting to learn auto mechanics, metal shop, woodshop, electrical, plumbing, heating and cooling, cooking, or other vocational subjects.

Even under the current price system, these classes might gain some support from local businesses who might donate equipment or expertise on subject-related issues. Under our new energy certificate system, these businesses would draw their employees from the school system, not from work visa programs, so they will be more willing to support those schools.

The Local Office of Education:
Roles and Responsibilities (your school district)

1. This office works with the *State Office of Education* to register students.
2. It works with the parents to develop the schedules for testing various registered students.
3. It would provide the required personnel to test the homeschooled or private school students.
4. It would provide the building or buildings to be used as testing centers within the jurisdiction of the local government authority or school district.
5. It works with local churches and civic organizations that provide support for any students who need tutoring and cannot afford it.
6. It works with local libraries, local churches, and civic organizations to provide access to computers if necessary.
7. With state funding, the local office will hire the necessary teachers required to instruct under the public certificate system provided by the state.
8. The local office could, at taxpayer's approval, also hire additional teachers under the money system. The level of pay will be established by and governed by the citizens of the state. This is to assure wages do not become excessive yet at the same time remain in line with each individual's proven achievements.

The Office of, if you will, the Parents

This educational plan provides the parents with the opportunity to enhance their own education. This could be achieved through working with their own children at home. Perhaps the adults might benefit in their own occupations from going over this material with their children. If this happens this would help to raise all of our standards.

Parents will also have the flexibility of allowing their children to take the exams over the entire K to 12 time frames or to test at a more rapid pace and receive their certificates or diplomas early. These loftily goals will be subject to local and state oversight, so as to prevent abuse. The parents will continue to have the ability to homeschool or they can choose to hire a teacher or tutor to assist their child.

The state or local communities may elect to provide public teachers or make school rooms available for tutors under a public certificate system. Parents may even elect to send their child to a small private school where other students help to share the potential extra cost of the tutor or teacher. These teachers might be paid under the public certificate system, or they might be paid under a new, more downsized and controlled money system, or price system.

A curriculum based on the "Trivium" design
of grammar, logic and rhetoric.

Economically speaking, the main thrust of our education plan should be on reading and writing, science, and arithmetic. These are the principle disciplines; generally, all others build off these. Parents may wish to provide additional studies in other disciplines, if the state isn't in a position to provide them.

This would be something the parents and their children can determine. This program allows them to do so, on their own, as it only sets the minimum standard, not the maximum. The state might even provide higher-level program lessons; however, local offices may not elect to test them, if funding is not available.

Note that the above method of education reduces the need for the extensive use of publicly owned schools, buses, teachers, athletic fields, swimming pools, etc. It also reduces the expense of heating and cooling, lighting, and maintenance cost. This has a potential to lower the direct cost of education to the state and local governments.

The method's structure of testing one day a week provides the means to reduce school facility requirements by roughly 80%. Testing could be accomplished within a three-hour window. This would allow testing in both morning and afternoon sessions.

This educational plan could also lower the cost for the parents. This is because there is less of a need of cars, gasoline, and lunch money, if they homeschool. Parents who do not teach may also reduce their cost by jointly hiring a tutor or teacher so as to share cost.

Under our new economic system, the public work schedule should range between four and six hours each day. This makes it much easier for each parent to be available for their children. Homeschooling would become a more viable option. I think you will agree that there are a number of potential savings, inherent in most sharing ideas; this one is no exception.

If the local school community decides to revive some more of those old classrooms, they will still have that opportunity. They should however impose safeguards to prevent the private enterprise system from driving up their operational cost in those publicly owned buildings. If that were allowed to happen, we would end up as it is today, too many bills and not enough income. It is likely though that a true free market system will keep cost down all on its own.

Now, before you begin to feel sorry for the loss of some of those sports and music programs above, let me explain that it may not be all that bad. Some of these services could be provided locally through township or city programs, if voter-approved funds were secured. For example, the city or township might already have some active sports programs.

They might expand one of these existing programs to create city high school teams. Likewise, music programs could be developed by the cities or by private organizations if so desired. These activities would be outside the primary educational program abilities, but not necessarily outside local communities.

Public schools will have to arrange their teaching staffs to allow for the balance that our educational programs need. However, this will likely open up other opportunities for teachers. There will be an active need for tutors and teachers, as many parents will elect to hire their services.

Testing centers will also be in need of their services. Those teachers not employed, as teachers, by the state and local programs might start their own business or even their own schools. It is very likely that there will be more job opportunities for everyone as a result of the new shorter work schedules used by the energy or public certificate system.

If it made sense, we could assist small businesses engaged in primary and secondary education. Perhaps by allowing the sharing of public facilities with them, this could be studied. Alternatively, we might even rent out the existing structures, if a group of teachers can assemble to form a company; again, this would have to be studied. Remember that we the people would own the public education corporation, so we want it to be a solvent enterprise and not an excessive burden on us.

Today under the price system, teacher's incomes and benefits have, at times, gotten out of line. Tenure, for example, was a detrimental construct of the price system. Our new education plan will mend these issues in a fair and equitable way through the use of public certificates. These changes are necessary, in order to correct that failed system.

Those certificates would allow for perhaps ten different levels of compensation in our public sector jobs. This means that each person could strive to better themselves by seeking the position they aspire to. That can be in the public or private sector or both. In fact, opportunities should be better for people in all walks of life, as the employment situations should improve.

Our new educational design should provide a basic education. One that would teach the fundamental skills of reading and writing, science, and arithmetic. The quality of this education, at graduation, should be at a level that would allow students to enter a school for advanced education. This might be a college or a trade school. I might add that there already exist several on line high school and college programs.[3] So, at least that part of this plan has already been trialed.

What would these educational changes mean on a federal level?

I do not believe that the federal government should even have a full Department of Education.[4] It exists, under the price system, so that they can control the dynasty and use it for their purposes. Under our new system, education is opened up and free to expand where it sees fit, perhaps even into college level programs.

I believe education really belongs to the state and local governments. Therefore, the Federal Department of Education could be extremely scaled down. Their role would be reduced so much that it could be rolled into some other department.

The federal government's new role would likely be the following: they would study international educational norms in order to compile and suggest uniform levels of achievement. They would then provide the results of their studies to each state. Since the role of the federal education service is drastically reduced, fewer tax funds will be needed at the federal level. Those funds could remain back at the state and local levels of government.

At the state level

It is also possible that the new education process will require fewer funds at the state level as well. Taxpayers thus might use some of that money to hire tutors or toward higher education programs for their children. It would be up to each state to achieve or exceed those worldwide standards so any extra funds would help. The states need to understand that their students may want to receive employment in other states or countries so it is very important to meet or exceed that worldwide standard.

Reforms in the Insurance Industry

Insurance is a mixed blessing at best. Some might say a necessary evil. Like anything in the price System, insurance costs can get excessive as well. Think of all the crimes that can occur because of the way our insurance industry is linked into the price system.

This industry allows people to insure, not only themselves but also other people and things for vast amounts of money. Insurance then, in and of itself, provides an incentive for those inclined to commit fraud. Sometimes, these criminal acts hurt people directly. This occurs when large insurance policies tempt people to hurt or kill others.

In the price system, there is no limit on wealth. That approved of excessiveness gives incentives to evil people. One goal of evil people is to achieve that wealth anyway they can. This means there is also no limit on criminal intent. The price system encourages these attitudes, because it sets no limits. Could our need for insurance be accomplished in a way that doesn't promote the above criminal acts?

My first encounter with insurance was in junior high school. Of course, two or three bullies were selling it. Yes, you guessed it—they were selling protection dues. This is the way it worked. They would extract lunch money from the students by force; however, if the students paid protection dues, they were left alone. After accosting me and finding I had no money, they looked through my lunch bag to see what I brought from home. Fortunately, for me they didn't like peanut butter and jelly. I wasn't the target that they were looking for. Other students were not as lucky, that is, if you call having your lunch taken apart lucky?

I suppose this experience has tainted my view of insurance ever since. However, it is pretty easy to get a negative view when you're being threatened. Even today in our commercials, while we are not directly threatened, we are told that we should be afraid.

We are told we should fear dying or getting in an accident. This is because we then would be a burden on our families. Fear is also generated around losing your home to medical cost. The result is that we buy protection, only now it costs a lot more than lunch money.

It is hard to deny that fear is our motive for buying insurance. That fear centers around losing all of our money. So we take some money and buy insurance. This when you think about it is antiproductive. This quagmire is a built-in price system manipulation.

There is an even more confounding gift here from the price system. You see, fear of not having enough money actually also stimulates crimes. So the system provides incentive to create crimes and in so doing promotes the sale of protection dues.

The promise of a large inheritance has caused some people among us to even murder family members. They do this just so they can have a more secure and burden-proof life; at least, that is their hope. Crimes such as these do not happen as often as other insurance fraud, but it does happen.

The insurance industry knows how to handle fraud when it happens against them. Perhaps, there is more to the saying, "It takes a thief to catch a thief." I say this because the need for insurance is a price system creation. It is fraudulent in its nature. This is because it, all too often, is a means of extracting excessive amounts of money from people.

The price system sets up these conditions, and it works well for those who are in control of it. Here is how that works in the insurance industry. Private insurance companies use actuaries to sell insurance. Actuaries are a means to calculate statistical risk that people have for certain conditions that could happen to them. The actuary process is so good that the private insurance industry is extremely profitable.

In the price system, private companies dominate the industry. This leaves us at the mercy of their rate structure; remember that they have to make a profit. Since they have corporate advantages, as price system players, they can better determine what the rates need to be, to a large part. I would bet there is an actuary that defines at what point we would not buy their insurance.

Now, if you think that the private insurance company's rates are fair, then why don't other large industries always buy their insurance from them? You see, some very large companies have found that they are better off self-insuring their own employees. This occurs especially if they are a large company. The actuaries here prove that they are better off providing the insurance themselves, rather than by going to a private provider. Why pay those large fees when they don't have to?

If large corporations have discovered that truth, don't you think it is time that the American public did so as well? As a group, we are large enough to make the actuaries work for us. Rather than letting private industry over charge us, we can provide our own insurance or protection dues. I would feel much more comfortable paying those dues to myself. In fact, I would be more responsible in doing so for several reasons.

To begin with, in our self-insurance system, we would limit the insurance to an appropriate level. This level would be based on known actual costs to replace the object. The level would not be based on artistic subjective values. Those items of subjective value would be deemed priceless and therefore uninsurable in the public sector. Doesn't priceless really mean that it could not be replaced anyway? This would lessen the incentive for people to murder each other. It would also reduce the incidents for fraud.

Self-insurance would in the end cost a lot less because the size of our actuarial pool is so large. This would move our whole society toward a more compassionate stand on itself. It would help to eliminate waste, fraud, and abuse. Imagine the savings just in those residual benefits.

You might be asking, what about all of those workers in the industry? What would happen to them? Remember that I said insurance was a mixed blessing? The negative side of insurance we have already examined.

On the positive side, most of us will agree that insurance is a blessing when you need it. It can be a worthwhile thing, so the need of insurance workers would still be required in the public insurance industry. There might even be a private insurance industry set up to handle those artistic items, but as a group, we need to investigate that possibility.

What I am writing here is surely not going to be accepted by those upper-level insurance company executives. This is because they will be losing their eight-digit salaries. They will have to climb down from their pedestals and receive a normal pay, in line with their real worth. What they will gain is this—they will no longer have to buy off public officials to alter laws that favor their industry. Their lobbying efforts will no longer be necessary. Their fraud investigation duties would be reduced, as people would not be as inclined to commit those crimes.

These benefits would spill over into other areas of our lives. Our police departments would benefit by the reduction in these kinds of crimes. Our personal stress levels will be much better. Just knowing that we have all the insurance we need would create that condition. The savings in this industry again can be used to advance other more productive ventures.

A reminder here, the private insurance industry has always prevented what I am suggesting from happening. The existing price system has forces in banking, education, religion, and politics. They will do everything they can to kill the above idea as quick as they can.

They have done this many times before, so they have the experience and necessary assets all lined up to do it again. Those working to stifle this idea should consider that they may only be hurting themselves and their families. Sure, they are getting paid nicely today for stopping ideas like these, but look at the world and what the price system is doing to it.

If I could address them directly, I would say, Do you really want to promote a system like that? Aren't you really just more of a slave to it than you think? A new economic plan can be your way out of that old corrupt system.

True the new economic plan does cause us to become a slave to a degree. However, not to the extent that the current system does. Remember nothing we do can create for us a utopia.

Still, our new system should provide you with more time for yourself. It should restore to us the human rights that the price system had diminished for us. In time, we should even have fewer restrictions at the airports and more friends in other countries. We can return to being a good example for the world, so we can be revered as a force to reckon with. Sometimes, today, we are feared as a bully, when we should be respected for our strength in fighting bullies.

Identity theft again is another example of how the price system through the insurance industry sets up its victims. As you recall, the price system uses a debt system. This debt system is used to give out credit. Of course, if you want credit, you have to build an identity.

Your new creditor needs to be able to find you if you don't pay. You have to release, to that third party, all of your vital information in return for them giving you the credit. Your credit identity, due to loopholes in the security systems, is not guarded very well. The data systems have built in so many points of access that it allows criminals to steal your information, sometimes rather easily.

That weak security sets up a new price system insurance industry. They call it protection from identity theft. You are now afraid someone is going to steal your ID, and rightfully so. This fear is increased when you see honest citizens being questioned by police for crimes they didn't commit.

Here is something to think about. If there are safety defects in our automobiles, we recall the cars so that the manufacture can fix them. This happens because the price system's insurance industry gets hit with too many lawsuits otherwise. Now, if there are safety concerns with all those financial products we have, why don't they recall those services until the safety breech in that product can be fixed?

The price system, however, is not inclined to fix this. Currently, they are making more money by not fixing it. Once the lawsuits start, if they allow them, this could change. In the mean time, don't look for a quick fix. The additional money generated in the price system from fees and charges to straighten things out works in favor of the price system controllers. So it may be awhile before we see help.

Can we design a new basic economic system that doesn't need debt or credit to function? I think it is possible. In addition, I think we can build one that doesn't have an internal revenue system either. Wouldn't that be a blessing?

The IRS is still one more point where all of our personal information is put into the hands of a private industry. Yes, the IRS is a private industry. They are supposed to protect our information, but even there, it is at risk of being stolen.

With all of these people being able to see our financial information, we have become financially naked. Image screening at the airport just completes the picture. We truly have become naked, that is, if you honestly think about it. Is there no longer a need to have secrets, modesty, or shame? That seems to be their goal—to eliminate those things.

Being honest in a corrupt system, how does that work? The people who are honest get to pay the taxes—that's how. The people who are not honest offshore their money or use other types of loopholes designed into the corrupt price system to not pay taxes. The price system even allows money to be hidden in shell corporations.

The legal system works to make this possible at the behest of our controllers. The strong potential for corruption in the price system makes it difficult for many people to stay honest. There are far too many built-in opportunities to lead a person astray. In the end, for the honest person trying to live within this system, I think Jesus Christ would have recommended the following - render on to the price system what is the price system's.

Reforms in Our Trade Policies

Trade with other countries, if they are not member countries in our new plan, might be based on two levels. We could trade our public supported products and then our private company products.[5] By definition, free trade between countries is an agreement without tariffs.[6] The free trade system, under the price system, benefited the private sector over and above the common citizen.

Tariffs under the price system were frowned upon. Under our new system, we would likely want to consider reestablishing tariffs so that all citizens share in the sale of our resources. Yes, tariffs would now make more sense as they would benefit the common person.

Tariffs are something all countries who work to support the common citizen would want to do. However, there will be countries who will not support their citizens and who will not want to be part of our new effort. So, our tariff system would, at the minimum, match any excessive tariffs set on our goods by those globalist-controlled foreign countries.[7]

Our new trade process should consider several things. We should consider product quality, the nation's market size, our diplomatic ties or goals, and friendship levels in order to judge the size of the tariffs. These tariffs again would be imposed against the foreign corporations or companies.

For example, when a foreign product is a better product, with all other things being equal, then the tariff will be reduced somewhat, so as to protect our consumers. This will encourage our companies to improve their productivity. We do not want them taking advantage of their American marketplace with poor-quality products.

Some countries we want to trade with will have a larger economic market than we do. We would expect to pay a higher tariff charge in order to have access to their market. On the flip side countries with smaller markets should expect to pay us.

The system will be monitored to maintain a reasonable balance of trade so that it favors us, but not excessively. This is necessary, as our new system's capitalistic trade policy would demand that we make a profit as a country. We need to balance our economic wealth so that is doesn't get drained off by international corporations operating under the price system.

Just so that you have an idea of how trade can affect us, here is an example. Our trade deficit surged to $50.2 billion for the month of May 2011.[8] It is sad to say that these kinds of deficits have been continuing month after month for years. The wealth of our nation is being drained. It isn't just the money, but the jobs that are being drained away under the current price system agreements. Under the Trump administration, the rhetoric is suggesting that this is going to stop. We will have to wait and see just how much of a change will really take place.

Generally speaking, having fewer people with money to spend damages small businesses, so they have been losing their morale.[9] Under our new economic plan, the current free trade agreements would be made null and void, and new fair trade agreements will be established.[10] These agreements will not be allowed to be fast-tracked through government.

No trade agreements should force unfunded mandates on the states or on the peoples of the United States of America. Nor will they be allowed to supplant our constitution. Our new governmental leaders will be involved in the process on establishing trade deals. Science, not politics, will assume the major role in determining these fair trade deals.

Fair trade is as follows:

1. Trade where both sides reach agreements before any goods and services are passed between the countries.
2. Each trade contract is defined in size and scope, and a time frame is determined.
3. These trade deals will only use a third-party organization to arbitrate if they run into an impasse in their normal negotiations. In addition, this process would only be used if both parties agree to use it. If they don't, it will proceed to the courts or be cancelled.
4. Tariffs will consider the potential size of our American marketplace versus the potential size of the foreign market we trade with. Access to our large market has a value, and tariffs are a means of getting return value for allowing foreign access to our marketplace. Tariffs should help to equalize the playing field between workers in those countries. Countries that live under conditions with lower standards and codes currently take advantage of countries who want to maintain high standards; this has to be balanced.

    Those lower standards can also determine their ability and desires to work for less money. These conditions and codes subsequently can affect the ability of the American workers to effectively compete with foreign countries. In a sense, private industry, under the price system, is taking advantage of people on both ends.

There is no shame to want to maintain our codes and standards. We should not have to give up our building codes and safety standards so that we can compete with foreign nations. It is fair and just to charge a reasonable tariff fee for access to our marketplace.

Those poorer nations should be helped by some other means. We might help them to find ways to lift their own standards. That would allow them to trade in a balanced way.

5. A new federal trade commission would oversee all trade deals to confirm that these rules are met by all companies and corporations doing business with our country's businesses and consumers.

6. A new consumer protection agency (the CPA) with enough staff to monitor and inspect the trade goods and services could be established. Tariffs and fees will help to offset the cost of this agency. The defense department will also bear a part of the cost of this agency, as this is part of their national security duties. Funds previously given to the former homeland security department can be transferred to the CPA. These job positions will be worked into the energy or public certificate system. Those are certificates earned for work in our public service departments.

Homeland Security and Border Patrol

The following is offered more or less as a brainstorming exercise:

The duties of Homeland security need to be reviewed for efficiency.[11] We might find that the twenty two existing agencies there, perhaps should not have all been consolidated under Homeland security? There could be a need at times for a little more separation and secrecy to exist between them. We might however find that more consolidation could be done.

Multiple agencies doing the same tasks is nonproductive and would generally lead to reduced efficiency of the team. There likely will be some duplicate functions that can be eliminated. This should help pay for any transformation cost that are required and also, hopefully, lower future operational cost.

The border patrol should be beefed up, and those extra forces could now be positioned in more responsive locations. Those extra eyes and ears will contribute to the total team's effectiveness. The border patrol would operate with federal funds dispersed to all fifty states.

We use a matrix of the states' foreign border length and per capita allocations to balance workforces. This would add jobs to each state in a fair and balanced way. If border activity required additional manpower, agents from the interior states, or states with high populations and shorter borders, could be sent to the area in need. This could also work in the other direction if need be. Each state would have one director.

These directors would not be elected or politically appointed, but would come up through the ranks of the state organizations that they work for. This way, we assure that they are experts in their fields. This also assures that each state has some representation at the federal level.

These directors would all have to be continually vetted for security reasons and monitored and protected at all times during their time as directors. If these fifty directors held an election among themselves, they could set up a Border Security Council. This would provide for better oversight on our national boarders as a whole.

The council would interface at the federal level to improve the team's national security oversight function. If done right, this process could help to identify rogue agency operations and stop them from doing unauthorized activities. This process could be mirrored by the other agencies so their rogue activities could be more easily identified.

These are just ideas; if they do have merit, they could help to build a more efficient security network. The economic goal here is to reduce the cost of our security. There perhaps are already far too many agencies to allow for proper security measures to work efficiently.

We shouldn't be stepping on each other in times of need. Cost issues can also be addressed through simplification and riding ourselves of redundant or complex security protocols. These are things we should study.

Final Thoughts on All of the Above Reforms

Breaking out of the price system and implementing all necessary reforms would set us on a path toward a unified nation. These actions would help to restore the personal freedoms and power we were all supposed to have. Those would be the freedoms and power our Founding Fathers wanted us to have. The price system leaders have taken the power of the people and have redirected it to the 10% that run their system. The reforms discussed above would be key steps in helping to return the power to the people.

CHAPTER 8

──◆◆◆──

Planet Change and a New Twist on Energy

There are times when we know, deep down inside, that we humans cause nearly all of our own problems. However, we don't want to shoulder much of the blame for those problems. We tend to push the blame off on to someone else or better yet something else.

Generally that blame is pushed off on anything else, but what is the truth? Blaming everyone and everything else, but ourselves, is not going to solve our problems. We need to own up to it, and then, we will be more likely and more able to work our solutions.

It is time to man up to our involvement. We need to acknowledge that we, the inhabitants of earth, cause nearly all the numerous shortage problems that we face. In the process of creating these shortages, we have also created or added to several of the world's pollution problems.

Scientists have already told us that we are pushing the planet's resources hard. Oil is now said to have peaked. The oceans are being overfished. Existing land resources are being swallowed up by growing human populations. In the process, animals and plants are being destroyed to make way for human enterprises.

Regardless of what you believe about climate change, the evidence of "planet change" is very obvious. For example, one-quarter of the planet's land is above water, while three-quarters is below water.

Yet we humans, on that one-quarter of the planet, have impacted the other three-quarters so heavily that several food sources there are threatened.

Some species of fish have had to have quotas set in place on them. Certain fish have become endangered. Various forms of marine life are nearing extinction, if not already gone. We have heavily contributed to these things, because of our price system actions.

Some fish species that we eat today were once thought to be junk fish and considered unsellable because of their quality. Today, there is a huge demand for fish, so those standards have been lowered. Those lesser-quality fish have entered into our marketplace.

I will not go over all of the examples of our dwindling resources here on earth. I believe most of us have seen and heard the stories. Each of us, very likely, has had firsthand experiences of hard-to-get items ourselves.

Often, you can still get things, but they cost more. The extra costs, now, for those reduced resources are added to the consumer's bills. Those dwindling resources, you see, constantly affect the prices you pay at the stores. Here are a couple of extreme examples that should help to grab your attention.

You may have seen the articles in the news about certain fish being sold for record prices. In Tokyo, a giant bluefin tuna was sold in January 2011 for $396,000.[1] This single fish was 754 pounds, and while this was a big fish, it still comes out to over $525 a pound.

In February 2011, a critically endangered fish known as the Chinese bahaba was caught and sold for consumption for over $500,000.[2] This fish weighed only about 298 pounds, but here this works out to be over $1678 a pound. If nothing else, these stories should enlighten us to the fact that our fish populations are not as sound or strong as we would think.

Our human effect on the oceans is amazing. Considering again that three-fourths of the earth is covered with water and we humans only exist basically on one-quarter of the earth's surface. Yet we have had an impact, even here in those huge oceans.

We don't have to argue climate change because we know "planet change" is happening. If planet change can happen, it may also be likely that climate change could happen. We know that there are those businesses, which are betting against it, saying that it is all a bunch of hooey.

Perhaps the people that are betting against it realize that they themselves have little to lose. However, their family's futures might be at risk. That is a bet they are willing to take. It seems to me that if they are wrong, it wouldn't bother them anyway. It is more important for them to worry about the excessive money that they can make today. They worry only about the here and now. That seems to be a common price system dogma.

What if certain scientists are right, and there is such a thing as a "tipping point"? This tipping point is a point in time where our atmosphere changes enough to begin to threaten human life on earth. Some scientists believe that if we reach that tipping point, we might not have the means to reverse it.

There are some who think we might have some control. Perhaps, that is the gamble that those businesses are willing to take in order to make their money now. Is it wise to risk polluting our atmosphere when the earth is said to be nearing that point seemingly on its own? Are we aggravating the situation? Are we speeding the process?

Could we humans reverse climate change? Industries today are pushing for "growth." It is necessary so that they can secure their private business fortunes.

However, their "growth" strategy may be putting all of mankind at risk. It is true that some evidence of this, at this point, is a bit sketchy. However, common sense would suggest that we should error on the side of caution.

We should allow science a chance to confirm or reject the evidence. They can do this by collecting the necessary data needed to conclusively answer the questions. This ongoing investigation has had some time to do this already.

Today, certain price system businesses, on both sides of the climate issue, can make money by resolving the issue in their favor. They contend with each other at our expense. Scientists are being paid on both sides to generate reports to those ends. The common citizen is caught in the middle.

We do know one thing for sure—large businesses are there to make money, and based on their track record, they do not care about the losers. Losers are everyone but them. Because of this knowledge, one would think we would proceed with caution when dealing with them.

We are not far away from absolute proof on just how much the price system has been affecting our environment. Of course currently, we are blaming human activities not the price system. Our science is advancing pretty well and hopefully, it will resolve the issue soon.

In order to buy some time for the study, we might consider imposing moratoriums on certain aspects of our lives. I believe we have a moral responsibility to provide that time, if it is required and if we can. This is easy to say, but getting the whole planet to agree to moratoriums, ahead of time, is unrealistic.

The price system is sustained by "growth," and reducing it threatens the system. Moratoriums would suppress their growth plans. However, if that system collapses on its own, we should have an opportunity to, like it or not, try some restraint.

Moratoriums generally mean that some of us will end up giving up a whole lot more than others, at least during the learning phase. Absent a price system collapse, worldwide support might only be possible when scientists can conclusively prove their suspicions. Even with this proof, should it come, the people in control of the price system will still seek to advantage themselves over others. They are not above spreading lies and diversions to muddy the waters. This will reduce the effectiveness of efforts to reverse any global problems.

The central bankers and their cohorts have a damaging economic model called the price system. As a first step to improving our planet, their system has to end. Economic models that build their existence on the excessive use of resources, especially those that we are not able to replenish, should be avoided.[3]

We know that their economic system promotes population growth. This is required in order to increase customers and create product shortages. Those shortages allow for the excessive pricing of their goods.

Our mistake is that we tend to believe that their system is the only economic plan available. This is what they have always taught us. Do we have the will to find a different way for ourselves? How can you start that change?

You can start by owning up to your part in the problems that we all face. Consider that deep down belief mentioned at the start of this chapter. That is, that each of us helps to create nearly all the problems the world faces.

The price system's lifetime training should make you feel guilty about going against them. Since we have all gone along with their programs, we are partly to blame. However, our acceptance of this blame should give us some hope. We should have hope, because if we helped to cause these problems, we can also help to fix them. We start by acknowledging that our strong embrace to the price system is *wrong minded* thinking.

We have one major obstacle in front of us, and that is the central bankers of the world and their cohorts, a.k.a. the globalists. They have spent years educating us that growth is good and necessary to maintain our economies. More honestly, this education should be called indoctrination, not education. We need to take our eyes out of their book long enough to see what is happening around the world. With our eyes now opened, we can see that their economic system is destroying our planet.

Their system sometimes relies heavily on cheap labor, so they very often encourage population growth. They did and still do this all over the world. They do it especially in areas that didn't have their desired population growth.

Here, in the United States, we almost had zero population growth at one time. This trend was discouraged and disrupted by the globalists. Their news services promoted fear to counter the benefits of zero population. They said we would not have enough people to fill the excessive number of jobs that they were going to create for us in the future. That fear put an end to zero population growth. We never got those new jobs, instead we got *downsizing* and *off shoring* schemes.

Recently, with our economic wealth in decline, you would think that the price system wouldn't need to be as aggressive in pushing for population growth. However, they are always looking to reduce their expenses. When our population slows too much, they have several methods of supporting their extra growth requirements.

There are various kinds of visas (work, school, etc.) that their businesses request through our government to lower labor costs. In addition, they use immigration strategies coupled with a weak border policy to provide the extra bodies they desire. These businesses also use those people in a secondary way; they become customers.

Unfortunately, the general public doesn't profit from having these additional people. In fact, the general public suffers from lower-wage competition. Those larger populations also add expense to social programs. This generally means cuts in services. Our school systems become overextended as well. Another problem is that our hospitals and medical insurance have to find a way to balance their costs. That generally means they have to increase their fees, which results in those excessively high medical costs we are seeing.

The central bankers and their cohorts are part of the movement that we today call globalism. Globalists thus are the controllers of world activities and indirectly your controller as well. They pushed for loose border policies, high immigration, and substantial amounts of work and school visa programs.

Globalists also pushed bills to lower the budgets of the departments that have to monitor and control these programs. The globalist system had already, long ago, helped to grow the populations of many South American nations. That action there helped to deplete the wealth of their citizens.

The globalists have been and still continue to deplete the wealth of the United States of America. President Trump seems to be a thorn in the process, that is, a thorn they are likely to pull, unless he makes a deal. He is a deal maker so I would expect him to make one.

During the Nixon administration, relations with China opened up. The price system needed to pit China's huge population against that of the rest of the world's nations. This suppressed labor cost for the price system industries located all throughout the world.

The globalists then went on to commit the people of Western nations to compete with third-world nations. This was accomplished through lopsided trade agreements. The only way we can compete, under the globalist's system of economics, is to become third-world nations ourselves.

If you haven't noticed our declining economics, then you most likely are very young. If so, I suggest you talk to some of the older folks. Ask them what the country was like even forty or fifty years ago.

They will tell you that there were far more farms, vacant lots, fields, and forests to enjoy. The highways were smaller, and there were fewer of them. The public facilities, such as the parks, lakes, and rivers, also were less crowded. The employment opportunities in a variety of industrial base businesses were more numerous. The opportunities for higher-paying full-time employment were much greater back then.

Today, we are becoming more congested and more economically tested. So the living standards have dropped for a growing number of us, except for the upper class. More and more jobs have turned into part-time opportunities only. The population growth has expanded our highways into massive concrete systems that we can no longer afford to maintain, because our lower wages hamper our abilities to contribute.

While easy oil, some seventy plus years ago, seemed plentiful, the globalist knew that this condition would not last forever. They began a plan to involve our nation in the affairs of foreign countries where oil resources were rich. In fact, they involved many Western nations in their schemes.

These schemes economically tied Western nations to third-world nations in very negative ways. The price system operatives extracted the resources of third-world nations under protection of Western world powers. These actions cost the common citizens of the world dearly. This is because those actions led to several military interventions where lives were lost.

Today, we spend vast amounts of money and natural resources to protect those areas of the world, because we are told they are in "our national interest." Both us and our leaders are told this by the globalist. The greater truth here is that those resources are in the price system's best interest. That is the system where the bulk of any benefit goes to, at most, 10% of the world's population.

Let us think about that for a minute—if easy oil is polluting our oceans and our air, why do we want to spend money to protect it? Why do we really want to send our sons and daughters off to get shot at or killed to protect something that is causing damage to our food chain? The answer is that this oil makes those leaders in the price system millionaires and billionaires.

I do not mean to suggest that oil is not important to the world, because it is. I am suggesting that there is a better way of protecting that resource. We can do this and also protect the world at the same time. That way is to severely limit the power of the price system.

There was a time that the monetary wealth of many a Western nation was partly held by what is known as the middle class. This class of citizen has been seriously diminished in the West. Some of the wealth transferred to the extremely poor third-world nations, but the bulk has been transferred into the hands of the global upper class.

Roughly from 1940 to 1980, the pollution problems here in the United States grew excessively. To some extent, this encouraged policies designed to export our industries overseas. These policies were crafted by the globalist. Once again, these policies attacked the middle class. This is the short version of a long story. The point here is that the direction that our economics has been driven toward is that of a third-world state. The money drained off goes into the pockets of the globalist who control the flow.

It is true that our existing economy is locked into jobs that the globalists command. However, there is a way to loosen their grip on us and improve the world's environment at the same time. This suggestion involves *wars*. I am not saying that we go to war, but that we stop sending our armies to defend the assets of the globalist.[4] There is no denying that their assets have sent our children off to wars all over the planet. These are the same wars that have and are continuing to drain the wealth of the middle class and now the lower-class

American citizens. Besides this, globalist assets have and are continuing to pollute our world.

Could it be as simple as just stopping our brave troops from marching off to indirectly help those businesses? In a very real way, many of those military actions were not necessary, yet there was no way for the common citizen to have known that. The price system hides that well, when it needs to. We were fooled into fighting at times for some private companies that didn't deserve our help. There is a better way to use the military force of the United States of America.

The Army Corps of Energy

There are certain things we, as a society, have agreed to do in a socialized way. We have elected, as a group, to pay taxes to support our military. Thus, the military is a socialistic enterprise that we have approved of.

This is the kind of socialism that we should approve of, as it makes sense. We all have a common need for our defense, after all. When we have a common need such as this, socialism is acceptable. Suppose that we take part of this socialistic enterprise and channel it into a new kind of army.

We should remember that much of the money we spend on these foreign wars is money that is fired off, exploded, or destroyed, that, is, burned up, demolished, or stolen; and this happens over and over again. It is nonproductive money—money that we have spent in various parts of the world for decades. Worse yet, the bulk of the benefits have gone to the globalists complex.

Suppose we bring a major part of those troops home and enlist them in a new army called the Army Corps of Energy. This group of workers would be an army of energy workers. That portion of money that would have gone to those military wars would now go toward building our economy.

These workers will help to add to our new gross domestic product (GDP). This army along with other economic changes will improve our lives. Better yet, they can provide us an opportunity to positively impact the world.

We would be able to turn parts of our military's budget into doing some fighting to secure our energy independence, in a more productive way. This energy independence, in a sense, equates to the same function as securing foreign oil fields. Remember that old alibi? It's in our national interest. We now could truthfully say that we are doing it for our national interest. This time, instead of spending our money over in some foreign country, we can spend it here at home, which would improve our economy.

This army would build new power transmission lines, new solar arrays, wind turbines, and other renewable sources of energy. They would also work with our new Department of Innovation in doing research into these energy fields. They might even build canals between states to lower the energy cost for the transportation of goods.

Canals that could also be used in flood control. Now, instead of blowing up our money in some foreign country, we would be building new energy systems. These systems would then have several direct return benefits for our country.

Some people argue that those renewable energy systems are of no value, because they are not cost-effective. I ask you, how cost-effective is blowing up or burning up the money on war? What truly has been the common citizen's return on any of the recent military actions?

Here, in the United States of America over the past sixty plus years, what has been the cost of war? War has helped to reduce our middle class, lowered our overall economic wealth, caused pollutions and shortages, and exacerbated our government's financial meltdown. The biggest winners from war are the globalist.

Our renewable energies, here at home, might actually end up being cheaper. That is, cheaper than the cost of going halfway around the world to defend, secure, and then transport oil back home. Remember that just the cost of support troops is astronomical. The cost of blood is beyond measure.

Having an army here at home for protection is another benefit. I have a feeling that a new energy army would produce much greater rewards than most people imagine. Here is a partial list:

Jobs (In all fifty states.)

Cleaner air (In all fifty states and the world.)

Cleaner oceans (There will be less need to import oil so frequency of spills would be reduced.)

Oil (The length of time in which oil would be depleted will be extended.)

Lives saved (Workers would be less likely to be killed or maimed both physically and emotionally as compared to war.)

Medical cost reduced (War causes a whole host of short- and long-term physical and mental problems.)

Economy (Money spent here adds to our economy instead of someone else's.)

Economic lifestyles (Our lifestyles require energy to make them work and this plan focuses on these needs.)

Resources saved (Besides oil being saved, food, fuel, water, and other resources will be saved because they will not have to be sent halfway around the world, where they often ended up lost or stolen.)

One final thought, on this subject, a plan like this aligns perfectly with current efforts to clean up and slow the possible demise of our planet. The split decision of environmental scientists should not be the major focus that stalls our efforts. That diversion will be drawn out as long as possible; that is the price system way.

We need to quickly address our concerns for the cost of the cleanup that results from globalist business ventures. Those costs have always been passed on to the public. I should not have to tell you about the many toxic business properties that were left to taxpayers to fund the cleanup on. We know their record of environmental abuse.

What if the Environmental Scientist Are Right and the Planet Is Balancing Dangerously Close to That Tipping Point?[5]

What if scientists are correct about the tipping point and our role in it? How would we react to this news? The fastest way to help balance a horrific disaster like this is for us humans to consider "controlling ourselves." New, more restrictive policies for industries and for families would need to be developed. Will the price system force us to take these measures?

Restrictive policies are abhorrent to our price system controllers, so they would fight them. We shouldn't count on them for anything. We may be forced to be the adults in this situation.

An Environmental Breakdown Might Bring about a Financial Collapse of the Price System

We have talked somewhat about industries already and how they could be changed to help us recover from the collapse of the price system. However, there would likely be a need for families to take some action to help us recover from the economic collapse. Perhaps, a temporary moratorium on family size might be our first thought.

In an effort to secure a future for all our children, we might want to commit to limiting the size of our families to only three or four children. This might be for a period of, say, three years; I really don't know; our scientist will have to determine what would be necessary.

If a moratorium were established, it would provide additional time for our scientists to work on our issues and determine how best to reduce our economic problems. All potential parents should commit to this temporary measure. If we did this, then we would curb our population growth. The price system may not want this yet, but at some point they will; woe to us if they decide how to reduce our population.

These lower family sizes during the moratorium would benefit not only the nation but also the families. Families who can afford their children are not good for the price system. These families would be less desperate, so price system profit margins would go down. Family lifestyles however should improve.

We have to remember that each of us, rich or poor, leave our footprints on planet earth. Currently, the citizens of poorer countries are polluting more heavily. They do this in order to supply the goods and services to the richer nations.

These poorer countries have to remember that it is their laws that allow those goods and services to be made there. They then allow the conditions that add pollutants to the world's air. The price system is to blame for them being forced to do these things.

What good is acknowledging that the price systems is at fault? With this admission, we can agree that each of us, rich and poor, are also at fault. We all are at fault when it comes to pollution.

However, the main blame goes on the globalists and their price system. That is because they have made us live under their rules. People all over the world have to crawl out from under the old ideas of the globalists. We need to stop feeding their growth systems, which feed excessively off earth's resources.

Anyone critical of the price system should expect to find excessive opposition. Their well-entrenched support system will align against anyone who tries. They will not want us, the common people of the earth, to remove themselves from price system controls.

They will unleash their dogs of war on those that point out their errors. I know this sounds dramatic, but you should be warned that it will happen as long as they reign. Their opponents will be attacked by everyone that they control—by our own leaders, the press, the banks, and last but not least the churches, although not all members of each will attack, but more than you would think.

When their system fails however, we will have an opportunity to establish a new economic system. Unfortunately, our nation's economics will be in very bad shape. Otherwise, we would not be given the chance.

Consequently, at this time, should this opportunity happen, drastic measures would be required. Perhaps, ideas would need to be explored that heretofore where considered taboo. We already have roughly twenty trillion dollars of debt; and the debt ceiling is constantly being expanded.

That debt is likely to grow as debt is the staple of globalism. There is a breaking point, and if globalists had compassion, they would have already applied the brakes on their policies. Their plan seems bent on draining as much wealth out of the world as they possibly can. They have little regard for the aftermath of their actions. My guess is that they do not plan on paying for the destruction they caused. Sure they will give back what we would perceive as a huge amount of money. However, it is likely they have corruptly taken ten or more times that amount.

Our new economic system should not be based on the excessive use of our natural resources. Whatever would be left of them at this point needs to be secured. Somehow we will need to rebuild them.

To restore resources rapidly, a part of our plan needs to focus on slowing earth's population. Remember our temporary moratorium? This might be one drastic measure forced on us.

If further reduction is necessary, we would want to do this over time without the use of wars. This should be done by the will of the people of earth themselves. If common sense prevails, wars could be a thing of the past.

Foreign countries, who also want to accept this new economic system, should be welcomed to join. They should understand the need for adopting new policies, even those temporary drastic measures. Their thorough understanding of the new system will support their success in it.

We of course would want to establish trade policies with those countries who also share the new economic system's plans. Just as in the past, countries that join might be supported in other ways. The goal is to expand the system worldwide as a more compassionate replacement for the old price system.

Countries that do not join us should understand that they will be left alone. We however will have extremely limited trading connections with that old price system. Open trade would simply allow that old system a pathway back into our society.

From our point of view, those countries will suffer the consequences of their own actions. Those consequences will be at the hand of the price system. They likely would continue to produce excessively large families that they cannot support. We will however have to protect our borders as those countries will desire to feed off us or use us.

There will be a strong need for tough love on our part. Why? This is because we will have to allow them to produce those excessive populations—populations that they will have no way of supporting, except by violence. This tough love will require us to stay out of their lives and let them learn for themselves what their behaviors lead too. Lessons from the past suggest extreme poverty leading to aggressive behaviors.

Hopefully, their coming to reason will not take long, if they see the success of those in the new economic plan. Our hope is that they will agree to adopt the same drastic measures we had to. They live in the same world and should share the consequences of previous actions just as we have to.

Some churches will want to intervene and help them, but those churches will not be doing the earth any favors. Those churches would be putting the planet at greater risk. If the gloomy predictions are correct, they will be responsible for helping to speed up or aggravate the tipping point. If so, rather than saving lives, they will be making matters worse.

If some churches do intervene, they could very well be responsible for pain and suffering beyond our wildest imaginations. This would be more human suffering than has ever been seen on earth, over our entire human existence. Try to recall all of the images of those thin framed starving people that we have seen on television. Put all of those images together and they would not compare to what could happen if we do not begin to think responsibly. Will our immature emotions cause these gloomy predictions to come true?

I am hoping however that we might somehow have a chance at affecting a reversal of those potential environmental problems. I would rather take some prudent actions in advance to give us time to explore the reality of things. Let's hope our condition never gets to this dreadful state where really drastic actions need to be taken. Those would be actions even more awful than what I have already suggested.

Humanitarian efforts should be concentrated within those countries in our region. That is, those countries who accept the new economic systems and its policies. This will help to encourage non-participating countries to join with us. These actions will support troubled nations without encouraging them to over populate their resources.

Easter Island had a system that relied on one primary resource—wood. This resource, as a result of their population growth, was eventually used up completely. This island became unable to support their huge population.

Without the island's main resource, many islanders met a terrible and untimely end. This end might have been averted with some tough love. It seems no one was up to putting limits on anything, so that hastened the end.

Today, there exists what I call unnoble noble causes. Those "do-good" religious organization, who claim to help people, may not be all they are cracked up to be. They should look into the history of Easter Island or other such failed states.

Those religious leaders should try not to repeat the mistakes of history. Perhaps with that review of history, they would then realize that they are fighting to support a corrupt system. In so doing, they are actually increasing the pain and suffering of those trapped by it.

They also are indirectly supporting poor cultural values. Their economic support furthers the price system's methods of control, deepening it. Their actions thus end up aiding the enemy. This then causes them to sin by their own religious standards.

Today, we have a growing number of failed states. These failed states are marked by their absence of the rule of law, by their over-populated conditions, and by their lack of natural resources. If you can now identify the economic system that leads to these problems, there is still hope that these conditions can be turned around.

It should trouble us now as to just what those controls over the size of our population might be in the future. Are we making it worse with our unlimited policies? Each of us wants as much freedom as possible. However, if we wait too long to address that issue, we might be forcing our children to impose even more austere population controls on themselves.

This issue of population, for now, is not being addressed; thus, we can only hope for the best. Let us hope that perhaps those gloomy predictions are not as glum as some scientist think. Further, let's hope that we will come to our senses.

We need to crawl out from under our current system of economics. Let us work toward a system that doesn't rely on depleting our resources. For now, that is the kind of system that we have. It exists so that a small percentage of people can be excessively wealthy.

The actions of energy, environment, and population link together these days in very perverse ways. They do not, however, have to continue to work in those negative ways. We as humans can be responsible.

We can take the necessary actions required to plan a better system. We can use our reasoning skills to develop a new system. Such a system would put the world back on course. This would be a course away from the destruction of the planet. Our path should take us toward a balance that serves the majority of citizens and not just a few of them.

I would like to remind the reader here that these are just ideas. They are submitted to you, so as to give you a reason to think about these things. You need to be involved in this process, should things in our future turn to the worse.

CHAPTER 9

Our Alternative Modified Plan

A Modified Version: Additional Ideas

In our new economy, we need to find ways in which to pay for all the changes that have to be made. We can do this, in part, by paying people a little differently. The social system of technocracy has already laid the ground work for this idea. I don't know about you, but I am not above borrowing good ideas wherever I find them. In the system of technocracy, they use what is called energy certificates instead of money.[1] With just a little modification, their idea could be used in our system as well.

In short, your labor earns you these certificates. They are exclusively yours to be used to purchase items from a list of basic needs. All citizens would have input as to what is on that list.

Originally 'Technocracy' called for collectives, each made up of several nations. The collective, which included the United States, was called the North American technocracy.[2] The idea behind this collective was simply this—the nations therein were found to contain all the resources necessary to provide the things that people needed within that region. Under their system, the people would own the resources.

Today, the private corporations in many cases own those resources, and they use their price system to sell those things back to us. They also own the machines used to turn those resources into goods. Under their system, the majority of these two main benefits belong to those in the top 10% group. These are the two major reasons why globalists are so advantaged over everyone else.

The scientist of the North American technocracy, long ago, made the case for how machines should have changed our world. At the advent of the industrial revolution, the claims were made that eventually the machines would remove the burdens of life from us. Machines thus would make all of our lives easier and more rewarding. Scientists believe that machines are capable of making more than enough products for the population and at a considerably more affordable price.

Those machines however were at odds with the already existing price system. If the citizens owned the machines, that would jeopardize the price system's control. Consequently, the idealistic view of a utopian world was blocked by those in charge.

Technocracy pointed out that today, those corporations, who own the machines, can allow them to be idled. This is because the price system uses its supply and demand principle to drive up their profits. Things like this along with other price system dictums prevent the more favorable public ownership options from being realized. You see their wealth gives them the power to control us.

It is true that machines do offer some relief to workers. So in a sense the workers do have some benefit even under the price system. Unfortunately, the benefit level of the machine owners far outpaces the rewards that the laborers receive. This works to make life a utopia mostly for the private corporate owners.

The North American technocracy scientist suggested that "we the people" should own and operate these machines. We then could run these machines around the clock to make the products we need for each other. Further, if we improved the quality of the products, we could make them last longer and increase our savings even more. Just these two things would afford several advantages to the common citizen and to our planet.

Using the full power of the machines to provide our basic needs makes better economic sense. Tapping the full potential of our huge labor force to run the machines would generate another great benefit, one that we have long strived for—full employment. Logically, these things together should work to make our system operate with greater efficiency.

Now, that old idea of using energy certificates should not be taken lightly. It has tremendous value. That idea alone actually will tend to reduce the importance of money, as we know it today. That reduction in the power of money should be a major goal of ours.

These certificates would provide our basic food, clothing, shelter, and security. Security here includes the following: our military, police, and fire departments. It also includes insurance for health, life, and property, as well. This means that we would all work for energy certificates and not just money. In return, we would get the basic items that we need from the areas described above.

Now, those energy or public credits would be given out by name to each worker so that only they could spend them. You might be asking what the difference is between money and certificates. In a nutshell, the difference is that these certificates have specific limits.

The certificates would expire, perhaps in six months or a year. They also, can only be used by the person who earned them. One other difference is that they can only be used for basic living needs.

The certificates greatly help to reduce the importance of money. This is because with certificates, everyone would have a roof over their head, food to eat, clothes to wear, and all the basic insurance they need, granted they would only be given their basic needs and not everything a person might want. However, since money will not be required for these basic items, the importance of money will be diminished.

With the efficiencies we talked about already, we should be able to reduce the work hours required to pay for these basic needs. This then would allow more free time for everyone to pursue other means in which to better their lives, using the money they earn to pay for a bigger house, more clothes, food, insurance, or whatever. In this system, people might even be able to retire earlier in life.

I really haven't presented the technocracy plan in the same way as they explain it on their Web site. I have added ideas to modify their plan. For a more detailed explanation of their original plan, I suggest you go to their Web site and investigate their ideas for yourself. It is worth the visit. Their site is http://www.technocracyinc.org/about-us/.

In short, the machines that we are capable of building today can really be made to work for each and every one of us instead of a select few. In a sense, these robots would be doing a substantial amount of work for us. On top of this, they can be made to run more efficiently and effectively once they are not tied to the old price system.

These machines will afford each of us more time for ourselves so that we can start to enjoy our lives more fully. We might pursue other goals to improve our lives—goals such as higher education or to create or invent. Some might just decide to live with the basics and lead a very simple life.

I do not wish to mislead you because while this system sounds good, it will never be perfect. Nothing we do will ever achieve that status. Generally speaking, our flaws tend to spill over into our activities. However, I believe a system like this would be a far better idea than the current system.

I do not believe we could implement technocracy's exact system, as they originally describe it themselves. Just as we have problems with aspects of socialism and capitalism, parts of technocracy do not sit well. In my opinion, it is unlikely people will except its original design. One big problem, in my view, would be centered on getting the other necessary countries, in our region, to buy into this system.

Remember that a few other countries are necessary to complete their resource pool. I also feel that their system fails to properly address the human need for the spiritual aspects of our lives. Of course, being that the plan was developed by scientist, one would expect that. Faith is hard to quantify.

This is why I believe a modified plan needs to be developed. Even with the changes, our new system will still have flaws. Further, we also might not be able to get all the seemingly required countries to join. In the end, I envision a hybrid plan, a mix of two or more plans, which could be trialed.

The industries that deal with the resources that are necessary for life would be owned by all the people. These would be the industries that produce our food, clothing, shelter, and security. The entire population would provide the labor pool for this. This means we will have nearly full employment as all able-bodied citizen will have work.

We citizens provide the labor for our public sector jobs already. Those jobs are however patterned after the private sector. Our labor here in the new system has some redeeming qualities over the private enterprise system.

First, it offers full employment, instead of private profit-driven downsizing schemes. Downsizing, as you know, resulted in working those remaining employees harder to make up for the shortage of employees. This generated more profits for those in that 10% group. That is the nature of their system.

Another advantage is that our new labor pool will be paid across the nation at a predetermined rate scale. This is a scale that matches the basic needs that a person would receive at the various efficiency levels. None of these levels will be excessive, compared to today's price systems standards.

Our new scale would be limited perhaps to as many as twenty levels of pay. These pay levels would depend on the job responsibilities along with other to be determined standards. This means that executive pay will be held in check; no more salaries hundreds of times more than the average employee.

If we accept a twenty-level system, a person at the top would still be allowed to make substantially more than the starting-level position. By some standards, this could be viewed as excessive. I believe we need to see how it works first before making our final decision.

We should note here that there will also be a private system in which people can, on their own time, make money. This system would likely mirror this potential twenty-level rule, making it technically possible for a person to make double their income levels, depending on how the money system is structured. If material things are important, the levels that are possible here should provide for very wealthy, but healthy, lifestyle.

Second, because of the number of workers we will have available to us, we can work to reduce the hours required per day. "Many hands make light work," as the expression goes. Fresh workforces should help to increase our quality and improve our production. This workforce will be making the products they themselves use. This ownership should help to make those products stronger and better. Stronger and better products should help to save our resources and our environment.

The technocracy plan only required roughly four hours a day and then only four days a week, and it included an early retirement process. The efficiencies of the machines, our hard work, and some sharp thinking on our part might still make this possible in a hybrid system. We might have to start out with an extended work week until we work out the details. Remember that we will also have to deal with the devastation resulting from the previous price system.

We will need to balance this public systems labor against the quantity of basic needs and services paid out. Remember that our design starts by planning for a minimum basic needs objective. This would be matched up against available resources. Our hard work will in part determine our success here. Lazy, corrupt workers can negatively affect the system. We can design conditions to lessen these affects.

We as a people should find that labor unions should not be as important to us. However, we should know that where people exist, conflicts have a potential to happen. Some sort of mediating authority will always be necessary.

Our new system is fairer in its very nature, so those labor issues should be easier to resolve. It is fairer in that the workers would own the public buildings and the public machines. If someone has a dislike for their job in one industry, they might apply for a job in another public sector. Shorter hours and work weeks should also reduce the conflicts.

In the hybrid system, labor would become more important to the small businesses in the private sector. These are business that will spring up to supply those items above and beyond the basic needs of each person. The role of the laborer is more important now, because small businesses would have to encourage people to devote their spare hours to them.

Private businesses, as a result, should tend to treat employees more respectfully. Labor in the private market will also be better able to switch jobs should they need to. Job mobility is enhanced, because they will have their public sector work to fall back on. This makes it easy for them to look for new private employment. Their lifestyle might drop for a time, but they would not become homeless or without food.

While money would lose some of its importance, it will still be used in the private business markets and for foreign trade. In order to control this money, the people will also have to own the bank. Our bank will not be allowed to directly align with the worldwide banking system. It has to remain completely independent. We do not want to get sucked back up into the price system again.

The fact that our hybrid system will most likely contain a scaled-down less powerful price system suggests that we might still have some problems. It is likely that any new system would be vulnerable to the price systems operating in other countries.[3] We are also vulnerable because we will have to continue to use a modified version of the price system in our own economy as well.

We will have to make some other changes in our hybrid system. They are required to address that potential price system danger embedded in our private market system. I will be getting to those changes a little later, and those changes should help to make our hybrid system work better. Just keep in mind that we will need to place restrictions on our private market system. If we are not careful, we will likely return, over time, to be ruled by the select few.

If we start this process of building a new governmental economic system, other people will have ideas that could improve the system even more. We should be open enough to consider those ideas as they are presented. For example, you might suggest that the energy or public certificates should provide at least 225 square feet of basic housing for the entry-level individual. Things like this will have to be determined.

If 225 square feet holds for the entry level, that is, level 1, what might the other levels look like? Levels 2–40 housing allocations might or might not incrementally increase. Level 10 might provide an individual living space of 1225 square feet, while level 40 might top out at 4900 square feet. These higher levels might be too ambitious, so studies would have to determine what is possible.

Each of our other basic needs would have to be addressed separately as well. There will be incremental changes in those needs, which would occur as an individual progressed up the levels of pay. I do not foresee drastic changes in any of the basic needs.

Basic levels would pretty much remain constant with only slight improvements throughout the levels. The housing allocations will be the largest differences between levels. Why the austerity you might ask? We need to see how things go. We can't foresee how this is going to work exactly. We don't know how much damage the old price system will do to us, in its failure, until that failure happens.

Basic levels mean that in those levels you only get basic things. Cable television is not a necessity for life. Basic cell phones would be supplied for security reason, but a smartphone might be considered a luxury. Those luxury items can be left to the private secondary price system market. We must first determine if we can afford those basic items for life, before we try to add benefits.

When we can do more, we should work to add benefits to everyone as technology advances. The goal would be to balance our system as much as possible. Once we determine how people adapt to this system, we will know if we can give people more under the public sector.

We do not want to unnecessarily stifle a person's personal growth. We should understand that healthy people generally want to improve themselves. This human attribute is paramount to money, in our design, as it is a healthy ingredient.

Unfortunately, as stated, in our hybrid system, we would have to accommodate a system of money; so far, I do not see a way around it. Trade with other nations most likely will require it. Unfortunately, any system of money will put our whole system at risk if we don't put in safeguards. If the primary public system of living is based on energy certificates, then the money system's influence will be weakened, but that alone will not be enough.

The public sector improvements should help a great deal. However, this will not be enough to prevent abuses from that secondary system, that is, if we don't place additional controls over that system of money.

We will need to limit the size of private companies. This is required so that they do not overinfluence and corrupt our populations back into the price systems pitfalls. We should not allow private ownership of corporations as this would open the door for abuses. I have already addressed in previous chapters some additional ideas for control measures here.

I understand that not everyone is the same and that some people have needs and desires for things that others have no plans for. Our public system should be designed so that people are only employed roughly four hours a day, four to five days a week. They will then have time, if they desired, for other work activities.

Those could be activities in the money-based system if they desired. People want opportunity to enrich their lives. Sometimes, that means enriched with additional material products.

Individuals also seek power, and excessive power corrupts; we know that, or at least, we should by now. In order to prevent excessive power, we have to put limits on material things, or people will use those material things to secure excessive power. This is just common sense, and yes, it is socialistic as well, so we have to be cautious with this. This means we would impose limits on private income levels.

We could choose to use a twenty-level private sector system in parallel to the public plan. To avoid a return to the original price system, we could cap the two main wealth definers such as housing and income. This might mean that at the private level a cap of $1,000,000 a year and an additional 2450 square feet of individual living area. The rewards would only hold to the individual and expire at their death. This is necessary so that individuals will not be in a position to unduly influence our political processes as they do now.

These ideas are by no means a complete private sector plan design, but only just a bare-bones plan. The details could be worked out once we are clear about our system. We can manipulate it to fit the constraints we have and expand it when we resolve our issues.

Our scientists will determine projects we need to work on. They will look at both domestic and worldwide issues and make recommendations to our system councils. Ultimately, those ideas will be addressed by responsible leaders. Our leaders should serve short limited terms and then step down. They might spend a short term to assist their replacement, if need be, before returning to their normal life.

So as you read about some of the changes needed to make our lives and our economy work better, think about the benefits that a modified plan could mean. For example, in the field of education, a revamped education system might appear to weaken the teacher's economic status, but remember that they will be compensated for this by the energy certificate system.

Good teachers are very important and should hold a high value in any system of economy. In fact, we can start to think about how we would rank the different professionals in our society. We are accustomed to having pay levels define these things anyway. These levels should be based, in part, on a person's documented training experiences and the quality of their work experience.

Regarding their work record, their employer might rate their service by awarding their employee with a quarterly experience credit. This would be given out for each quarter that they successfully serve in public service. This would be like a time-in grade experience factor. It could be used to develop a supporting path to the next pay level. It would also carry with it an incremental mount of energy credits to be added to their account. Poor service could result in loss of these credits as well.

The housing department will work with the private sector to accommodate their demands, within the legal limits. Housing units could be provided based on whether the housing is for single or multiple individuals. In order to enhance life events, people will also be able to combine their housing credits.

People might choose to pool their credits together. Under certain conditions, families might want to do this. For example, elderly parents could combine their credits with their children to secure properties up to, perhaps, five bedrooms in size.

Housing would be provided for a variety of purposes. Our public sector housing options might include simple shelters, apartments, and one- to five-bedroom houses. Mobile homes might even be a choice, just as group homes are also a possibility.

Housing units would be supplied for those individuals who are societal dropouts. These are people who are deemed to be mentally and physically healthy, but choose not to participate. So as to not let them take excessive advantage of us, their allocation would be just the very basic minimal units.

System economics will impose restrictions for house sizing. Housing credits will be portable; however, excessive damage to their existing housing will be deducted from their account and will not transfer. Private sector credits could be used to make up for this.

Generally, new housing will be factory-built homes–homes built by workers in the public service. There will be a selection of designs and styles to choose from. Some of the existing excessively large mansions might be converted into medical housing units for group patients or for elderly care or nursing facilities.

We should define ourselves by roles and functions, putting these into ranks as best we can.[4] This is required so that we can determine pay scales. This system would influence the housing options available for the various levels. There will be a diversity of income levels, but these levels will not be in the extremes that we see today.

Under the price system, some CEOs were getting hundreds or thousands of times more pay than their lowest-paid employee. Another example would be entertainers making immensely high salaries, where other workers in the same category make far less. Sports professionals are still another example of excessive scales.

We need to get away from these price system influences and begin to think rationally again. The ranking system we develop should be as simple as possible so that everyone knows how to improve their lot in life. It should also explain why different people make more money than others so that everyone understands without begrudging those that do make more. Again, this will not solve all the problems, but it is a start in the right direction.

Cable news reported on July 10, 2011, that the June 2011 jobs report showed that the economy had added only 18,000 new jobs. They also reported that millions of jobs had been lost since 2008.[5] Further, they said that the economy needed at least 300,000 jobs per month just to put a dent in the current job slump. Reports such as this have been going on for a long time now. Economies based on growth are prone to receive this kind of reporting.

Now, what did this jobs report tell us about our population? It suggests, or perhaps tells us, that there are at least a couple hundred thousand new people entering our job market a month. These would be students exiting college, trade schools, high schools, visa workers, or just younger people looking for work. Not included in this are those illegal immigrants also seeking employment.

Shouldn't we consider that our population is growing at a clip far greater than their price system has capacity for? Without telling us directly, it suggests that our population increase is at least part of the problem. It is the part that the controllers do not want us to think about. If we really did think about it, then the cheap labor would go and part of their customer base as well.

We can look at this problem many ways. The view, which is generated by our controllers, tells us that it is a problem with government regulations, because they are stifling the businesses. More private businesses are necessary to provide new jobs, they say. However, if the population continues to grow, that will mean we need even more businesses and so on and so on, continually. That loop only goes to continually serve the 10%.

If businesses use resources that we cannot readily replenish, are they not using them up? Of course, they are. Along with this issue of depleted resources, we, as we deplete them, create most of the other problems we face. You need to ask yourself, how long will their growth answer work? Better yet, do you really think that it works now? We know it works for them.

Globalists who try to get government out of their hair remind me of children wanting to get adults out of theirs. They are like juveniles wanting to get their parents out of the house, so they can make mischief. They want government to cut taxes on their businesses and reduce the regulations.

The carrot being held out to us is that this will spur job creation. If you understand the problems that limited resources impose on us, then you know that their promise is in the end empty. Growth, the way they want it, is destructive. It is Easter Island on a grand scale. That growth actually causes nearly all the problems we have in our world. Of course, we all want jobs, but isn't there a smarter solution?

Another unappealing solution that they, our controllers, come up with is to cut payments to social security, Medicare, and other such programs and use that money to pay the debt. The debt is that money we borrow from them. The debt is also that money that they, the controllers, petitioned our government to spend. They asked for those foreign interventions to enhance their worldwide enterprises.

The debt is based on growth. In their minds, if there is no borrowing, there is no growth. You can see that they need growth to survive. They really care little about helping people in need. They plan to milk this system as long as they can. It will fail, and it will take us years to rebuild. They're hoping, by then, that we will have forgotten what all their destructive behaviors caused. If we do, they will return to reinstitute their system all over again.

There are alternative views on how to help our economy back into a balanced system. Perhaps first, we should face the idea that growing our economy, in the same fashion that they have in place today, is a tragic and unrealistic solution to the jobs problem. Our resources have and will continue to run out if we continue down the path they have chosen for us.

Tragically, this is not the only problem that their system has given us. The debt, they have us in, keeps us from fixing the things that need fixing. Being in debt prevents us from spending our money on things that would serve us, instead of serving them.

There are ways to get out from under their oppression. Oppression is not too strong of a word to use; however, you may not, quite yet, agree. If you study their system more closely, I believe you will eventually agree.

One thing we could accomplish, if we tried, is to slow our population growth. Slowing our population growth would allow jobs to eventually catch up. Instead of allowing large amounts of immigration, encouraging large families, and illegal immigration, maybe we should put the brakes on for a bit.

Would a moratorium on immigration be wise? I think so, at least until we figure things out. Why continue to dig ourselves deeper into their growth solution when we know in the end we cannot grow forever?

Besides, they use huge populations for cheap labor; do we really want to be part of that? Do we want to help them out in their plans to take advantage of people? Their price system encourages people to multiply beyond reason.

The writing has been on their walls for years now. Corporations want to take jobs to other countries where wages are lower and the rules on their businesses are substantially absent. They, our controllers, are often welcomed in third-world nations. This is because they can generally find people needing a job so badly that they will accept any conditions.

We ourselves are now being taken into despair. They are creating the atmosphere of a third-world nation here in America. How well have most third-world nation done in dispelling these controllers? It is necessary that our controllers do this to us so that their businesses can operate more efficiently with lower wages and lower standards.

They are doing all of these things under the disguise of capitalism. However, theirs is not true capitalism, but might be better called corporate communism. It is a perverted capitalism that is extreme and not humane or planet friendly.

However, on their march to get what they want, the controllers will promise us anything, but give us the minimum. They want us to help them perpetuate their system. It is a system that basically makes the top 10% of our population royalty. They are the lords, kings, and nobles that rule over the remaining 90%; haven't we seen this before?

CHAPTER 10

Is This the End?

Here, I am referring to two possible ends. One is the end of the price system as we know it today. The other is the end of this earth age.

There isn't anyone who can truly answer these question, yet. The price system has time after time found ways to extend its life. It will likely find a way to survive a little longer.

Are we approaching the end of this earth age? I believe the answer here is tied to the price system itself. I base this on my current understanding of prophecy. However, I will have to get into that a little later. First, I would like to ask you this question: Are you starting to feel that we would be better off without the price system as it exists today?

There is a very old song that asked us, "To dream the impossible dream."[1] Well, think about a world without money. It may be a lofty idea, but it certainly is not a new idea. The dreams for that world are ancient. To many of us that is a world without evil. I hope this book has provided some clues to the connections that money has to evil.

Certainly, those in charge of the price system would abhor any idea that makes money less important. This is not something they want us to think about for any extended time. Yet their system compels them to make money by any means. In fact, they will generally find a way, even for that very negative discussion of money to make money for them. Everything has a price, and they truly believe they are right.

Turning our alternative system into a communistic plot is the best way for the price system to make a villain out of this new plan. The trouble for us here is that there is some truth to that argument. Any society that undertakes such a plan would have to be careful not to slide into the communistic trench. However, we should face up to the reality that our current capitalistic system has already fallen into that communistic trench.

Our current "corporate communism" is in fact a lot more evil than the perceived semisocialistic ideas, which I have presented so far. Remember that our plan would not call for a party leadership or ruling elites who have excessive wealth and power. Still, we need to be vigilant. We do not want excessive socialism or excessive capitalism.

What can we do to prevent our new system leaders from doing the same thing the corporations are doing to us now? How do we limit their influence and power yet allow our government the strength it needs to be reckoned with as a world power for the cause of good? The answers lie in our ability to create a balance.

This book, for sure, won't give us all the answers we need. Some of you who read it will, I am sure, have some improvements to add. The book was intended to offer suggestions, which you might be inspired to improve upon.

For example, it alludes to a large pool of scientists becoming a major ingredient of our leadership. It also revived the need to have an ever-changing hierarchy of leadership. Term limits or term lengths were another very old revisited idea that the price system generally objects to.

Keeping the leadership constantly revolving is key to keeping it honest, that is, keeping it for the people and by the people. With these limited terms comes a need to have a depth of leadership so that experience will not be depleted with those changes. This means we need a larger stockpile of shorter-term leaders with terms that overlap. These terms might last for perhaps a 4–8-year time frame. We can vote on it.

I have also suggested that there is an alternative system of commerce, other than the price system. The price system managers have a vested interest in keeping us in their system. They have stifled several attempts by people around the world who have tried to establish new forms of bartering currencies.

This book also touches on how religions have been influenced by the price system. *That system* has tried to silence the words in the Bible which attempt to dampen *their* business goals. They have gone as far as altering the religious texts. This has affected both the Jewish and Christian faiths.

Even the Muslim scriptures have had verses perverted from their original meanings. Our protagonists have laid waste to the words in these books, which have tried to turn mankind away from the love of money. We should note that the Bible is full of stories where mankind, in essence, always fails to stop their worship of money or symbols of it. The price system today is that old corrupted materialistic system still worming its way into our lives.

I say this because, here we are today, still not united as a body of people, a human family. Money, in its excess, has replaced God, thus making unification less likely. What we are then is a body where 10% of us have 90% of the money and 90% of the body has 10% of the money.[2] Some have said the ratio is 1% versus 99%.

However, even using the lesser figure, 90% of us have little to lose from trying to lessen the power of money, if that is possible. Unfortunately, for now, we don't see the world as a place where this is possible. Our minds are not conditioned to see it.

The excessively wealthy have seen to it that we do not see it. For if we do wake up and see it, their excessive lifestyles could vanish. They would have to live as we do, and they truly believe they are too good for that.

Those who look to have extreme wealth, fame, or power by taking excessive advantage of others do not represent the bulk of our population. They are a small percentage. Their greed is only matched by their cunningness.

These qualities are necessary in order to get us to believe that they need all those objects of wealth. In fact, in their minds, they do need these things more than everyone else. Therefore, taking a little from each one of us in order for them to have more makes all the sense in the world to them.

To our shame, many of us end up going along with this. The money system thus is designed to allow only a small percentage of the population to live in excess. Should we really favor a system like this?

In reality, we unfortunately nearly always fall for the money system traps. This is because we have the potential, through our human weaknesses, to be corrupted. Although when we are healthy, we do not go to the extremes that those in the top 10% do. Still each and every one of us chases that carrot, which the price system dangles.

We were and are taught that this is just the way it is. It is life, so get used to it. This conditioning makes it all too easy for those in the top 10% to push their system's *drug*. This drug is known as money. The main side effect of this drug is "a desire to have more and more," a condition known as greed. When we give in to greed, the controllers end up being able to take excessive advantage of us.

What is likely to happen if we were to enact a new economy, as suggested in this book? How long would it take for those who hunger for excesses to start bending the system toward their goals? They will push for the levels of excess, between individuals, to be widened and then widened again until we are back to their old system.

It does not take a lot of contemplation on our part to conclude that mankind is not truly humane, at least not yet. It is not civilized enough to do what is necessary to completely clean up the world's problems at this time. We are, however, civilized enough to try.

We may not be able to implement a better economic system, because of our immaturity of ethics. However, we still should be aware that we alone make that decision as to whether we try or not. We create our own fate.

Our fate is set for both our physical and spiritual natures by us. Both are created by the choices we make individually. Will you be swallowed up by corruption here on earth? If so, you will become a slave to your money.

One thing about money, if you love it, you generally don't want to share it. This causes a lot of unhappiness. Your chances for true happiness will be better if you don't love money. It is your choice as that is what we are all here for, to make choices. How else can we be judged?

This book expressed many ideas from contributors who are found among the living and the dead and among the known and unknown. While I believe most of these ideas are basically sound, I cannot claim that they are all rock-solid facts. They do, however, represent the minds of a great number of people over a vast amount of time.

These views represent both past and present efforts to figure out how our existing economic system really works. Basically, this price system has been found to be a closed system. It is a design that champions, to excess, a select few. In their excess, these "few" create conditions on earth that punish not only the vast majority of society but also the planet itself.

Unfortunately, there are those who are bought and paid for who will thoroughly disagree with me. They are fringe players in the system, well paid, but without complete knowledge of its evils. They have suppressed truths, for money, which should have been told.

Deep down, you know they are not reporting everything. You have likely learned this through experience. My guess is that a lot of that shallow reporting gives you an ill feeling inside. Somehow, you know that you are missing important parts of the stories, parts that "their" networks just are not telling you.

The views expressed in this book are certainly not mainstream views. However, in my opinion, for the most part, they are far more accurate than that of your local network news. I may not have convinced you of this yet however I bet you agree, at least a little.

I make this claim, in part, because my local news didn't even want to cover the protesters in Detroit who were trying to get an audit of the Federal Reserve in 2010.[3] If they didn't feel that this was important, well what else did they deem unimportant? They covered a minor house fire in Pontiac instead; go figure.

I confess that many people have influenced me. While I may not have copied their ideas word for word, I have used their thoughts. I could imagine someone accusing me of plagiarism; this was not my intent.

For sure, I haven't given credit to the originators of many of these ideas. However, this is more a matter of me not knowing who the first person to use these ideas really was. It is not like the mainstream press has been covering most of those opinions, so documentation is often missing.

Truthfully, I don't think the ideas expressed here are ideas that should belong to any one person. Many of the ideas have been orally carried forward for years and years now. In any event, the idea of this book is to make the world a better place. How could you do this unless you share ideas?

Of course, the current price system would want to put a dollar value on these ideas. It is no secret that we are all stuck in this system. The rulers of the existing systems want us to believe that money is everything. A system that takes away money's importance also takes away their importance. You should know that there are other ways in which to reward people.

The primary flaw of the price system is that it focuses on *money*. So much so that it plays on the human tendencies of greed. Money in the price system has no limits. The system promotes it as the more, the merrier. Money of course can bring power. This power today has been used to set up the old feudal system again. It, in a sense, brings back the kings and queens of yesteryear.

Many of our elected officials tend to see themselves as "royalty" as well; and this is how they want to be treated. Romantic as some may wish to portray this, it is a fact that the common people of yesteryear didn't like that system. Many kings and queens were very abusive, so much so that the people fought for their freedom.

Today, these kings and queens are corporate kings and queens. From my position as a common citizen, I would agree that these leaders are back to their same old tricks—stealing from the poor and giving to the rich, that would be themselves.

If we think about it, are not these people just self-appointed masters of today's large kingdoms? These would be the kingdoms of oil, of finance, of trade, and so on and so forth. We have become their subjects again. Through the price system, we have allowed certain elites to become our masters again. This is the control that *money* has over us, because it causes us to lose sight of the principle cause of our enslavement—*the price system* itself.

Good and bad, right and wrong, yang and yin, no matter how some may describe our human propensities, money has a tremendous influence over our human frailties. Money can push us rather easily in the direction of crime. A system based excessively on money is, in the end, just asking for trouble.

In excess, money provides, promotes, and rewards the opportunities for corruptions to occur. One could easily say that we reap what we sow or that we are doing it to ourselves. We are making the world corrupt by employing such a divisive system. We need to take the emphasis off money, in our new system. Lessening its power will reduce the likelihood of abuse.

Most of us have heard the saying, "Money is the root of all evil." Those of us who contemplate this generally end up agreeing. We then go on to agree that well there is nothing that can be done about it. The reason for this, after all, is that we all have to have money to live, right?

I think some of the ideas of technocracies do however offer us an option. If their idea of energy certificates could be employed, this would go a long way in curtailing a root cause of evil. Would it get rid of all evil? I think we would generally agree that it wouldn't do that.

Still diminishing the importance of money surely would make for a better world. The reason for this is that this would reduce the number of excessive abuses in our world. These are unhealthy excesses of greed that are allowed to exist today, as if they were appropriate behaviors.

Gold-lined swimming pools, gold bathtubs, gold this and gold that, and hording excessive wealth—none of this is really honorable. Shame on us for buying into that idea. However, we have been trained well to desire these same things.

Deep down, we know that these are not healthy ideas. If we learn constraint, we learn to be better neighbors and friends to each other. To a healthy mind, good friends and neighbors are much more important than gold-plated pools or bathtubs.

Money can allow corrupt individualism to flourish. This kind of individualism when applied to our economy generally causes us to end up with dictators, fascists, or monarchs. The simple act of reducing the importance of money, in our new system of economics, will help tremendously.

It will help to improve the likelihood that our new system would be directed toward the majority of people, instead of just a few. The idea again is that when more people can share the fruits of their labor, the country as a whole will be healthier and stronger. Individualism when taken to extreme, or excess, leads to the systems of dictators, monarchs, and oligarchies.

Those systems are enemies of the common citizen and need to be avoided. However, we still need to nourish a healthy form of individualism. We can do this if we try to work for balance.

Some people have suggested that once people have their basic needs taken care of, such as food, clothing, and shelter, then those people will not be motivated to do anything more. Studies have shown however that people do still continue to be motivated by other things. There are at least three other main things that motivate people.

The first thing is autonomy. Autonomy is our desire to be independent and self-governing. Part of the training that our parents give us helps us to achieve this goal. However, we struggle our whole lives to maintain this ability.

The second thing that motivates us is the desire to master a skill, trade, or a task. There is a sense of creative accomplishment that works in us here. In fact, this desire hints also at the idea of competition. We all know how this can help to motivate a person. This motivator also helps to support our autonomy goals, as well.

Now, a third thing that motivates us is a sense of purpose. We need to feel that we can contribute to our world, as this can give us our value to others. That value is something each individual needs, as it adds to our internal strength of spirit. The attributes here really make life worth living.

Today, people often attempt to use money to achieve these things, but they shouldn't have to. If our system can give each of us autonomy, a means to improve ourselves, and a sense of purpose, we will be able to relocate money to a minor position. Money alone does not have to be the reward for our actions.

Under the current system, those with the money can manipulate everyone else rather easily. That is why they want to keep their system. They can take away your autonomy and your sense of value.

However, if your basic needs were taken care of, they would have a harder time taking advantage of you. Without you to support their excesses, they have a problem. The problem for them is that their multimillion-dollar excessive salary would not be possible. They will fight hard to keep their advantage and thus those salaries.

Controlling Devices or Tools

During our thinking process, we can be, and often are, easily swayed from looking at the true reason for why something happens. This can be done by simply turning the focus of our minds toward something other than the real cause of the event. For when we refocus, our attention begins to wane on whatever the original thought was.

We can easily become confounded if that substitute cause, thought or reason, is a type of perplexing dilemma. These dilemmas are ideas that require more reasoning time than we are typically allowed during the discussion. This then makes our minds wane or wander even further from the original idea of the discussion. Some people employ this technique when they argue gun control.

For example, consider this argument. Guns kill people; therefore, the guns are the problem. The solution is to take all the guns away. By blaming the inanimate object, the gun, we are diverted from the true reason as to why tragic deaths occur.

Let's take a minute to consider this issue. When we do, we eventually admit that, with few exceptions, someone generally has to be interacting with the gun in order for it to fire. This basically means people kill people.

If we look at guns as being the whole problem rather than people, we neglect the major cause as to why people are injured or die. Thus, we are not really looking at the problem. We were diverted from solving the issue by being asked to accept a perplexing dilemma instead.

If we take the time to consider the issue, we find that guns, by themselves, normally don't kill people. We find that more often than not, they have the help of a human. The larger truth is that humans kill people; guns are just one tool they use.

Other tools are knives, forks, spoons, wire, poison, and on and on. Just taking away any of these things from humans does not really solve the problem. A better approach here would be to offer humans better mental health programs so as to avoid the need for so many guns in the first place.

Money is often found to be the cause of many deaths, in one way or another. Using the previous logic of blaming an inanimate object, such as a gun, for the deaths, we should also take money away as well? Somehow in the case of money, we don't come to that conclusion. Still, money is not just another inanimate object. No money is much more powerful than any object could ever be. Yet despite its lure, or because of its lure, this world has it to deal with. If we were wise we would see that people who excessively want money are the real problem.

Can we control human greed? Not if it is left to run rampant and to excess, as that is like giving in to an addiction. We cannot continue to treat excess as normal behavior. If we ignore its negative influence we are only fooling ourselves. When we do that we are just escaping reality.

Here again, we divert ourselves from solving the real issue by pushing it off on a difficult dilemma instead. Is it possible that these dilemmas, of or over our human shortcomings, could be reduced? With a solid mental health program for our entire population, many problems can be reduced.

We know that people are involved in the money process. Instead of deflecting our minds off our human frailties and pointing blame on guns or money, maybe we should be looking at the process that aggravates both problems. Could it be that the price system is the process that we should be asking questions about?

Simply put the price system creates the excessive desire for money. In doing so it sparks the incentives for money to do "evil." These are the "evils" we pretty much all agree are a major problem. Those incentive, inspired by the excesses that the system allows, push people into criminal behaviors. It seems to me that if the price system's importance was reduced, many problems would also be reduced.

There are other occasions in which changing the focus and switching the blame are used against us. Generally, these techniques are used to win us over on many controversial government issues. They can also be used to change our morals. Yes, it is in their best interest that our morals are lowered. Why? It is because this causes more expense on our parts and more profit for them.

Who Places the Controls over the Price System Who Makes the Rules?

Despite claims that there are rules and regulations over their system, these claims are superficial. One only has to follow the money, and you soon come to the conclusion that the system is heavily stacked in favor of the corporations and other large businesses. They can afford teams of lawyers to battle with. They can lobby for their cause. They have a voice that can be heard.

Think about it, if those with the money make the rules, wouldn't they tend to make those rules so as to favor themselves? Our government tells us that those large businesses have controls placed on them. These controls are said to prevent them from unfair practices. If that were really true, why do venomous scams and cons occur so often? Why are there so many loopholes in those controls?

Those businesses pay a lot toward reelection campaigns. Do you think they might have a reason for doing that? Perhaps, they get to write a few bills into law that support their businesses. I bet you have heard that this has actually taken place. The Affordable Care Act is just one example. They wrote the bill, and it was a disaster. In free market pricing, we are told the following. If the corporations and large businesses charge too much, then the customers will not buy the product. However here the health-care costs were already too high before the act.

People were already not buying health care. What the act basically did was have the government start paying part of the bill. The government quickly learned that even they couldn't afford the payments.

Without compensation, the health-care companies made sure they could withdraw from the market. They wrote it so they could not lose. Their pricing is still so high that fewer and fewer people can afford health care.

The government however still wants to keep the same health-care industry in place, even if we cannot afford it. The system's design hurts large businesses far less than their customers. This is because while they have fewer customers, those that can pay are paying exceptionally high fees. The price system thus is not suffering, and the industries overall health is intact.

In regard to research, our government says that large businesses must be encouraged to innovate. It is the only way they can compete with the rest of the world. In fact, subsidies, to these businesses, are often doled out for carefully worded funding requests on just about any topic you can think of. Again, who prompted our government to do this? The controllers we have been talking about here in this book, of course.

In regard to supply and demand economics, select corporations and large businesses are more frequently the predominate source of our goods or services. When this happens, the prices can more easily be fixed by those companies. That generally means that prices increase substantially for consumers. In fact, the prices can outpace the average incomes of the customers. The health-care industry is a good example of this, at least in part.

The public cannot even tax these industries, in an effort to gain parody. If we tax the large businesses more, they just add that cost back on to the product, and we end up paying that tax for them anyway. In the end, we have to conclude that large businesses actually control things, not the government.

The price system was, after all, set up long before the government; so in its view, any government that interferes with it is not a good government. Since they control the money and money controls the government, can you guess who wins? Why is anyone surprised that we cannot do anything about controlling big businesses, the banks, or Wall Street? If those groups pay for the government, shouldn't they get what they want?

These possibilities are just a glimpse of the problems that the price system imposes on our society. Their system of course cannot be sustained if they allowed everyone to be part of it. Unfortunately, for most of us, only a small amount of our population can fully participate. The price system will pick those who will participate in their system. That is, most of the time, they control it, but sometimes people come into it by chance.

How does one get into the system? You can be born into the system; this is the biggest and best way to get in. The other major way is to find a way to be useful to the system. If you by chance have a skill they can exploit, you are in. Note that you have to make them money or you are not going to stay. If they force you to fail, well that is just business; it is the capitalistic way, nothing personal. That is what we are told, at least.

I think we all know that if you're human, that it is personal. Allowing only, at best, 10% to enter their system makes it a crime against our society. The system is detrimental to over 90% of the people on earth. I call that a crime.

It affords those at the top luxuries beyond imagination. Those however not included in the upper ranks must share the crumbs that fall to the floor. Those that are on top, they don't seem to have a problem perpetuating this corrupt system. Living the life of luxury can do that. Oh, if they only had a conscious.

How the Leaders of the Price System Use Our Earth's Resources as if They Were Their Own

The price system allows privileged corporations from various countries to use other country's natural resources, as if they were their own. One example, among many, is a certain central European country that has little resources of its own. This country however has managed to command an extremely large economy. Their means to do so has been the price system.

Those in control of the price system have used the system's rules of globalization to secure resources they do not have. They secure them from other parts of the world. Under this new world-order system, resources can be treated basically as if they were located in their own country. This allows some individuals (private corporation owners) to benefit unfairly in a lopsided fashion, instead of the general population that lives in those resource-rich countries.

Corporations send their tentacles out all over the world to set up extraction centers for the resources they require. Their globalization deals have been structured in their favor. The fact that their economic wealth is so strong and the common citizen's economic wealth is so weak confirms this.

There is a question the news services fail to ask far too often. How could the corporations of small resource poor countries in Europe make their country's world leaders? Many people say that they are just naturally smart.

True these are smart people, however that idea is not the reason for their success. Remember there are often more people of these nationalities here in the United States than in their native countries. No, intelligence is not the reason. We need only to look at the price system for our answer. It has provided them with the tools to succeed.

Here in the United States, we have seen many business deals afforded to several countries. Those businesses have used the price systems power to obtain those contracts. Through these deals, our U.S. resources such as gold, oil, various minerals, water, and even physical structures have been handed over to foreign corporations.

The citizens of our country could and should be in control of the mining, drilling, and capturing of those resources ourselves. We then could be selling those commodities to those companies at an honest value to us. We can't do that because then we would be taking business away from them. *They* are after all in charge, not us.

So, our government has allowed those private corporations direct access to our resources. They can come here and predominately cut the U.S. citizens out of the process. Our government has thus allowed foreign middlemen to intrude on our resources.

Remember that those resources belong to the citizens first. However, in the price system, that is not the case. The price system treats resources as if they all belong to the private sector. Nothing really belongs to the people of our nation or any other nation where resources exist.

Why should resources belong to the people? There are several reasons as to why they own it. Generally, those people have set up some form of collective government. They generally pay taxes or if not at least protect that nation's territory. Sometimes, the citizens protect their land with their lives.

They paid additional taxes for infrastructure. They did this to improve their own businesses and communities. In the case of the people here in the United States, taxes are paid to keep the water and air clean and usable. Don't they deserve an honest return for doing so? Instead, the bulk of the profits go to some worldly corporation.

Further, in the case of oil, we can more easily extract it ourselves, because we are already here. We could easily drill our own oil at a much lower cost. Instead, our government sets it up for us to pay foreign corporations, at times, for the oil they extract from our own oil fields.

The same case can be made for all of our other resources. We can do these things ourselves and cut those private middlemen out. Those private corporations, by the way, have a track record of corruption, excessive salaries, and neglect for the environment.

Today, with the price system in place, we have venture capitalist and private business buying up the next great sources of energy. They do this so that they can continue to exploit us. They want us to once again come to them for our needs.

They reap excessive profits off our labor and resources. There is no need for "we the people" to allow them to extort us. They do this through us paying them for what we can simply do more fairly for ourselves.

What I mean by "for ourselves" is we as a whole body of citizens. This would also include the few local citizens who currently help to control things. They of course would also be included in with us. However, not as excessively paid pseudo royalty, but only treated in a more deserving fashion, under our new system.

Those individuals who imagine themselves as something special need help. They really believe that they need to be treated excessively grander than nearly everyone else. Yes, they really need to examine themselves. I believe that if they truly were honest about this exam, they would agree they need help. Their excessive greed might just be the reason they have this opinion of themselves.

Sometimes, businessmen claim that their good fortune stems from being in the right place at the right time or being born into it. Is life a crap game? Is being in the right place at the right time or being born into it really an honest justification for making excessive salaries? Obviously, they think it is, but this is only their subjective opinion.

The price system not only allows this kind of "gambling" attitude, but it also encourages it, because this is how debt can be forged. It is forged on the weakness of greed. It is this debt that makes nearly everyone slaves to those who are ruthless enough to follow the price system to the top. That debt however can also be the destroyer of systems like theirs.

Their system makes only a few people wealthy and most people poor. Without their excessive greed, the majority of the world would be better off. We need to remember that greed is a weakness.

It stifles the progress of individuals within the multitude by depleting their resources. It aggravates the pollutions we see. It degrades the environment, and it even seems to possibly be diminishing earth's resilience.

Now for sure, no matter what system of economy we use, there will always be some people that do not fit its basic mold. Even in this money-driven economy, there are those who would prefer to drop out and not participate. This is generally because of the stress that the price system brings. Actually, this stress is more apparent these days.

More people are beginning to understand how the current economic price system works or should I say doesn't work. You may have noticed that there are a lot more people these days that could be paying taxes that just don't. Many people haven't been able to find work for so long now that they have basically given up. For a growing number of people, the only jobs left have been criminal in nature. Under Trump, there does seem to be some relief, but how long will it hold?

No system will cure all the problems with this world or please every single human being. Since humans are not perfect, whatever we have done, and will do, will not be perfect. However, this does not mean we should not try.

We should strive for those desires to be better and to have a better world. Even if, as a group we haven't tried hard enough to establish it. This most likely is because we all like to think that our leaders are trying hard for us, so we don't have to. We have put our faith in humans.

This thought of putting our faith in humans prompts me to consider an alternative. I would be remiss if I didn't at least provide you with at least a few paragraphs on a religious alternative. The major religion in the United States is Christianity so we should consider the Bible's view on the price system. Just what should the general Christian view be on the current money system we have?

The reality is that most so-called Christians haven't really given it a thought. That is, at least at the level they should. Most of them know at least this much—the price system hasn't offered them much hope lately.

They might perceive also that it seems to lack faith in a supreme being. Students of Christianity understand that a completely perfect system isn't possible while we remain in flesh bodies. Prophecy from the Bible explains that near the end of this earth age, a one world system will control the world. We are not exactly there yet, but that one world order has developed considerably.

Eventually, this one-world system will start to fall apart. Horrible events, for those in charge of it, will begin to unfold. Then, there will come along a leader who will seemingly find solutions to bring it all back together.

A good part of the people will believe in this leader. However, a portion of the people will see him as being very deceptive. You will likely take a side here, but religious confusions will hamper many from a sound decision.

There is no real solidarity among the Christians. There are far too many denominations that fracture our unity. So the above events might change a little depending on the Christian telling it. Generally, however, I think the above version should cover the basic idea of this prophecy.

I should point out here that the current price system has helped to create those various different versions of the end-time stories. In fact, it has helped to create the many different versions of the bible itself. I say this for the following reason.

They, the controllers, have encouraged through their system a multitude of theological publications. You may have seen all the different kinds of so-called Bible translations that are out there to be purchased. They add confusion and some might say purposely. There have been so many translations, and each version seems to change things just a little. It is a wonder that on the subject of the end-times prophecy, we can still find some agreement in those different books.

Generally, they still agree that the corruption in the world will end in a violent and quick way. Some hold this violence will not necessarily be at the hand of man, but by God himself. It is also commonly held that just preceding the end, a false messiah will come. He will pretend to bring our one world back together, back to justice. However, his deception will be exposed when the true Messiah returns to rule until God comes to judge us.

After his judgment, a new earth age here on earth will begin. When this happens, we will not have to worry about building a new economic plan. Money will not be important at all.

Most Christians seem to have not taken to heart that money was not important to Jesus. He fought the price system many times. We can see this clearly, even from the few stories that we have telling us about his life.

A Christian view that is also widely taught is the following. God is a loving father. So we should expect to be treated fairly. However, if you don't love your father, you cannot expect him to love you forever. Even God has a limit on tolerance, as there is a certain future period of time, called the millennium, where those who persist to ignore him will not be allowed to exist at its finish.

Not that God wants to kill any of his children, but if he doesn't kill these few, he would have to suffer mankind to return to a world where these *parasites* would continue to plague them. He loves his children too much to allow that. By the way, these parasites are often identified as the sons of Cain. Christians must try to follow God's commandments, and to do this, they need faith in God.

Well, that was a brief synopsis of what some Christian prophecies teach. It is basic, and it is general in nature, so be aware of that. Christian teachings require mankind to put their faith in God, not humans who pretend to be gods.

In the meantime, none of us knows when our current economic system will fail and fall. However, we still need to face the fact that we are here on earth facing this potential issue together. Regardless if you believe in the Bible or not, we still have a need for a good honest economic system.

Most of us want a system that doesn't just benefit a few people at the top. So, we would be wise to look at building a new economic plan. Who knows, we might just use some of the ideas in this book to build it.

We really do not know the timetable of events to come in the future. It may be that "we the people" come to an awakening and want to change our economic plan. We might even have many years with a relatively good honest system before it gets turned back into corruption; who knows?

There are all sorts of things that can happen. One thing we are pretty sure of is that the current economic system is going to eventually fail. Before that time arrives, we need to start thinking about what would be best for us, our country, and yes the world as a whole.

There are roughly seven billion of us using the price system. We are constantly seeing people from all walks of life trying to use the system to their advantage. They pick at the various parts of the system to work their schemes. We try to set up defenses; we hire guards, security agents, and institute penalties. We spend a huge amount of time and money trying to figure out how they cheat the system.

When we do figure it out, we spend a huge amount of time and money trying to send them to jail. There seems to be no end because each and every day, more new scams or crimes occur. We keep doing the same things over and over again thinking we can make a difference. Doing the same thing over and over again thinking that you can get different results is said to be the definition of insanity. It seems we are so busy watching the individual parts and pieces in the system that we forget that perhaps it may instead be better to replace the whole system.

This truly is a matter of not seeing the forest for the trees. Could it be that by addressing the price system directly, as a whole body, we can find a way to minimize its loopholes so that they do not impact us so grievously?

Could we lower the volume of corruption simply by removing the power that the price system has? I think it is possible. However, this would require us to have the will power to wrestle control of the system out of the hands of those few who are perfectly happy with the design it has. These people would be the ones that seem to make the most money from its purposely poor design.

If we manage to reform the price system into a less cancerous instrument, we still have to contend with our human natures. Here, we might look at adopting a solution to the price system promoted by the Christian view. We have to look deeper into our individual selves or souls.

This is where each person has to apply common brotherly love to every action we take, day in and day out. If we could do this, we would not follow the price system's corrupting nature. This however is hard to do from within our flesh bodies where the price system's design has such power over us.

Still, Christians are to try as this provides the path to avoid the corruptions. Those who try, day in and day out, will find that in time, it will become easier and hopefully ultimately their nature. This nature would make the world a better place.

If we revamp the price system and take away most of its power, we will have a lot easier time respecting others. "For we wrestle not (just) against flesh and blood, but against principalities, against darkness of this world, against spiritual wickedness in high places."[4] Our task is not an easy one.

As you have seen, there are a number of ideas out there to get us started. There are very likely many more that were not addressed in this book. These short condensed reflections of extremely complex issues are, I am sure, going to leave a lot of questions.

Questions on just what our new economic design should be. We need to focus on the issue of complexity. It should be the goal of our new system to reduce the complexity of things. With a weak price system in place, it would be a lot easier to do. We would be better off doing it.

Freeing ourselves of the price system completely doesn't seem likely however. The necessary changes to the existing economic system are likely to be hard fought. However, if we succeed, the common citizen would benefit.

Those making obnoxious amounts of money however would have to take a pay cut. I'd guess that's about 2% of our population or perhaps as high as 5%.[5] Under our new plan, if we designed it right, far fewer people would suffer even during the reconstruction phase. That suffering would stem mostly from the aftermath of the price system's failure.

If anyone should suffer the most, shouldn't it be the ones who used a corrupted system to prosper the most? They used as many people as they could to achieve their excesses. If we are successful in our new system, those corrupted individuals would suffer.

They will suffer because they would no longer be able to take excessive advantage of others. They would have to work like everyone else. This means living off the achievements that we all share on a more equal footing.

Their suffering thus would be self-imposed, that is, until they learn that taking excessive advantage of people was never the right thing to do. Some of them will never admit that they were wrong. They after all are better than everyone else, in their minds.

Yes, these people will still exist, both rich and poor; and they would, if given the chance, work toward a system where they can freeload off the hard work of others excessively. Let's hope that our safeguards will be strong enough to protect "we the people" from their pressures, that is, assuming that "we" do have that chance to set up a new economic system.

Reports of Stress on the Planet

On July 16, 2011, a report on WDIV Channel 4 Detroit high-lighted a triathlon schedule that morning. It was for the St. Clair Shores-Pointes Adventures Triathlon's first annual event to raise money for charity. A triathlon is a three-sport event—swimming, biking, and a 5K run. The problem was that Lake St. Clair was having an E. coli problem at that time. So no swimming was allowed. Instead, they switched the event from swimming to kayaking.[6] I mention this because E. coli issues are a problem these days.

On July 11, 2011, an article on Yahoo News (see file) titled *Once endangered, eagle population soaring in Michigan*[7] sounds good until it points out that with a little more than 700 pairs flying around the state, their room has run out. According to the U.S. Fish and Wildlife Service estimations, bald eagles have run out of prime habitat—typically cottonwood trees near a body of water with ample fish. Eagles normally live miles apart, but occasionally nest closer together, if there are enough resources to share.

That old report from 2011 suggested that with just 700 nests, the prime nesting locations were basically gone already. Somehow, their growth will have to depend on finding more nesting areas. What is troubling here is that the state of Michigan has the second largest coastline of any state, yet prime locations are no longer available.

What happened to all the old prime locations? Did they get destroyed? Has our system of commerce destroyed those old sites? Have they paved paradise? The story didn't go that far. That is the kind of news they would want to avoid reporting on. We are left to consider what the real story is, by reading between the lines. Most of us are not conditioned to do so.

To support the idea that perhaps we have commercially built on most of that habitat area, we need only look to the news again. Over the years, there have been thousands of stories about this or that new business under construction. Developments of all sorts spring up, which we have been conditioned to believe are saving our lives. Remember their mantra is growth, growth, growth—that is their cry.

If we really stop to consider the side effects, it is easy to see the damage that is being done by their system. Sure that beautiful mall looks nice, but those woods also had beauty and a purpose. With all those parking lots, it is hard to remember the beautiful fields of grass or prairies full of wildlife. Now, the runoff from those parking lots helps to flood our basements and pollute our rivers.

The price system has put this stress on the planet, through its encouragement of excessive populations. Their money scheme requires growth, and this calls for the depletion of resources. Look closer and you will find that the system controllers have self-serving goals. They want to live at a higher standard than the bulk of the population without regard to the negative effects on the planet or its people.

I would rather the whole body of citizen, not just some, live at a higher standard. I would rather that we minimize the abuse to the planet as much as possible. I would rather we do on to others as we would have them do to us. This golden rule is what we should strive toward, as it encompasses a "One heart" concept.[8]

Christ Jesus didn't like the money changers. He wanted us to fight, to rid the world of those people who used that system to take advantage of others. He fought to release the people from the oppressions of those evil ones.

What did they do to him? Here we are 2000 years later, and the price system is still here. It is doubtful we will ever learn the error of our ways in this earth age, but that doesn't mean we shouldn't try? Try to be better, try to do the right thing. Try to look for a better economic model.

Bankruptcy

Another devious practice of the price system is actually one of the price system's methods of perpetuating itself. That would be through the bankruptcy laws.[9] These laws, I will argue, are a crime in themselves. The mainstream price system advocates of bankruptcy tell us that these laws save millions of people.

They don't explain, however, that the price system itself generates the conditions for people to have those problems to begin with. In this sense, bankruptcy bailouts are just as dubious as those huge bailouts we had in 2008. The only thing here is that these bankruptcies are spread across hundreds of thousands of smaller businesses and individuals. The bailouts of 2008, on the other hand, were given to a select few large banks and corporations.[10]

Debt is what the price system runs on. Bankruptcy is a means to recycle the debt and start the whole process all over again.[11] In a very real way, bankruptcy has a lot in common with an older way of bailing out your business. That method was, and is, as follows.

The corrupt individual would take out a rather large insurance policy on their property and then burn it down. They then collect the money and build a newer and better property. Long ago, this used to leave the insurance companies holding the bag on that bad debt. Since insurance companies are a major part of the price system's mechanics, ways had to be found to protect them.

A close examination of the insurance industry suggests that basically these companies are often just as corrupt as those individuals burning their businesses and homes down.[12] The reasons for the corruption are due to the various practices that the insurance industries use to make money, but that is another matter. The topic here is still bankruptcy.

Burning down your business or house of course damages the price system's profits. They had to find a way for people to have an alternative. Now, I am not saying that two wrongs make a right here; both are wrong for doing what they do. You of course already understand that one has the law on its side, while the other doesn't. Bankruptcy is a way of providing a legal alternative. It is a lawful way for those corruptive actions to happen.

The laws of bankruptcy can be different in each state. Businesses and even individuals still continue to use those laws to their own advantage without examining the roots of the idea itself. Desperate people often don't care. The price system here provides an option so people would be less likely to revote or commit crimes.

We all understand that some people tend to overextend themselves to the price system. Bankruptcy laws are a designed in vent for this. The price system likes these laws for another reason.

Instead of some lesser but crafty people taking advantage of the insurance industry, these people are now allowed, under these laws, to take advantage of the whole body of citizens. This allows those working the system to get richer. It is a means in which the system can bleed the wealth out of the populous and funnel it into the hands of the people that run the system.

Those that oversee a bankruptcy proceeding greatly reduce the financial debt owed. The company assets are sold for pennies on the dollar.[13] This makes it very convenient for wealthy individuals to pick the bones of each other and grow their businesses.

It also sets up a way to have third parties repurchase materials and properties at discount prices. The collusion in this scheme is always murky. However, over the long run, it seems competitors appear to be helping each other out during these sales.

Tax payers and consumers all too often pick up a large share of the misfortune. Local, state, and federal tax revenues are appropriately realigned back onto the taxpayers. Consumers might enjoy a slightly reduced product cost, but the majority of the sales profits goes to those crafty competitors.

The End of the Earth Age

It is said that the Bible is a book of examples. These examples tend to repeat themselves so that we, in the process, will learn what to do and how to act. Today, in a very real way, we, the common citizens, live in bondage just as they did at the time of Moses.

Our taskmasters have given us jobs to do and very often without enough time or resources to do those tasks. Examples are their work phrases such as "You have to do more with less" or "You have to learn how to work smarter." The pharaoh, as you may recall, asked the Hebrews to make bricks, but he didn't supply the necessary ingredients to do so.

Despite the pressures, the Hebrew people were not all united in their desire to leave Egypt. Today, the same can be said of our unity in regard to the price system. Do we have any other commonality?

If this story of Egypt holds true as an example or type, we should expect to experience plagues similar to those the Egyptians saw. AIDS and Ebola perhaps should cause us to wonder, but I don't think we are there yet. One thing for sure, at least in my mind, is that we are oppressed. However, I will understand if you don't want to admit that yet. Truthfully, even the price system elites are in bondage, though they may not see it, they are in bondage to money.

Today, we are also taught to ignore the corrective actions of Jesus Christ, which were expressed in the New Testament. This clever manipulation has prevented us from seeing the price system as a principal cause for all of the world's hardships. Jesus set an example for us, but it seems we haven't been able to see it.

We have concentrated or have been led to be fixed on his kindness and goodness, and in so doing, we have minimized a major point in his teaching. We should not be worshiping money. Money is not the most important thing in the world. Yet we have the price system.

In Conclusion

I hope by now there is at least a little crack in the armor of your love for the price system, although I know, deep down, that this little book doesn't stand much of a chance against the years of training you have had. I understand that most people do not see the price system as a thing to fight against.

I hope that I have conveyed the idea that it is an evil system and one that we should stand up against. I have given you worldly alternatives for our fight to control that evil beast. I have also alluded to you fighting this beast with your spiritual power as well, if only for your individual self-interest.

Whether you believe in Satan or not, you certainly have to admit, that this is the sort of system he would devise. He would lull us into being so comfortable with it that we wouldn't want to change it. We don't seem to want to change, even as we are being drained, not only of our wealth but also of our moral values.

When Satan comes to save the day, by saving the price system from its collapse, will you see him as our savior? Knowing what that system is will help you decide. I hope I have awakened you to the deceptions of the price system. If not, I hope I have at least roused you enough to consider its negative nature.

I commend you for taking the time to read this book. However, no one is perfect, my opinions at times may be flawed as well. Use your own mind to test those accusations, which were made. I remain open to change, if a good argument is made. We all should be open to change.

Epilogue

During our lives, there are times when we do desperate things. I realize that it is unlikely the price system will ever change, yet I wrote this book. There is, after all, a chance that this desperate act will effect a positive change on someone. With any luck, that someone might be in a better position to make an even bigger positive change.

I know that many people will scuff at this book. It would be easier for me to not publish, rather than go through the scorn and contempt that some people will generate against the dream. It is truthfully a dream, because some people, well entrenched in the current system, will sabotage any effort to make changes to their system of commerce.

I based my proposed efforts to reform our economy on the premise that the current price system will fail horribly. My wish is that we could climb out of this corrupt system without that happening. Some would even call this a dream.

This book likely will not have the answers we can all agree on. Still, it does help to point out why some things happen the way they do. The alternative perspectives brought out in this book should help in that understanding.

In the price system, things happen because man sets those things up. Man determines what is right and what is wrong. From where I sit, man is not making very many wise choices. In fact, most of those choices are selfish in nature.

We should allow God's spirit to set the standard for what is right or wrong, not man. If we did, that standard would not be changed to fit the whim of the day. Standards that change often are not standards at all. How can we know right from wrong when things change so much? God's standard is the one we should hold ourselves to as he points us in the right direction, that is, on a path to self-improvement.

References

Introduction

[1] Hollywood Salaries
http://www.hollywoodreporter.com/news/hollywood-salaries-revealed-movie-stars-737321

[2] Willaim D. Hartung - Only the Pentagon Could Spend $640 on a Toilet Seat - April 11, 2016
https://www.thenation.com/article/only-the-pentagon-could-spend-640-on-a-toilet-seat/

[3] Dr. Keith Smith - Episode 3: The Story of the $100 hospital aspirin - July 11, 2014
https://www.youtube.com/watch?v=y9H0CGgMnAM

[4] Carol Teaberry - Competition cure for what ails health care system - April 26, 2017
http://www.dailyadvance.com/Letters/2017/04/26/042117terryberrylet.html

[5] Aaron Kesel -High-ranking-cia-agent-blows-whistle-deep-state-shadow-government - Sept 14, 2017
http://thedailycoin.org/2017/09/14/high-ranking-cia-agent-blows-whistle-deep-state-shadow-government/

[6] 1 Thessalonians 5:6, The King James Version

Chapter 1: A Review

1   The Price System - https://en.wikipedia.org/wiki/Price_system
2   Patrick Pepper -In his own words: U.S. Rep. John Dingell - May 29, 2011- 'The News Herald' - www.thenewsherald.com/news/in-his-own-words-u-s-rep-john-dingell-with/article_3e777770-6715-535d-b97c-73d71d51f5c7.html
3   Webster's Online Dictionary. http://www.websters-online-dictionary.com
4   Technocracy Study Course, page 129, http://www.archive.org/stream/TechnocracyStudyCourseUnabridged/TechnocracyStudyCourse-NewOpened#page/n141/mode/2up
5   Technocracy - https://en.wikipedia.org/wiki/Technocracy
6   Alaskan glaciers melting - https://climate.nasa.gov/climate_resources/4/
7   Earth diameter- https://www.thoughtco.com/essential-facts-about-the-planet-earth-1435092
8   Technocracy Study Course - Technate Design - http://www.technocracyinc.org//wp-content/uploads/2015/07/Study-Course.pdf

Chapter 2: How the Economy Is Negatively Affected by the Price System

1   Eisenhower's farewell address. January 17, 1961. youtube.com
2   Kennedy's speech to the Press 1961. youtube.com
3   Dave Gilson and Carolyn Perot - *"It's the Inequality, Stupid"*, March/April 2011 issue- Mother Jones
4   *Wealth gap widens between whites, minorities*, Hope Yen, Yahoo News
5   Benjamin Franklin, "A republic if you can keep it" www.ourrepubliconline.com/Author/21
6   Bernie Madoff's Ponzi scam. http://youtube
7   Technocracy Inc.- http://www.technocracyinc.org/

Chapter 3: The Influences of the Price System on the Economic Groups in the United States

1   Dave Gilson and Carolyn Perot - "*It's the Inequality, Stupid*", March/April 2011 issue - Mother Jones
2   "A Wealth of Entertainment Channel" - awetv.com - Excessive lifestyles
3   Drug War Clock - http://www.drugsense.org/cms/

Chapter 4: Influences on Government

1   Abraham Lincoln. A house divided speech.
1   Matthew 12:25, Luke 11:17. The Bible
2   Lobbying. – http://www.answers.com/topic/lobbying
3   Fiat money. Wikipedia
4   George W. Bush racks up $15 million in speaking fees. Rachel Rose Hartman. Yahoo News. 5-21-2011 by
5   Barbara Slavin, *Iran's political process*
6   Robbie Cooper, *Five Monkeys – Congress*, August 27, 2010
7   Terence P. Jeffrey - "1,665 Pages; GOP Spending Bill Longer That Obama's Stimulus - May 1, 2017 - https://www.cnsnews.com/news/article/terence-p-jeffrey/1665-pages-gop-spending-bill-longer-obamas-stimulus

Chapter 5: Why Our Governments Always Run Amuck

1   A government is: - http://quotegeek.com/television-quotes/firefly/6313/
2   Kathy Henry - "Shortcomings of Human Capitalism"- Ezine Articles - http://ezinearticles.com/search/?q=shortcoming+of+human+capitalism

[3] Corporate welfare-wikipedia.org; The United States of subsidies: The biggest corporate winners in each state - Nlraj Chokshi - Mar 18, 2015 - https://www.washingtonpost.com/blogs/govbeat/wp/2015/03/17/the-united-states-of-subsidies-the-biggest-corporate-winners-in-each-state/?utm_term=.55a21ded07cb

[4] Four Hidden Dynasties of the End Times - R. Christopherson - https://www.theseason.org/topical/4_hidden_dynasties.htm

[5] They're Watching Eddie Brown July 2011

[6] The Century of the Self. – Adam Curtis - BBC Documentary - youtube.com

[7] *Dan Rather Reports*, HDNet, The Mother Lode Orig. 4-12-2011

[8] Mark Twain, *Politicians*

[9] military industrial complex - youtube.com

Chapter 6: Reforms in Justice, Corporation, Trade Laws, Lawsuits, and Medical Care

[1] Matthew 7:12, The King James Version

[2] The Law. Wikipedia

[3] Concerned Citizens Against the Patriot Act- http://www.scn.org/ccapa/

[4] Insanity: Stimulus Bill passes House but no one has ever read the contents - Pat Battlefield -Feb 13, 2009 - https://www.wackbag.com/threads/insanity-stimulus-bill-passes-house-but-no-one-has-even-read-the-contents.103752/page-2

[5] How can a corporation be legally considered a person?-Cecil Adams - Sept. 19, 2003 - http://www.straightdope.com/columns/read/2469/how-can-a-corporation-be-legally-considered-a-person

[6] Colossians 3:28, The King James Version

[7] Romans 2:11, The King James Version

[8] Private prisons. http://en.wikipedia.org/wiki/Private_prison

Chapter 7: Reforms in Education, Insurance, Trade, and National Security

1   The US Government Is Bankrupt - Doug Casey- Jan. 13, 2012 - https://www.caseyresearch.com/us-government-bankrupt/

2   "Problems and Weaknesses in the American educational System" - Nicole Smith - Dec 15, 2011-http://www.articlemyriad.com/problems-weaknesses-american-educational-system/

3   Degree.Net. http://www.degree.net/degree/net

4   Abolishing the Department of Education is the Right Thing to Do-Julie Borowski -Sept. 19, 2011 - http://www.freedomworks.org/content/abolishing-department-education-right-thing-do

5   Trade Balance, Balance of Trade - Economy Watch - June 29, 2010 http://www.economywatch.com/international-trade/balance-of-trade.html

6   Free Trade - see Business Dictionary - http://www.businessdictionary.com/definition/free-trade-agreement.html

7   Tariff Table-United States History - http://www.u-s-history.com/pages/h963.html

8   U.S. trade deficit surges to $50.2 billion in May- IBT Staff Reporter -July 12, 2011 - http://www.ibtimes.com/us-trade-deficit-surges-502-billion-may-471201

9   Small business morale falls slightly in June -Lucia Mutikani -July 12, 2011 - http://www.reuters.com/article/us-usa-economy-confidence/small-business-morale-falls-slightly-in-june-idUSTRE76B26020110712

10   Free Trade Vs. Fair Trade- Jason Gillikin - Chron - http://smallbusiness.chron.com/trade-vs-fair-trade-1683.html

11   Homeland-Security Business Still Booming Ten Years Later - Constance Gustke - May 29, 2011- https://www.cnbc.com/id/43185358

Chapter 8: How Energy Can Add to the Economy

1. Bluefin Tuna Sells for Record $396,000 at Tokyo Auction-Paula Forbes-Jan 5, 2011 https://www.eater.com/2011/1/5/6703367/bluefin-tuna-sells-for-record-396000-at-tokyo-auction

2. Downcast: Critically endangered bahaba caught and sold for $500,000- John Platt - Feb. 16, 2010-https://blogs.scientifi-camerican.com/extinction-countdown/downcast-critically-endangered-bahaba-caught-and-sold-for-500000/

3. Central Banking Conspiracy-https://www.youtube.com

4. Cost of national security - https://www.nationalpriorities.org/cost-of/?redirect=cow

5. Tipping point (climatology)https://en.wikipedia.org/wiki/Tipping_point_%28climatology%29

Chapter 9: Our Alternate Modified Plan

1. Technocracy study course page 238 - Energy Certificates - http://www.archive.org/stream/TechnocracyStudyCourseUnabridged/TechnocracyStudyCourse-NewOpened#page/n251/mode/2up

2. Technocracy study course page 213 - The American Technate - http://www.archive.org/stream/TechnocracyStudyCourseUnabridged/TechnocracyStudyCourse-NewOpened#page/n225/mode/2up

3. Technocracy study course page 130 - Rules of the game of the price system - http://www.archive.org/stream/TechnocracyStudyCourseUnabridged/TechnocracyStudyCourse-NewOpened#page/n143/mode/2up

4. Obery M. Hendricks, Jr. - The Politics of Jesus - The Church's hierarchy page 88

5. Bailed out banks - List - http://money.cnn.com/news/specials/storysupplement/bankbailout/

Chapter 10: Is This the End?

[1] The Impossible Dream from Man of La Mancha by Mitch Leigh & Joe Darion

[2] *"It's the Inequality, Stupid"* Dave Gilson and Carolyn Perot, March/April 2011 issue - Mother Jones

[3] About Audit the FED - Campaign for liberty - http://www.campaignforliberty.org/audit-fed/

[4] Ephesians 6:12, The Bible

[5] Excessive CEO pay. http://www.aflcio.org/corporatewatch/paywatch

[6] WDIV Channel 4 Detroit, 7-16-2011

[7] Yahoo News, 7-11-2011

[8] Obery M. Hendricks, Jr. - The Politics of Jesus - One heart or mind - page 110

[9] Bankruptcy laws. http://en.wikipedia.org/wiki/Bankruptcy

[10] Bailed out banks - List - http://money.cnn.com/news/specials/storysupplement/bankbailout/

[11] Chapter 11. http://en.wikipedia.org/wiki/Chapter_11,_Title_11,_United_States_Code

[12] http://www.cnn.com/CNN/Programs/anderson.cooper.360/blog/2007/02/insurance-companies-fight-paying.html

[13] Pennies on the dollar savings. http://dallas.rjabankruptcy.com/articles/creditcardsandchapter13.html

Note: Some Web site references may have expired.

Other Suggested Readings

G. Edward Griffin, *The Creature from Jekyll Island*
Ralph Nader, *Only the Super Rich Can Save us!*
Lou Dobbs, *War on the Middle Class*
Ron Paul, *The Revolution*
David Wallechinsky, Irving Wallace, *The People's Almanac #1-3*

About the Author

The author received his bachelor of arts degree from the Detroit Institute of Technology in 1973. On the way to that degree he attended classes at the University of Kentucky, while also serving in the U.S. Army. In the army he served as a sergeant in the Vietnam War.

Following his military service and college graduation he worked, as an engineer, for a major telephone company. His work there often took him to the headquarters of major corporations, where he worked in a supportive role. His thirty two years of service and experience here, in several business capacities, nurtured an understanding of how "*things*" in our world work.

His expertise on the material in this book were, in part, gained through years of active awareness. That is, he was, in a sense, home-schooled, in these matters; after all this material is not really being taught in our schools. It has, however, been the discussion of many independent minds, over the years.

The author admits that over the course of his life thousands of people have influenced him. The material in this book, in essence, is an assembly of their collective ideas. These are thoughts that were meant to be shared, but were often stifled.

As for his motive for writing this book. It was his desire to help, not only our country, but also our world; that prompted the effort. Things need to change if they are to get better. His hope here is that issues in this book will inspire you to help in this quest.

CPSIA information can be obtained
at www.ICGtesting.com
Printed in the USA
FFOW03n0841160418
46223954-47568FF